ALSO BY TODD SENTELL

*Toonamint of Champions—How LaJuanita Mumps Got to Join
Augusta National Golf Club Real Easy: A Particularly Allegorical
Comedy of Real Bad Manners*

*The Stairway Press Collected Edition of Toonamint of Champions
and Why Golf is so Exciting! A Novelty!*

3/15 DOROTHY — HERE'S A GREAT MIX OF SPECIAL EDUCATION AND JOURNALISM! I HOPE THE SAME FOR YOUR GREAT FUTURE, TOO!

Can't Wait to Get There.

Can't Wait to Leave

GO BE SUCCESSFUL.

A Schoolhouse Memoir

Todd Sentell

CAN'T WAIT TO GET THERE. CAN'T WAIT TO LEAVE

A Schoolhouse Memoir

FIRST EDITION

Portions of this book originally appeared in the online magazines Hippocampus and Smiles for All; the web sites Education Week Teacher, Education Week, Edutopia, and A Dixie Diary; and Flag Research Quarterly, the scholarly periodical of the North American Vexillological Association

ISBN: 978-1-941071-11-3
eBook ISBN: 978-1-941071-12-0

www.stairwaypress.com
1500A East College Way #554
Mount Vernon, Washington 98273

Cover Design by Guy Corp www.grafixCORP.com
Front cover illustration by Rick Geary www.rickgeary.com

To SUSAN SANDERS
The best principal ever

The schoolteacher himself come after you, the stranger said, and got shot in the leg and the ear for his trouble.

—Flannery O'Connor, *The Violent Bear It Away*

In the deep glens where they lived all things were older than man and they hummed of mystery.

—Cormac McCarthy, *The Road*

CAN'T WAIT TO GET THERE.
CAN'T WAIT TO LEAVE

AUTHOR'S NOTE

THIS BOOK IS the schoolhouse account of a teacher who thinks kids are the most important people on Earth and that teachers and headmasters and principals and assistant principals and academic deans and counselors and coaches and janitors and lunch ladies and certain parents—as sneaky as they are—are pretty darn important to the educational process, too.

I became a teacher when I was old enough to have ear hair concerns, backed up with a whole lot of life and work experience in big buildings near subways. The classroom gave me a whole lot more—pesky ear hair included.

I began as a wide-eyed substitute teacher and ended up as a full timer with very wide eyes. I was exactly a middle-aged man, in other words, when this particular mid-life thing began. During another moment of middle-age, I totaled my first crotch rocket motorcycle, and when I could walk again I bought another one. Whenever I pulled into the school parking lot on the rocket, the kids thought I was about the coolest teacher they'd ever had until I started giving out assignments and homework.

The independent schools where I taught were established exclusively for kids with a single or any number of learning, behavior, and emotional disorders, including Asperger's disorder; pathological narcissism; Angelman syndrome; rhinotillexomania; mucophagy; bipolar disorder; autism; dyslexia; attention deficit disorder (ADD); attention deficit hyperactivity disorder (ADHD); "Ring of Fire" ADHD; electronics addiction; work avoidance; disorganized-type schizophrenia; Tourette syndrome; dyscalculia; dysgraphia; dyspraxia; dysphasia; dyssemia in all of its forms; aphasia; auditory processing disorder; visual processing disorder; hyperactivity; over stimulation; low, or slow, functioning; eating disorders; trichotillomania; dermatillomania; self-injury disorders; fetal alcohol syndrome; obsessive-compulsive disorder (OCD); generalized anxiety disorder; social anxiety disorder; school refusal; articulation disorders; receptive and expressive language disorders; nonverbal learning disability; disruptive behavior disorders, which include oppositional defiant disorder and conduct disorder; fragile X syndrome; Rett's syndrome; selective mutism; and ear wax eating. I don't know the scientific word for ear wax eating. I don't think there is one yet. I looked.

Some students also exhibited sociopathic, and even psychopathic, traits. Some students exhibited deeply authentic qualities. Some students were right there in the middle, watching both extremes try to outdo each other.

A few times I've named for the reader the disorder in the vignette. In the rest of the vignettes I've allowed the disorder to speak on its own. Sometimes it speaks softly. Sometimes the disorder roars all day long and even into basketball practice.

Everywhere I taught, I taught with humor, even while knowing that most of my students don't understand humor. But I never let that worry me. I'm glad they were in the classroom with me, and so many other understanding teachers, while we taught them how to understand us, too, and the confusing world outside of the schoolhouse. For all of my students, though—struggling or thriving—I attempted to keep class time funny, knowing I was teaching *and* entertaining them at the same time...also hoping that the time they spent with me, learning about whatever it was at the moment, might have lifted their weary spirits. Their quirky personalities and ways of thinking sure lifted mine.

I think I knew what I was doing. I was hired without a teaching certificate and a master's degree. I was hired, pretty much, on potential and personality, and gained extreme ability and confidence while actually doing the job. On my first day as a substitute teacher, my psychology degree diploma was twenty-three years old. I was the walking-around definition of learning on the job as furiously as possible. My students never knew I wasn't degreed-up and certified, and they wouldn't have cared if I was. They just didn't want any homework.

I understood the kids and their disorders pretty quickly. I had collegial fun with them, and they had some serious fun with me, too—because I let them. I still got a finger waggled at me from time to time anyway. Some administrators loved how I ran my classroom. Some scratched their heads. Some parents thought I was a life changer—for the better. Some couldn't quite figure me out. But I think it might be that way for all confident teachers. We really don't spend too much time worrying about the popularity contest—or changing our style—especially when we know what we're doing is working.

Everyone's names in the book have been changed except mine, as well as Jeff Morrison's of Unseen Underground; Marie, Christine, Sylvia, and "Shenanigans" of my local

Waffle House; Bernard the Washington, D.C. grifter/con man; and Mr. Warbird's cats.

Here and there, various identifying information of the people and places in this book have been changed, but the messages of the stories are still faithful.

All of what's recounted, spanning many years, comes directly from extensive notes, or from writing the vignette while the scene was actually unfolding, or from writing the vignette later in the same day the action occurred.

The names of the various schools where I taught, their specific locations, and their ferocious mascots are intentionally not noted. The schools are real, however, and they're important and necessary places.

Todd Sentell
In the teacher's lounge. Where, apparently, there's no smoking anymore

PART 1

GENTLY HERDING CATS. OR, GENTLY HERDING ROLLING-AROUND LIVE HAND GRENADES. OR, SUBSTITUTE TEACHERS ARE HUMANS, TOO.

"Lady," the man said to the children's mother, "would you mind calling the children to sit down with you? Children make me nervous."

—Flannery O'Connor, *A Good Man is Hard to Find*

ONE OF THE greatest educational accomplishments of my life was in sixth grade when I led my team of classmates in running off a substitute teacher. Her name was Miss Stackhouse. Wanda Lynn Stackhouse. She sang for money at a lot of local churches, too.

I know this because my parents made me go to church every Sunday and sometimes even on Wednesday nights and sometimes Sunday nights, too, even when we'd already been there that dang morning for Sunday school *and* the church service. Don't get me started about the horrors of vacation Bible school. Anyway, Miss Stackhouse sang love songs very

Todd Sentell

loudly into a microphone to Jesus.

Beginning while we were mangling the Pledge of Allegiance, we delivered for the next two and a half hours a highly coordinated psychological attack on Miss Stackhouse...and then she sort of had a nervous breakdown and then she trotted out of the classroom with her purse and her coffee mug. Before lunch, too. The pride we felt for ourselves was palpable. Miss Stackhouse had come to the belief, which she verbalized to us that morning a number of times, that we were all possessed by Satan. We took that as a compliment.

After Miss Stackhouse clomped out the door we ran to the windows at the back of the classroom and watched her get into her car and drive off. Miss Stackhouse had put her coffee mug on the roof of her orange Corvette while she fiddled with her keys and when she peeled out of the parking lot the mug tumbled down the back of her roadster and busted apart on the asphalt.

After we stopped cheering, I strongly suggested to my team that we read books and draw and color and play our educational board games while we kept real, real, real quiet. I tiptoed to the front of the classroom and eased the door shut.

Forty-five minutes after Miss Stackhouse took herself off of the substitute teacher list, the assistant principal, the real cheerful but one-legged Mrs. Nix, an expert with crutches, bopped by to see how Miss Stackhouse was doing. After looking around the classroom, and then by asking us a couple of questions she demanded we answer because we were acting pretty puckered up, Mrs. Nix found out that Miss Stackhouse had left the building. Mrs. Nix made a funny face.

She asked us how long Miss Stackhouse said she'd be gone.

I told Mrs. Nix, with a dramatic wave of my arm, that we *all* felt Miss Stackhouse would not be returning. Ever.

Thirty-nine years later, and just a few short miles away from my elementary school, home of the Incurables, I was sitting on the front porch of a crappy house for sale on an open-house Sunday afternoon, trying to be a patient real estate agent. The only people who came to see the house were other real estate agents, looking for free food.

All of a sudden I got a good and curious and remorseful feeling in my gut and heart and mind and soul and started thinking about what it might be like to be a substitute teacher at the school near where I live for kids who have learning, behavior, and emotional disorders, and then I decided I wanted to do that for a while and that's how it all got started. The thought, random or ominous, was just as natural as thinking about some of my golf swing problems. Of course, I figured I could make a lot more money being a substitute teacher than what I was making as a real estate agent who didn't sell anything.

I called the school. I used my sales skills, which most of the time is simply being a nice guy who uses his manners. A few days later I had an interview with the headmaster and the human resources lady. I filled out a bunch of forms while I smiled a lot and acted like I was not a wanted felon.

Two weeks later I got a call from the human resources lady at the school and she told me my application was accepted, that my police check came back clean from the police station, and that I was now on the on-call list. Your name and number is on the list, she said, and every teacher and principal and assistant principal has the list, even the athletic director. But let me make absolutely sure we have the best phone number for you.

I told that human resources lady I had only one phone and it's always in my pocket.

I think I made a difference as a substitute teacher. I think just showing up is half of it and the other half is getting home alive. I got scheduled in advance—days, weeks, and even months in advance. Sometimes I got called the night before. Sometimes I got called the morning a frantic principal needed me to fill in that day for a sick teacher or for a teacher with a sick kid of her own and I had to get cleaned up real fast and speed over to campus.

I was untrained for what I did—if you can call sixteen years of going to school—untrained. I didn't make a lot of great grades. I was more of a student of *school*. I loved school, especially being on that crazy third grade cross country team of a little Episcopal school in a Civil War town. We ran crazy fast and raised historic hell. Just look at the pictures on our cross country page in the yearbook.

I was voted "Wittiest" my senior year. My best friend, in an underground poll of our pals, was voted "Most Likely to Become a Circus Geek." I was more proud of him.

I loved my teachers, too. I appreciated their inexhaustible toleration of our inexhaustible goofiness. Deep down I knew what they were trying to do and I knew they cared. I knew they did. I still do today, more than dang ever.

While I was substitute teaching one day, a regular teacher said to me about a sixth grader, who was standing right there beside us in the great room of the middle school, "You

4

Can't Wait to Get There. Can't Wait to Leave

should have seen Debbie when she got here two years ago." And then the teacher put her hand on the sixth grader's shoulder and said in a tone of voice as if it would be the last thing she'd ever say, "Now she's my miracle. My *miracle*." I found out that teachers get to have those moments a lot. Even substitute teachers.

Some people say teaching is a calling—that if you don't feel you've been called to teach definitely don't dang do it. I got called a whole lot more than I thought I would.

SUPER GREAT DUMB IDEA

It's my first day of being a substitute teacher at the school near where I live for kids who have learning, behavior, and emotional disorders. It's my first day of being any kind of teacher at any kind of school.

At this school they also have a smaller school-within-a-school for about twenty-five kids who have a whole lot more learning, behavior, and emotional disorders than the other kids on campus. The school's principal, Pam, walked me to a social studies classroom. Her ancient little drooling bloated dog followed us down there; his yellow toenails clicked on the floor. Pam said his name was Bluto and he was dead but Bluto just didn't know it yet. The dog looked like Winston Churchill.

At this school, I was told, the students get to call the teachers and principals and the headmaster and school dogs by their first names, and even by their nicknames. Right before Pam shut the door behind me she said sort of funny, Good *luck*...and run down the *hall* if you *need* anything.

5

Bluto yawned. It was hideous.

To get things started, I thought it would be a super great idea to ask the kids where they lived. Break the ice. Get them talking to the new substitute teacher. I really thought it was a super great idea.

I got to a super serious kid named Karl. I asked Karl where he lived.

He said he couldn't tell me.

I said why.

Karl said he couldn't tell me because he didn't want to get tortured and raped.

OLD BURRELL'S ALL WET

Today I'm over in a different building on campus with the regular kids, but they're not regular at all, either. We were having an open-book test in a seventh grade literature class and a kid named Spurlock wasn't working on it.

Spurlock was sitting way in the back corner of the room against the wall and was poking a push pin into the wall and taking it back out and pushing it back into the wall somewhere else on the wall.

I asked Spurlock to get to work on his test, please.

He said I wasn't Old Burrell, the *real* teacher.

I swear to God they call the teacher Old Burrell without getting into any trouble at all. I asked Spurlock what he meant.

He said I wasn't Old Burrell again, the *real* teacher.

I said he really needed to explain that one better.

Spurlock said that since I wasn't Old Burrell then he just

wanted to wait and do the work for Old Burrell when Old Burrell came back.

I got up from my desk and went back there and took the push pin away from Spurlock and then I went to the front of the classroom and said I'm Old Burrell for today as well as tomorrow because Old Burrell ain't here. He's on a field trip with some other kids at the ocean.

Spurlock rolled his eyes and then he said he can't *wait* for Old Burrell to get back.

I almost said—Me, too—but didn't. Instead I said that the assignment for today was given to you by Old Burrell. That Old Burrell even wrote down on paper what he wanted you all to do while he was at the ocean and I read it to you guys not ten minutes ago.

Spurlock said I like Old Burrell a *whole* lot better than *you*. And then he rolled his eyes around some more and made a loud huffing noise.

Another kid in the class said, God-*damn*, *Spur*-lock.

I walked back over to Old Burrell's desk and called the principal of the school, a lady named Lurlene Bougainvillea, from the phone on the desk and said I'd like to bring Spurlock to see you. He's in big trouble.

Lurlene said come on.

This school has about ten principals.

I brought Spurlock over to her office and she said...*Both* of you sit down.

ATTENTION, PLEASE

Later today, in another one of Old Burrell's classes, while

Butch was taking his open-book test, he started making fart noises with his lips.

I let him make the fart noises for a while without saying anything because he was making them sound so grossly accurate that I was truly impressed. I used to do the same thing in class from pre-kindergarten to about my junior year in college.

Butch kept making the fart noises...for a long time.

I finally walked up to the front of the room and asked Butch if he needed some attention.

He looked at me like he didn't know what I was talking about. But at least that made him stop making those gross fart noises.

I said did you know that when kids make noises when they're supposed to be quiet that what they're actually doing is screaming for attention? I said I read that somewhere. Or like people who drive real slow in the left lane of the highway. They're just screaming for attention. I was sure a real-world analogy would work on Butch.

Butch looked at me like I was a circus freak.

WINTHORP HAS A QUESTION

Yesterday I didn't wear my glasses but today I did. Today, Winthorp said are you wearing your glasses for emphasis?

CLASS OF AMERICANS

On my first morning substituting in the school for fifth and sixth graders I watched as the principal and the teachers gathered all the kids in the great room before classes began. Everybody put their right hand over their hearts and we recited the Pledge of Allegiance.

The Pledge of Allegiance to the United States of America. That one.

Imagine the sound of fifty fifth and sixth graders innocently and sincerely saying those words. They sounded like baby patriot angels.

DO YOU SMELL WHEN U R AN ADULT?

If you're real eager to know what's on the minds of 11, 12, and 13 year old boys concerning the best bodily functions, then go get yourself a job substitute teaching at a school where they ask you, after determining you're not a world famous serial killer and actually have a natural knack for mesmerizing hyperactive children, if you'd also be willing to become a guest lecturer on fascinating adolescent health and hygiene topics in our fifth and sixth grade middle school on Tuesdays and Thursdays right after they come off the playground and are pretty much amped up and freaked out anyway. You'll get paid for it, you're told by the middle school principal. Seventy-five dollars. Your daily rate for just forty-five minutes of talking.

So what you do is say...Uh, okay...and go find a book real quick on adolescent health and hygiene topics, which fascinating, and get all geeked up on everything in your free time and make your handouts and then teach a bunch of guest lectures to the boys and girls of the middle school on health and hygiene. They are extremely curious, mostly about hygienic issues. And there are about fifty to sixty of them. Sometimes it feels like thousands.

So after a few riveting lectures the principal of the middle school sort of angles up to me one day and says real nice...It sure would be...real nice...uh...if you could teach our sex lecture this year.

Did the middle school principal just say A SEX LECTURE?

She's smiling at me, with a hopeful expression on her face.

The middle school principal *did* say A SEX LECTURE!

Not the one about how to tell the difference between apple tree sepals and stigmas, which is pretty hot stuff, too. No, this middle school principal is talking about the you-know-what and the other you-know-what lecture and how the you-know-whats work together...to make middle school principals.

Oh, Lordy Jesus help me.

The middle school principal said you'd just be talking to the boys in the great room and me and a couple of the other teachers will talk to the girls in another classroom. What memories you'll have of this. Thank you for what you're doing for the children.

I asked her why she wanted me to do it, seeing as how I was a new substitute teacher still winging it.

She said Guido the science teacher won't ever do it. He's been here for years, but this is the one lecture he just won't do.

I whispered...Is there something wrong with Guido?

She whispered back, I think so. Anyway, she said brightly,

Guido will be standing in the back of the room while you give the lecture. Right there with you every step of the way. Yep.

I gave each of the boys a three-by-five index card and asked them to confidentially write down at least two questions about all this stuff that they've been wondering about, and want honest answers to, from your sex guest lecturer. Then they could go running like their hair was on fire to third period and then we'd convene again on the dreaded day the fascinating topic will be delivered.

Here's what I got handed back, in their own words:
•

- Why do we laugh at gross things?
- Does dressing appropriately effect how you smell?
- How do you get sleepy?
- How did you win?
- Where do your zits go after you wash them?
- What is an erection?
- What causes an erection?
- Why do a hormones change?
- What does your brain look like?
- Do you smell when u r an adult?
- How do you grow zits?
- What is the name of the school?
- How many years does it take to become a man?
- Why do you grow hair in those places?
- Why do girls mature faster than boys?
- Where does hair grow quickest?
- What should you do if you want to do something and your friends don't think it's cool?

- How many showers should you take?
- Why don't you get treated differently when you don't take a shower?
- Why do the girls like you better if you are clean?
- Why do my balls hert sometimes?
- Is there a way to avoid hair?
- Do all old people have a lot of hair?
- Why do we get smelly?
- How do we get her?
- Talk about girls
- Always believe in yourself
- Have a positive attitude

Exactly, fellows. Have a positive attitude. That's how you win; that's how you get her; and that's how you get through a forty-five minute sex lecture.

Me, not you.

LUDICROUS LUNCH

I'm substituting for a teacher who had field trip lunch duty today. He's a math teacher and the school's soccer coach. He's got quite a few religious icons in his classroom. I wonder why.

Anyway, I'm back in the school-within-a-school and I'm driving a beat-up school bus full of high school guys. Every one of them has Asperger's disorder. We're on our way to the local Steak 'n Shake.

Pam told me to make sure they all calculate the right tip, and then actually *leave* the tip on the table. Pam said the last time the boys were there they didn't get the concept of tipping quite right while the regular teacher was in the bathroom and later that day the Steak 'n Shake manager called the school to complain.

And here I am a substitute teacher for only a month and these guys have already given me a nickname. Driving this clunky, squatty bus for the first time, every time I turned the bus to the right I chugged over, or scraped against, a curb. Now they call me "The Curbinator."

I immediately assumed a school bus full of high school guys with Asperger's disorder is supposed to be real loud. I gave into the assumption pretty quickly. They are all deeply interested in a wide range of topics and they were making their points with each other as verbally as possible. I assumed for as long as I could stand it. The inside of the bus must be made of tin. I asked them could they quiet down a little bit so I won't hit any more curbs.

They quieted down for about three seconds, and then cranked it up again. I heard vigorous conversations about the Atlanta Falcons cheerleaders, Minecraft, a girl named Petal, and presidential politics.

I asked them again. Same result.

A fellow sitting behind me tapped me on the shoulder. He said if you want them to shut the hell up then turn on Ninety-Five-Five The Beat. That'll do it.

The radio station?

Yeah, turn it on and watch what happens.

95.5 The Beat is a radio station that plays rap and hip hop music. Most of the songs are about sex, guns, women with fat butts, and how to control your woman, fat butt or not. I turned it on. They instantly shut up.

That guy behind me said...*Told* you.

After a minute I asked anyone why you guys shut up. These songs are so bad they're good...know what I mean?

A kid in the back yelled...Because our *parents* won't let us *listen* to the *radio*.

I understand. At the time, a song was playing called "What's Your Fantasy," sung by a fellow named Ludacris. I'd heard the song before, a bunch of times, and it has a way of sticking in your brain and it won't come out. It seems to be about a man who loves a woman very much:

> I wanna, li-li-li-lick you from yo head to yo toes
> And I wanna... move from the bed down to the down to the flo
> Then I wanna, ahh ahh, you make it so good I don't wanna leave
> But I gotta, kn-kn-kn-know what-what's your fan-ta-ta-seee!

From there, Ludacris sings about how he'd like to have intimate relations with his woman in a huge number of additional and different locations around town. The list is extremely long. Ludacris must have a lot of energy, time, and money.

Anyhow, the fellows tipped real well this time. And on the way back we got to hear the song all over again, cranked up even louder. That fellow behind me tapped me on the shoulder as we were pulling into the school parking lot. He said thanks a lot. The regular teacher...he's a prude *bitch*.

THE BUNNY IS CURIOUS BUT NOT RAMBUNCTIOUS

I have been substituting so much they finally gave me an e-mail address. I guess this means I'm bona-fide. Now I can really see what the adults are up to around here. I got my first e-mail. It was sent to all the teachers and students from a student in the high school:

> **I have a young male bunny rabbit that I am giving away to a loving home. I am not giving him away because I don't like him but because he is costing a good amount of money and I do not have a job at the moment. He is easy to fall in love with. He is free and will come with a cage, bottle, food dish, some food, timothy hay, hay holder, litter box, some litter, and a couple of toys. He is a very calm bunny. The bunny is curious but not rambunctious. He is less than 6 months old. He likes licking things and hopping around on the carpet. If you are interested and would like more information, please e-mail me back. Thank you, Rachel**

I know what you're wondering, of course. Me, too. What's timothy hay.

CLOCK WATCHING

Instead of substituting, I was asked to come in to do a one-on-one session with that Spurlock kid.

A one-on-one session is where a kid's teachers and principal and assistant principal take a big break from each other for a full day, or sometimes for two or three days,

15

because things aren't getting any better for anybody and undone work is piling up or his attitude is sucking the life out of everybody...or both at the same time. In other words, it's the big time-out. The school's substitute teachers are the ones called to perform one-on-one sessions.

I was asked to do the one-on-one with Spurlock in the conference room in the administration building.

There's a real nice conference room in the high school building where some other substitute teachers do their one-on-ones and I had asked Spurlock's principal, Lurlene, if we could do it down there but she said no because the conference room in the administration building was closer and it was easier for her to check on us in there. She said if we were in the high school conference room then she'd have to walk up and down that big hill and she didn't want to walk up and down that big hill.

This is how the mind of a common-sense principal works.

Lurlene also said to me if Spurlock doesn't get his act together then she was going to start the kicking-his-fanny-out-of-the-school process. This Lurlene woman said that to me in the privacy of her office and I figured if she started to use even mild cuss words with the school's new substitute teacher then that meant I was making my bones around here. I hope so. She scares me, too. She's what you call a tough love giver.

The conference room in the administration building has a couple of big tables shoved together and a bunch of chairs and a microwave and a refrigerator. On the wall is some artwork from some students that went there fifteen years ago that's still extremely abstract fifteen years later.

In a one-on-one you sit there with the kid and help him with his work if he asks you to from 8:15 to when the bus leaves at 3:15 or when one of their parents picks them up. Sometimes babysitters or nannies or driving services pick up kids.

In the one-on-one session the kid is supposed to settle down and shut up and get caught up on their work. You can't even go have lunch with your class. You both have to eat lunch right there in the room. Man, do you start looking at that clock on the wall starting around 8:30 and wonder how in God's name you're going make it to 3:15.

I had already read the newspaper and had started in on a book about Duane Allman of the Allman Brothers Band. You can be a genius at a lot of things in life and he was a genius at playing the guitar.

Spurlock was doing his work real hard and he was being real quiet and I felt proud of him.

Some people say they can see the grace of God wash down over people who need it real, real bad. I pretended seeing the grace of God washing down over Spurlock because if he didn't hunker down over the next couple of days and if he got kicked out by that Lurlene then he'd probably have to go to some huge public school and they'd beat Spurlock up during the first few minutes of homeroom of his first day. He's that annoying.

I swear to God my eyes teared up just a little because I thought the grace of God really did wash over him a few moments later—it looked like someone had sprayed room spray over his head from about six feet above him—and even before then I still knew Spurlock was special and he could do it.

But I think sometimes you don't need God or room spray or whoever to help you do something. Just up and finally dang doing something yourself can work just fine, too.

WOMEN ON DIETS

It was a long time before lunch time and a whole bunch of women who work in the administration building were already coming into the conference room and taking things out of the refrigerator and putting them into the microwave. The door of the microwave clanked when they opened it and clanked even more when they shut it.

They seemed embarrassed about coming in there a lot to get food.

While it's being microwaved, macaroni and cheese does not smell as good as it does when it's sitting in a big bowl in front of you at your grandmother's house.

One time a woman who had already fixed herself something to eat came in there a little later and fixed herself another something else to eat. It still was a long way away from lunch time. She said to me you must think that all we do around here is eat.

I said you read minds real well.

The lady said...Well just *look* at us. She got her food out of the microwave and walked out.

Spurlock said...What if those gourmands got paid for the amount of food they ate.

SALES PITCH

A little later the guy who does all the computer stuff for the school came into the conference room with a man and a woman and asked me and Spurlock if we minded if they had a short meeting in there.

I looked at Spurlock and he shrugged his shoulders.

I said okay with me and kept reading about Duane Allman.

I was amazed at how loudly the man and the woman talked to the guy who does the computer stuff for the school. The man was a salesman and the woman seemed to be in training to be a saleswoman. She'd chime in every once in a while with a comment like, I'll e-mail you what he just said when we get back to the office.

They were telling the school's computer guy about some computer system they thought would be good for the school.

When the computer guy said that's what he'd been looking for and he'd make a decision next week the man and the woman seemed real happy.

After they left, Spurlock said to me…Listen to this. On his laptop, Spurlock had transcribed pretty much the entire conversation between those salesmen and our guy. He read it to me.

I couldn't believe it. I said even though you're supposed to be catching up on your work for Old Burrell and Smithson and Billy and Morty and Cassie and Mamie that I have to admit I'm impressed. I told him I knew he was smart.

Then Spurlock said that man was being mean to our computer guy.

I said that man was the salesman and sometimes salesmen talk a little loudly and that he was just trying to convince our computer guy to buy his stuff.

Then Spurlock said that he thought the salesman was weird.

I said he wasn't weird. That he was just from another country and it wasn't his fault that he looked and talked different than us. That he just had to do a lot of convincing real fast and sometimes it seems real aggressive, especially when you were watching it from the side like we were.

Spurlock looked at me for a moment, and then started doing his work again.

CATCHING UP

Later in the day, Spurlock's math teacher, Billy, came in there and gave Spurlock some papers and told Spurlock he'd like for him to try real hard and get this done. The teacher said it was work from August. The month we were in was November.

THEY BROKE SPURLOCK

I heard he got that work from August done. He started acting nice again in his classes toward his teachers and the other kids and generally got his act together so Lurlene didn't kick him out.

But it's a day-to-day thing with some kids and everybody knows that and is cool with it. Sometimes it's a moment-to-moment thing and everybody's cool with that, too. Alert for it. Alert as hell for it. But cool about it. Can't get all panicky.

Good teachers and principals are like combat squad leaders, I'm learning. Cool and constantly watchful and caring all the time. That's what I think because that's what I've seen so far. From every one of them.

LOWER SCHOOL ITTY-BITTY DOLLS

Beulah is the principal of the lower school. She asked me if I could do a one-on-one with a first grader named Benjy on Wednesday.

I said sure...and what's *he* gone and done.

Beulah said he's been real disrespectful to his teacher. Philomena, Beulah said, is about to pull her hair out.

I conjured up a picture of Philomena pulling her hair out. I cringed.

Beulah said Benjy's real smart and he's never done a one-on-one so be ready. Then Beulah said real shaky, I'm not sure what to expect.

I said I look forward to meeting him.

You have to be real confident with kids. Even the itty-bitties. That's what they call the lower school kids around here. Itty-bitties. Fifty pound itty-bitties can raise holy hell just like the rest of them. You'd be surprised. On Wednesday morning I walked into the lower school building and Beulah was sitting in her office. She motioned for me with a yellow pencil to come in there.

I walked in there and sitting on an old wooden chair was a little boy. He was crouched on the seat with his legs and feet underneath him looking up at me with big, almond-shaped eyes.

The first thing I thought was that he was a porcelain doll.

FLY TRAP

We walked to that conference room in the administration building and I didn't tell Benjy he looked like a doll but he could have fit into his own backpack. Benjy said in his little doll voice that he'd never been to a one-on-one before.

I said I'll be with you all day to help you get your work done.

He said he didn't need any help because he was a real fast worker.

I said that's okay, too. Just let me know if you need me. I'll be right there.

When we walked into the administration building the receptionist and another lady were standing around talking and drinking coffee and I said ya'll meet Benjy.

They said real sweet...Hey, Benjy.

When we walked into the conference room Benjy said he'd been in here before.

I said what for.

He couldn't remember but he was sure he'd been in there before.

I said okay.

There was a fly in the conference room and Benjy started focusing on it instead of the pile of work he needed to work on. He said that looked like the fly that was bothering him yesterday in the lower school.

I said are you sure it's the same fly.

Benjy watched it fly around and then it landed on the table in front of us and then it would fly around some more. He was really watching that fly. And then Benjy said he was pretty sure it was the same one.

KILLING FLIES

It was hard for Benjy to concentrate on his work with that fly flying around.

I rolled up the Living section of my newspaper and wanted to kill that fly so bad. I roamed that conference room with bad intentions. The fly wasn't letting us get our job done. I knew Beulah might appear at any moment and this would not look good—me and Benjy watching a fly fly around.

Benjy was watching me try to murder that fly. He said a one-on-one wasn't that bad because he was finally getting some peace and quiet.

Breathing heavily, I asked him what he meant by peace and quiet.

He said down at the lower school it's so loud he can't concentrate. He said it's noisy down there.

All I knew was he was not being nice to his teacher. I figured he was probably the cause of some of the noise, too, but that was me conjecturing.

He said he had come to Georgia from Kansas.

I watched him work a few math problems while I chased the fly around. He did the math problems as fast as that fly was flying around. I said something about how fast he was doing his work.

Benjy said I'm a fast thinker, too. He said I'm good even when I do my work fast. Benjy said he was the fastest worker in his class. And then he said I can tell if someone is fast or slow by looking in their eyes.

When he spoke he pronounced every letter of every word. Precisely every letter. I have never met a seven year old who was more articulate than him. He was so articulate it was unnerving, especially with that doll voice.

But he didn't look in my eyes when he talked and we talked a lot. All day he looked just off to the side. Like he was looking at my right ear. I asked him about it later because it was bothering me so much. I said you're not really looking at me are you. You're looking right over here. I held my hand up behind my right ear.

He said that's right. I'm not.

SIGH OF DISBELIEF

That afternoon, after Benjy's father picked him up, I asked Beulah if she noticed he didn't quite look you in the eye when he talked.

Beulah didn't say anything. It looked like she was trying to recall if she ever noticed.

I told Beulah I was sure of it.

She said you know…I think you're *right*.

Then I said he's one of the smartest kids I have ever met.

Beulah said he was. But boy can he sure raise hell.

I opened my notepad and read Benjy's answer to a question he was supposed to answer for me by the end of the day. He was supposed to tell me—Beulah, ultimately, through me—what he would do differently tomorrow. The first thing he said was, I don't know.

I told Beulah I said to him you need to do a lot better than that.

Beulah smiled.

Then Benjy had said: I'll try to behave as much as I can. I'll try not to argue. I'll try my best when working. Be the best I can. I'll help others if they need it. I'll show courtesy and respect.

His very words. From out of that child's mouth.

After I was finished reading all of those things Beulah took a huge breath and let it out real slow.

FRACTIOUS

Debbie is a fifth grader with freckles and brown hair with a pink ribbon in the back that helps keep her pretty hair out of her face. I think Debbie might be a little tall for her age. She has a high, sweet voice I don't think I'll ever get tired of hearing it's so cute. But when she starts whining in her other voice I want to gouge both of my eyes out with a spoon.

I was substituting in Debbie's math class and Kathy the math teacher left a pile of worksheets on fraction problems for them to complete. When I looked at the first page they were supposed to do and at those million fraction problems I started feeling woozy and I turned pale.

I understand that a lot of people in the world think math is important.

When Debbie started in on how hard these fraction problems were over and over and over and over I felt a deep and instant kinship with her...until she started slapping the page on her desk over and over and over while she was saying real loud and whiney how hard it was over and over and over. Debbie also asked me real loud wasn't the *nu*merator supposed to be greater than the de*nom*inator or did she ask me over and over and over was the de*nom*inator supposed to be greater than the *nu*merator and that's when I started twitching and my body fluids started pouring out of all of my seven orifices like the Ogeechee River and I became a moist and creamy blob of quivering, useless, steaming biomatter in the real teacher's desk chair with two glazed-over eyeballs staring up at the ceiling and if there would have been a math poster on fractions stapled to the ceiling then that would have been an incredible comic and ironic touch but there wasn't a math poster stapled to the ceiling above Kathy's desk thank the Lord God almighty.

Gilligan finally said...*I'll* help her.

I said *thank* you, Jesus. Uh, I mean Gilligan.

INSTANT RESEARCH

A bunch of seventh graders were taking their open-book test. The class was real quiet. All of a sudden Larry went...*Hup!*

Real loud.

I was startled—sincerely and truly startled.

My heart was thumping but I tried to keep my cool. I was reading a book on Mark Twain at Old Burrell's desk and I kept my head down for a second or two and took a deep breath and tried to figure out what just happened. Then I slowly looked up at the classroom.

Larry was working on his open-book test. They were all working on their open-book test. No one was looking at Larry. No one said a thing.

Hup!

Larry's body jumps and his head snaps back a little when he makes the noise. I saw the whole thing this time. Then he went back to working on his open-book test like nothing happened.

I wiggled Old Burrell's mouse (I know that doesn't sound right) to make the computer screen come back on. Then I keyed in Tourette's syndrome and while I experienced watching it in real life I learned about it on the world wide web.

Larry finished his open-book test in one class period. You had two class periods to do it in.

FEAST OF FEELINGS

Fifty kids are sitting quietly in their chairs at the place they'll come back to after they go get their food. Standing around the great room behind them are the teachers and a few parents who came in to help get everything set up and the food served and the whole thing cleaned up later.

The principal of the middle school asked each kid to tell everyone what they were thankful for and then the next kid would do it until everyone was finished. Even the parents and the teachers would say something. Then we could eat.

Standing next to me was Soozi's dad and her mother was on my right. When the time to speak got to Soozi, she said in a loud voice that she was thankful for everything in her life.

Before Soozi, most kids said they were thankful for their video games.

Next to me, I heard Soozi's father make a soft, moaning noise in his chest. It's the sound you make to yourself that comes naturally—when you're overcome with deep sweet emotion for your child.

CHICKS DIG...UH...WHAT?

I had Larry in another class. I asked him what he did over the weekend.

Larry said his mother bought him some bongo drums. Larry said his mother said that learning how to play bongos would help him with his Tourette's.

I said I had never heard of that but I'm not one to question it. I also told Larry I would have to believe that chicks dug guys who played bongos?

He said...Well, I just got them yesterday.

I asked him did the bongos come with a DVD or a booklet to tell you how to play them.

He said no, but as you beat on the drum closer to the middle it makes a lower sound.

That made sense to me. I mushed my lips. Larry is tall and sturdy for his age and has a huge head of black, thick, curly hair. He wears oval-shaped glasses without rims. His teeth have braces on them, but he still smiles a lot, naturally, quickly. Everybody likes him.

Then I thought of Larry in his college dorm room, years from now, in a tie-dyed t-shirt, playing his bongos for a bunch of cute girls, sitting cross legged, looking up at Larry with great, romantic affection...because another kid said to Larry, Hey, so what *if* chicks dig guys who play bongos?

Larry looked at his classmate as if to say that would be okay with him.

AMERICAN PICKERS

Now I know why you find a box of tissues in every teacher's classroom. It's not there for sniffles and sneezes.

A box of tissues, within rapid reach of the teacher, and substitute teacher, is there because of the frequency and urgency of some students to dig around in their nasal cavities with a crooked finger and with tremendous and shock and awe-inspiring determination to pull something out.

Some parents and teachers and stand-up comics call this digging for gold. They are not digging for gold. They are digging for a lottery ticket that has already been determined to be a billion dollar winner. They are digging for pages of homework and final exams with all correct answers.

I watch them dig and I am stunned.

They dig as if in a trance. If you are teaching them about Western Europe they don't care. That the other name for The Netherlands is Holland and they export a lot of flowers...they don't care.

They are digging. Digging with a crooked finger stuck way up in there.

If they perform everything else in their future lives with the concentration they use to pick and pull something from out of their noses then their emotional, physical, personal, financial, familial, and professional success is ensured.

I am also convinced they are concentrating so much during the digging that they don't breath. That if a blue-faced student faints onto the floor after pulling an enormous booger from out of their nose I will not be surprised.

I will go over to them, of course, and poke them awake with the toe of my shoe or a crooked finger, but I will not be surprised.

THE STUDENT'S RESPONSIBILITY

One morning just after I sat down at the history teacher's desk I was substituting for I noticed over on the left side of his desk three rubber stamps. The word the stamps would produce when the device was pressed hard on a piece of paper was displayed in all caps and in red on the top of the stamp. The three different words on the rubber stamps were, INCOMPLETE, LATE, EXCELLENT.

SIGNS OF LIFE

One morning just after I sat down at another teacher's desk to substitute for her...a math teacher...I was sort of whacked out by the posters on her wall. Well, you really couldn't see the walls because they were covered by colorful posters that screamed:

Integer Rules!
Basic Fraction Circles!
All Math Work Must Be Done in Pencil!
Watch These Factor Trees Grow!
Primes and Composites!

Helpful Graphing Info!
Fraction-Decimal-Percent Equivalents!
Rules of Divisibility!
Complete Homework Has Three Parts!
Metric Weights and Measures!
Rules for Multiplying and Dividing Negatives!
Respect is not a gift! You have to earn it!
God Bless America!

I liked this teacher even before I hunkered down in her classroom for the day. She's serious about her job and about math and about being a good citizen and person. And these posters were like a warm blanket wrapped around us all day. The exclamation marks are mine, however. God bless those common polygons, too!

WHAT MORE DO YOU WANT

I saw Benjy the other day. After I finished the day in a class in the junior high school building I walked down to the lower school. I was going to find Beulah and see how Benjy had been doing.

Outside the door of the lower school Beulah was sitting on the bench. Beulah and the other teachers sit on that bench with the itty-bitties when school lets out while the itty-bitties wait for their ride.

Benjy was standing there with his backpack on his back waiting for his father or his mother or his babysitter. I didn't know.

He is so tiny.

I sat down next to Beulah and asked Benjy how he was

doing.

Good.

Really…are you doing okay?

Good.

Beulah said, Benjy, he really wants to know how you've been doing in your classes and with the other kids. *Talk* to him.

In that sweet little seven year old porcelain doll voice, Benjy said…*Good.*

I'LL TAKE IT!

The headmaster raised the substitute teacher's daily rate by $15!

SPLITTING HAIRS

I was warned.

The principal of the school for just the seventh and eighth graders, Lurlene, told me a while back that a lot of the kids just don't get your witty remarks and oddball humor and scholarly sarcasm…and since you're a real expert at all three don't be surprised if you get a few blank stares when you lay some goober head remark out of the blue on one of the kids.

I almost said something scholarly sarcastic to her. But didn't. I had it all ready, though.

On Friday I was substituting in the middle school and the kids were coming into the classroom all excited and glad it was Friday.

I was glad it was Friday, too, but I was glad to be there

with them because Fridays are real easy in the middle school.

Guillermo walked in there and I have always liked Guillermo and his hair. He has a big, thick head of dark brown hair that curls up in the back a little bit and the hair on the sides of his head he puts underneath the frame of his glasses and the bangs come down to his eyebrows. In a nutshell, his thick head of hair looks like a helmet but it's also healthy and rich looking. There are women who would love to have his hair and a lot of grown men have his hair all over their backs. I'm a member of a health club near where I live and you see things in the locker room.

Guillermo also wears braces on his teeth and is about as cute as they get right before they become teenagers. Guillermo was standing in front of the desk looking at me. I was sitting in the regular teacher's chair. The regular teacher's name is Jilly and she teaches math and was at some sort of doctor's appointment all day or something. I told her kids she was in Nebraska duck hunting and none of them thought that was funny or believed me.

So then I told them Jilly was actually a CIA agent and she was in Bangladesh installing a security system. They scrunched up their faces and looked at each other.

Guillermo was still standing there looking at me. I said, Guillermo, can you tell me what hair products you use because I'd like to purchase some for my own hair care.

Guillermo looked at me some more.

Your hair products. What do you use, babe.

I was getting no reaction at all. This was what I had been told to be on the lookout for. So I decided to take it to a whole new comedic level—never before seen in fifth grade

American education—instead of changing the subject to Lemuel's hair, sitting over there, which looked as if he had combed it with a gasoline powered mulcher.

I said, Guillermo, do you wash your hair with bleu cheese dressing?

Guillermo said no I don't.

I asked Guillermo did he dry his hair with a blow torch.

He said he didn't dry his hair with a blow torch.

By this time a number of other fifth graders were assembling at Jilly's desk—more like surrounding me like in that good movie Children of the Corn—to find out what in the heck I was talking about with their pal Guillermo.

One of them said real serious that Guillermo *didn't* wash his hair with bleu cheese dressing! That he used sham*poo*...or *soap* probably.

I was carefully watching Guillermo. And I was smiling to let him know I was trying real, real hard to be funny and to be his pal. It was Friday in the middle school. I was really feeling it.

Then Guillermo said I want you to start calling me "Dude."

WILL WORK FOR HUGS

I saw Benjy again the other day. In the nice sunshine.

I was walking back to the junior high school building after lunch and he was walking to the lunch room with his class. I stopped and said hey, Benjy. And then I leaned down and hugged him. At that moment I felt like hugging him so I hugged him.

Sometimes teachers hug kids. Sometimes kids hug teachers. You don't want to do it a lot, but when you do it for the exact right reason there's nothing on Earth that compares.

MEDICAL ADVICE

To be real clear on the difference between burping and barfing and urping you have to understand that a burp is a burp and it's really more of a wide open mouth sound situation and barfing is when your total food package comes flying out but when somebody *urps* that's when you burp and some food bits go flying out but not as much as a barf. This was explained to me today in a hugely scientific tone of voice by a kid named Beauregard.

STICKER SHOCK

This school is what you call a laptop school. What that means is that starting in fifth grade you're required to have a laptop. Just like a pencil, you have to carry this thing around with you to each class except P.E. and Art and Band because the school wants the kids to learn how to use a computer and to be able to use it for research and to learn how to write essays and book reports by using the QWERTY keyboard. Teaching kids how to type on a keyboard is called keyboarding. We all need to know how to type.

Even fifth graders know how to put together pretty good PowerPoint presentations, too. It may be about how an asteroid is going to hit the Earth next Tuesday afternoon, but they're still pretty good.

Anyhow, the cover of a laptop has a big space for communication type opportunities with the rest of the student body, the teachers, and anybody else who looks at it. In other words, a lot of kids put stickers on their laptop covers.

If you don't have a degree and experience as a psychiatrist, psychologist, behaviorist or wide-eyed substitute teacher or any other job where you're able to figure out kids, the easiest way to figure out kids is to look at the stickers they put on the cover of their laptops. This is a way to figure out kids without badgering them with questions and them having to even look at you or act like they're listening. One way to get to know a kid better is to know what they're interested in and have a conversation with them about it...or even base your early relationship with them on their interests. So look at their laptop computer cover stickers to determine their interests. It's sneaky and fun.

Adults put stickers on the bumpers of their car or trucks, you know. Support Free Speech, But Carry A Gun Anyway!

A lot of kids at this school like either Georgia Tech or the Georgia Bulldogs. There's no grey area on that one. Some like the Wolverines of the University of Michigan. One kid is loyal to the Army. One likes the Air Force. Symbols you've seen here and there but don't know what they mean but you know the kid knows what they mean. Most of them have to do with rock and roll or partying in general. Being a party animal. Obama rocks. I love apple head Chihuahuas! Bush Rocks! I'm a Jesus freak! John Cena! Batista! Hornswoggle!

Is that a sticker of a marijuana plant or the plant that's

not marijuana but sure looks like marijuana?

Got Milk? Peace! Got Sig? Peace!

Country flags of countries they have some affiliation with. The flag of Turkey, for instance. I ask...Why Turkey, Simon?

He says, My grandmother is from Turkey!

There's more: Jews for Jesus! Say yes to hugs! Hugs not drugs! Got Sig? Deny Satan! Coexist! Jesus Rocks!

HAW HAW MEE MAW

Every November a week or so before Thanksgiving the school holds Grandparent's Day. It's held for a couple of hours on one of those fall mornings that's usually bright and cool and overall just real nice meteorologically.

Mee Maws and Pee Paws and Maw Maws and Paw Paws can go poke around anywhere on campus and they dress up like crazy for this thing. Sort of visualize that all the Mee Maws and Pee Paws are Las Vegas mobsters and molls having a super big night on the town.

The Mee Paws and Pee Paws always smell so nice and are in real happy moods and are looking around a lot like they're a kid at Six Flags for the first time and if you're on the substitute teacher's list and you're not subbing somewhere on campus that day you get asked to drive a golf cart since the campus is real hilly and the school doesn't want any of the matriarchs and patriarchs to vapor-lock climbing up a hill to see what their little precious made out of lard in art class.

Seventy-five dollars to do this back and forth and back and forth between all the buildings at the high and low elevations for two hours. Afterwards, you're not even asked to stuff capital campaign envelopes for the rest of the day. You can go right on back home to bed.

So I get a nice gasoline engine powered four-seat golf cart that's real loud and blows smoke and within ten minutes the transmission ups and meets Jesus. So then I tell an authority figure I'll go clean out my truck and we'll just use that. Plus, the truck's got a heater that works and leather seats and a CD player.

A school authority figure who's real sarcastic but in a leadership-type way says please clean out your gross piece of crap truck real good. You're representing the *skoooo*-wull. That's exactly how the authority figure said the word school.

My truck is well known on campus. I perhaps have too many stickers adhered to it. A number of them are bullet hole stickers.

Anyhow. So here I go riding around campus, hitting all the hot spots, and these poor old folks are so used to getting a ride with the P.E. teacher driving around the other golf cart that I'm having to roll the passenger window down all morning and tell them they're not being kidnapped to be taken to a rest home but that I'm the other guy driving the golf cart but it broke and I'm just using my personal truck to haul you up the hill. Of course, by this time the P.E. teacher has already snapped them all up and here I'm sitting in idle burning up my gas.

A real old, classy looking Mee Maw comes walking out of the high school building all alone and I holler at her through the open passenger side window if I could give her a ride up the hill or wherever.

She looked at me like she thought that was a great idea.

Actually, I could tell that she had seen some adventure in life and wouldn't mind a bit more. I could tell by the way she held herself and the way she was dressed (Talbot's or Neiman Markup) that she used to probably have her man's drink ready when he got home from being the chairman of a multi-billion dollar international conglomerate situation. That her and her man had drinks before dinner every night, served by a butler. That she and her man probably summered somewhere every summer. Like Sea Island or Bermuda or Monte Carlo. I was really wondering who in the hell she was the Mee Maw of.

So classy Mee Maw gets into the back seat and immediately says something about how nice I'm dressed and that it's nice to see people dressed up these days...that you just don't see it anymore. Me, a long camel hair overcoat from the Brooks Brothers store at the outlet mall I couldn't afford so I put it on a credit card I couldn't afford. Then she asks me if I'm a teacher and I tell her that I'm a substitute teacher the school uses a lot.

The fragrance of her classy lady perfume filled up my truck and I was grateful for that. I started thinking about my mother who smells like that.

Then she says I sure must have a lot of courage and patience.

I said I guess that's what you call it. I'm not really sure what it is.

Mee Maw says you must know my *grand*son, Lester. The little bastard's really *some*thin'!

I look at her in the rearview mirror and she's smiling. I said I don't think I've ever had him. What grade's he in?

He's in *ninth* grade.

I said I haven't subbed in the high school yet this year.

All of a sudden Lester's Mee Maw starts laughing. Really laughing. Then she leans up and taps a bony finger on my shoulder and says...Well, when you meet *him* you'll sure as hell *know* it, mister! Lester's Mee Maw started cackling again.

Two months later I was asked to sub for a couple of months in the high school for a history teacher who had a baby. I had Lester in third period world history and Lester constantly made fun of how I did my hair and the way I acted even though I was a grown man. Some days I told him it took me less than three hours to get my hair like this. I had Lester convinced, and most of the rest of the class, that groups from the senior center near where I lived, as a senior center field trip activity, came over to my apartment every morning and watched me prepare my hairdo through a two-way mirror.

One fellow said to me...*You* should go to this goddamn school.

Lester made a lot of fun of me because I let him. I finally figured he used the opportunity to release his demons. Lester had a number of demons living inside of him. Some of the demons Lester had given names.

Today we were back making fun of my hair again, and I asked Lester, deeply hoping for more of a philosphical answer, what happened when *he* looked at himself in the mirror. What Lester said next was one of the funniest things I've ever heard from a student in my life. Lester wasn't a ninth grader. He was a comic genius, posing as a ninth grader taking world history from a substitute teacher. That's what he really was.

YOU WORK FOR ME NOW

That Lurlene Bougainvillea tracked me down while I was substituting in some godforsaken classroom in the high school full of real hilarious guys like Lester and offered me a full-time teaching job with her.

She said Jua-*nita*, her Georgia history teacher, who you have *subbed* for *many* times, just resigned, amicably, and is leaving at the end of the *year*...and now I need a *new* Georgia history teacher. We *know* you, she said. Kids all over campus are *crazy* about you. So just don't screw up between now and the end of the *year*.

I looked at her funny. Was I being hired or shanghaied?

She said...You *would* like to be a real teacher, *right?* Full time. With benefits. With your very own classroom? Even if it's full of squirmy eighth graders?

I said I...*think* so.

Good. You're working exclusively for *me* now. And you'll *like* it. Lurlene handed me a huge Georgia history textbook. She said here's your summer reading. Lurlene said that Jua-*nita* decided to go live out the rest of her life in a log cabin in the mountains with her *boy*-toy. Lurlene widened her eyes, and then said, who has made her a *bay*-bee.

I mumbled a thank you. I'm pretty sure I said thank you.

Lord have *mercy*, Lurlene said. *Tee*-chers.

PART 2

I HEAR SELECTIVE MUTISM

Hi Lurlene! I wanted to give you a heads up on something. Spike has told me several times that his teachers act a bit bizarre sometimes and it unnerves him totally. When I ask who...he says pretty much all of them except Sally and Mamie and Coco. I know you can't control everything at all times. At least I don't think you can...can you? Thanks for all you do!

—*E-mail from Spike's mom, forwarded by Lurlene to her teachers*

In his mind's eye, he saw the schoolteacher about to appear in it, lean and evil, waiting to engage whom the Lord would send to conquer him. The boy clamped his teeth together to keep them from chattering. The door opened.

—Flannery O'Connor, *The Violent Bear It Away*

ONE OF MY Georgia history students, Huckleberry, doesn't like to say anything. Even when I go ahead and tell him the answer to a question, and then ask everybody else not to say the answer when I ask Huckleberry the question, and then ask him to say the answer so he can hear what it's like to say

42

something out loud in class from his own larynx, Huckleberry will smile, but he still won't say the answer from his own larynx even when he knows the answer.

But during the morning and afternoon break and while he's waiting for the bus, Huckleberry's out there with his buddies and he's yakking away like Rush Limbaugh, with arm gestures and everything. He really does have a great smile, too, and a fuzzy wad of red hair with a life of its own. Huckleberry and another student named Flavio are best friends. In class and on breaks, Flavio is just like Huckleberry. The great smile included.

When I have to leave the classroom to take what I call a "teacher's break," with finger quotes, I usually tell everybody to please stay in their desks and work quietly. I drink a whole lot of coffee and then follow that up with a bottle of ATOMIC JAMAICAN STYLE GINSENG ROOTS DRINK WITH TIGER BONE TONIC OPEN WITH CARE I obtain in mass quantities from my local Publix. A vile, gag-inducing beverage, sure, but it makes me a better teacher.

Anyhow, Spike always gets up the moment I walk out and roams around the room and gives his horrified classmates a quirky commentary of some of the items I've used to decorate the classroom. If Spike isn't creeping around the classroom he's paying attention and answering questions and offering up some mighty good discussion questions. When he participates like that you wonder why he comes to this school about the time Spike starts creeping around all over again. Spike is inquisitive—in an other-worldly sort of way.

Most of the time Tempest is funny and generous and kind-hearted. Then there are days when she's just evil. Then they are days when she's back to being angelic and if golden wings made of switchblades popped out of her back I wouldn't be surprised.

Levon will cut enormous farts in class and isn't embarrassed about it. Not one bit. Levon's not even embarrassed when he's asked to go outside the classroom to fart after he warns us he's got a big one coming on. Even when he steps outside the door we can still hear Levon fart. Not embarrassed. About anything. I guess that's all part of Levon's quaint charm. Of course, that's a whole lot of quaint charm to enjoy and I admit—we do.

Petal will shut down completely and will turn around in her desk for the rest of class and won't look at you or acknowledge anything you say to her from then on. Not just for a class period—for weeks. But when she's on she's the very best at class participation of every one of my students. Probably in the whole school. But then there are those days when I wouldn't be shocked at all if Petal, with her green cat eyes blazing, jumped out of her desk and whipped out a machete and attempted to separate my head from the rest of my body. Not shocked. I would not be shocked one bit.

Johnny can hardly read. Watching him try to read out loud is so agonizing you finally have to look away. But the effort he gives in trying to spit the words out is profoundly inspiring. I know Johnny knows how much we all admire him because we tell him so every day.

When Hoover forgets to take his medicine everybody else gets real nervous, too, because the possibility of Hoover flying out of his desk and crawling across the ceiling like a bug instantly increases. Funny, Hoover always apologizes for forgetting, so that sort of calms us down, too.

In homeroom, Spike also enjoys dropping onto the floor and rocking back and forth on his knobby spine with his ankles locked behind his head. While we watch and point. In mild horror.

Then there are all my other favorites, too. A whole bunch of them with a wide and wild range of learning, behavior, and emotional disorders they bring to school with them. During the day, they're all trying hard not to do what their mind and body are furiously telling them to do, usually when it's not quite the right moment in the noble process of knowledge seeking to do it.

But all that's okay with me. Every bit of it. That's why they come to this school and that's why teachers teach here. You stay hopeful no matter what.

So is it patience a teacher of kids with learning, behavior, and emotional disorders possesses?

No.

Patience means you're waiting for some big payoff. Just getting them through the day with some knowledge in their heads is a payoff, and most days that's satisfying enough.

So what's the secret to getting them through the school *years?*

It's durability and understanding is what it is. The durability of a battle tank and the kindness of human understanding. I learned that when you're in the same classroom teaching the same subject every day and every year, instead of butterflying around campus as a sub, you get into a real knowledge groove. Familiarity breeds experience.

Kids and teachers—sometimes it's a cantankerous

combination, but when we understand each other and the reasons why we're in school together, there's a pretty good chance we can all learn something. Even when kids don't talk...even when some kids crawl across the ceiling like bugs...and even when some talk too much.

Teachers included.

SYMBOLIC LEARNING

The first morning of being a real schoolteacher with my own classroom I was already so high on caffeine when I got to school my eyeballs were the size of BBs and my brain was screaming Yeehaw.

At 8 o'clock in the morning, which is not a particularly attractive time of the day at all for doing anything except teeing off, the first schooly thing I see when I get out of my truck is the grizzled veteran of educating seventh and eighth grade boys and girls and their teachers, Lurlene Bougainvillea, our principal and my new boss, standing in front of the building with her video camera.

Lurlene was photographing the seventh and eighth graders while they were getting out of their cars and walking into the building. Lurlene was smiling and waving and giggling and screaming in her Appalachian Mountains-infected accent...Welcome to skooooo-*wull!* We're so glad to have *yooooo!* Lurlene aimed the camera at their heads as they walked by, and then she'd aim it at another kid's head and scream the same stuff. Welcome to skooooo-*wull!*

By this time I had juked out of Lurlene's way. Now I'm standing behind her watching the kids' expressions. I have to tell you, Lurlene was enjoying these precious moments a whole lot more than the seventh and eighth graders. Sweat was already running down my back. I'm really looking forward to working for Lurlene this year. I've got the rest of my life ahead of me to see what being a real schoolteacher is like. What the heck, I'll start today.

Welcome to skooooo-*wull!*

God forbid I was planning to give them a test on the first day of school on the eighteen most popular Georgia state symbols. I just had this deep-down, full-time, rookie teacher's feeling that they'd appreciate it. One of the state symbols is a largemouth bass.

We started in on the Georgia state symbols. Jasper noted that you can kill and *eat* the Georgia state fish symbol but you can't kill and eat the Georgia state *bird* symbol.

All of a sudden I figured they needed to know the big difference between a game bird and a regular bird and animals you can shoot and eat and those you're not supposed to. They still didn't like the idea that the poor state fish was fair game and the state bird wasn't.

Petal, a girl with blazing green eyes, asked me what the state bird was. She hadn't opened her textbook yet. I had asked them to twenty minutes ago.

I said the mosquito.

Petal mumbled...No *shit.*

Now everybody's looking at me with their eyes bugged and their ears perked as if they would run out of the room if they could, but they are frozen in awe. I'm pretty sure it's awe.

After a second or two of rookie teacher introspection, I

figure I must seem like an enormous doofus. But it feels about right to me. It gets their attention. And on my first day of real school, for them and me, I'm wondering what I deep-down think of kids and children and young people…learning, behavior, and emotional disorders or not.

They're still looking at me. All with a certain expression on their faces. My decision's been made.

CLASS ROOLS

My classroom particulars are sensationally doofy, too. I know this and embrace it. I had all summer to allow my imagination to do things.

The best thing about teaching, and sometimes the worst thing about teaching, is that you're left alone most of the time to do what you think's best. I learned that my first day of subbing for Pam and Bluto. Sometimes good deeds go unpunished.

The name of my classroom…*your* classroom, I said…is The Cozy Room of Learning. I have designed and decorated it with the hope that its coziness might make you want to learn a bunch of things without complaining. I said I hope you like my lamps and my maps and some historical prints I've had in my room since I was a kid.

Tempest moaned…*Creee-peee!*

I had been to School Box, the teacher's dope store. I held in my hand a fake pencil, two feet long. It's bright yellow. I said…This is The *Teaching* Stick, and I'll probably be whipping this thing around a whole lot this year to punctuate the air with knowledge. Touching The Teaching Stick is unholy, however. Don't do it.

Spike yelled...Can I touch it!

I ignored the question. I had to. I knew I had to get through this as quickly as possible before I changed my mind on every bit of it. On the wall I have placed in big letters, I pontificated, that I bought at an arts and crafts store and that I painted in a school color and the words are Seek Knowledge. I pointed The Teaching Stick at our class motto: Seek Knowledge. When in doubt, I said, seek knowledge. I gazed at them dumbly for a moment or two.

They gazed dumbly right back at me.

Yes. They seemed to think having a class motto was okay.

I moved over behind a lectern my father had made for me out of old wood. Wood that had seen some things. I said this is The Lectern of Speaking. I said I'll be blowing hard from behind here a lot this year. I said when I really want to deliver some awesome stuff I'll probably step behind The Lectern of Speaking and I will probably be holding The Teaching Stick, too, and whipping it around.

Petal moaned...This is *so* lame. Petal and Tempest high-fived. Petal said...There is definitely something *wrong* with you.

And in the back, near my desk in the back, I said, is not a *globe*. It's The Globe of *Happ*iness. After you push the northern hemisphere up you will see that inside The Globe of Happiness, in the southern hemisphere, is a whole bunch of candy I discovered is real expensive to buy. Do good deeds. Say good things. Work hard, I said, and you'll get candy, and lots of it.

All eyes were now on The Globe of Happiness. Four of five of them, especially Spike, were already lurched forward, ready to leap out of their desks for an inspection.

I walked back there and lifted the northern hemisphere on a globe on a stand with wheels that's actually a bar. The southern hemisphere holds ice for adults who drink cocktails.

Three kids, at that special moment in the early history of The Cozy Room of Learning, said that I was their favorite teacher. Spike said he'd catch a bullet for me anytime, and at this school, he said, it could be any day.

I think bribing kids with wads of Snickers, Butterfingers, Smarties, Twix, Milk Duds, Milky Ways, Blow Pops, Gobstoppers, and Chupa Chups, Twizzlers, Swedish Fish, Dum Dum Pops, M&M's, Sour Patch Kids, Tootsie Rolls, and bubble gum cigarettes, to do and say nice things is fine because it works. I also asked them not the chew on the carpet or lick the walls. Class discipline must be maintained.

BUTTSING HEADS

We're still getting organized. All of us. Students and adults.

We finally got to that deep and sentimental moment where I told them it's important as a Georgian or a resident of any state to understand your state and its role in the development of the nation and its history and regions and who the governor is and how he or she got to be the governor. I said I feel so strongly about this that if I moved to Kentucky I'd immediately want to know more about the history of Kentucky and its state symbols and all that.

Then Tempest says that she's got a great-grandmother who lives in Kentucky and if she brought her great-grandmother to class could she get extra credit for it?

As politely as I could, I said not really.

Then Tempest blurts out did I know there was a county in Georgia called Butts County!

I said, yes…there's a Butts County. I did know that. You're looking at the big map of Georgia over here, aren't you.

And there's also a Coffee County and a *Ba*con County! Can we go there, Tempest shrieks, to drink coffee and eat bacon and see how big people's butts are in Butts County!

Petal said all this was making her butt and her head hurt.

She wasn't trying to be funny. I could tell.

Earlier today I was in Lurlene's office asking her a bunch of inane questions and all a sudden she asked me to make sure I gave her any and all handouts I've handed out in class this week for her to see, so I moped back to my classroom and printed them out and gave her everything.

Later in the day I got an e-mail from Lurlene about my recent announcement about how you'd get an automatic F if you forgot to bring in a writing utensil on the day of a test or quiz I thought was a real super great idea that promoted responsibility under pressure. Here's her e-mail message:

Employee Person:

I would like for you to reconsider the policy you have for automatically giving a student an "F" on a test or quiz for forgetting to bring a writing utensil to class on the day of a test or quiz.

That strikes me as outside our mission and too punitive. I think the smarter and less negative approach would be to reflect the lack of materials

on their daily performance sheet, which is what the sheet is for.

Either just have a stack of pencils available or let them return to their lockers. If you have someone who is a constant offender, then let's deal with that person individually. Remember, if you, as an adult, needed a pencil, I would give you one without penalty. Please feel free to discuss this with me further until you see it my way.

Your Boss, Lurlene Bougainvillea, Principal, All Knowing and Always Right

I stared at the e-mail a long time. Then I blinked. Then I laughed. Then I felt light-headed.

Now, just three days of school are in the history books and I'm already wondering about the quirky academic motivations of every one of my students and the back-at-ya humor of my principled boss. She really does know how to write memorable performance reviews.

But at this early point in my rookie teaching career I honestly don't feel like I'm in command of anything yet, except turning the classroom lights off.

Before I run out.

SUCH NOBLE WORK THIS IS

To begin the school year I wanted the students to make a list of the reasons about why we study history.

One of the reasons is how much fun it is to compare how we do things now to how we did things a long time ago. For some freaky reason I asked...Do women have babies now the way they did a couple of hundred years ago?

They screamed...No *way!*

Nowadays, I said, if a mom's in trouble, and even the baby, the doctor would probably perform a cesarean section.

Petal screamed that she was born by cesarean section! Oh, my God!

Then Hap said he was, too!

And then Tempest said she was, too, by cesarean section, and that they ought to form a club!

I took a deep breath and changed the subject. I can just imagine them running and screaming down the hall to Lurlene's office and pleading and screaming with her to let them form a junior high school cesarean section club.

Enthused about the day's multitude of educational successes, I, for some masochistic and unknown reason, walked down to Lurlene's office and said in a happy voice that this was such noble work, teaching. It really was such noble work.

Yes, it certainly *is*, she said without turning around to see how happy I was and how noble I looked and felt. She's always doing something on her computer or talking on the phone or watching kids and other teachers out of the window by her desk.

I asked her why did you become a principal when teaching is so much more fun?

Lurlene turned around and said with a kindly wink and an iniquitous grin...So I can torture teachers.

THE EAGLE FLIES ON THURSDAY

They're still trickling in. Another new victim of learning today. Her name's Debbie and she's been a student here for several years, even last year, but the last two weeks of another school this year weren't going real good. So welcome back, Debbie.

Debbie knows the scene and she scoots into the classroom and asks me if I have seating assignments. I said you can sit on Petal's head if you want.

Debbie made a funny face...like ain't nothing's changed around here.

I gave the pack of first-day handouts to Debbie so she'd start to get caught up with the rest of the class. On the first handout in the pack there's a picture of Tomo-chi-chi and his little nephew who's holding an eagle in his lap. All that's right by my e-mail address on the page and my name so they know my name. You'd be surprised. In the heat of the passion of answering a question together with all the frantic arm and hand wiggling they sometimes forget your name even though frantic arm and hand wiggling always gets my attention enough.

I told Debbie Tomo-chi-chi's nephew was called Toonahowi (which is true) and I don't know if the eagle had a name (which I really don't) and moments after the etching was over they ate the eagle. They sure did eat that eagle.

Debbie looked at me for a long time, and then back at the picture of the famous etching and said...What a couple of *pickle* ticklers.

She must have learned that one at her old school.

THE BEST WAY TO A MAN'S DUODENUM

I got assigned parking space number 18 in the faculty parking lot. Lurlene and her husband, who I found out a while back is Old Burrell, always pull in about the same time across from me. Old Burrell's classroom is across the hall from me. He still teaches literature. He's one hundred years older than Lurlene who ain't a spring breeze herself.

They met while they were both teaching at another school back in another millennium. Lurlene said she was rifling through Old Burrell's refrigerator one night over at his gross apartment whose carpet was made of layers of stinky running shoes and Old Burrell was sitting at the kitchen table and she said he all of a sudden said...Lurlene, I *love* you.

Stunned still, gawking at something scary wrapped in plastic, Lurlene told me she just about gave birth to a Buick Regal.

This is the stuff you learn during teacher workday faculty meetings before school starts about your boss' personal life.

In the parking lot I said to Lurlene and Old Burrell...Don't it embarrass you that your county sticker on your car tag says Pickens. Ain't nothing comes from Pickens County, Georgia but drooling rednecks. That's what I said to her. Lurlene and Old Burrell live up in the north Georgia mountains.

So then I see Lurlene hauling a huge plastic grocery bag out of her truck full of huge plastic tubs full of rich, gourmet food she cooked this week for Old Burrell and had left over. She was taking it in for their gourmet lunch.

I said I bet all you two do every weekend up there in the

fresh mountain air is cook and chase each other around.

Lurlene gave Old Burrell a funny look and said all they do is *cook*.

SPIKE IN TOYLAND

On the last day of the week of the first week of school we come to the undeniable case of Spike, the former seventh grader who is now an eighth grader who is an elf.

Spike was an elf in seventh grade, I remember, from subbing around campus, and he is still an elf and he is ageless and changeless and brings fun and humor and mischief to the dreary world of the rest of us boring people. I have that certain funny feeling that we'll come to the undeniable case of Spike every day this year.

This year, Spike has no more—or less—freckles. He still has a million of them. His orange head hairs still stand on their ends. Like a mood ring, the color of his eyes still change from blue to green when he gets worked up. His voice is still squeaky. Spike has grown to a height of ten inches.

He is constantly moving, picking at something on his flesh…thinking, pondering, brooding, calculating, prognosticating, anticipating, commenting. His eyes are always open, watching for opportunities to please. His manners are natural and wonderful and instantly make me feel better.

Outside, during breaks, he'll have in his hands a string. Then the string will end up with two knots, one on each end. Then Spike will come show you how the string he's been playing with might be used to save civilization from evil. In several different and believable ways. Just him and a string with knots. I don't have a reason not to believe him.

He comes to school with a small ball covered with massage nubs. He also pulls out of his pocket a multi-colored plastic contraption that spreads out into a ring you can throw to your pals like a Frisbee. And when you're finished throwing it to your pals you can squeeze it back and you can put it back into your pocket...but Spike doesn't put it back into his pocket. He keeps playing with it in homeroom...while we're having our big group meeting on Friday morning where the teacher sitting next to him...me...has to constantly ask him to put it in his pocket.

Spike doesn't put it in his pocket. He puts it back there between the chair and his back. Next to his massage ball. Then he starts picking at something on his left leg with the metal ring of a pencil that would have held the eraser but the eraser has already been bitten off and the rest of it pulled out to be inspected and put to some use only Spike knows.

Spike brought to school this week a huge ball of yarn he keeps in his jacket pocket hand-warmer pouch and off of the huge ball of yarn he spins fibers between his fingers and in a few minutes he'll have a sturdy braid and later when you look again he's turned the braids into some kind of coaster or hair extension. Anything he makes he'll happily give to you.

He is in constant motion. Small, quick, constant motions, like a bug or a lizard. He has bright, darting eyes. A quick smile. Always a Yessir and a Thank you and a You're welcome. If Spike is not an elf he is a tree squirrel who drinks gallons of espresso.

I think he's an elf who has the genes of a tree squirrel.

He recently, in another class, probably under the cloak of the desktop, came into our afternoon homeroom class with dollar bills he had formed, origami style, into butterflies, onto which he had attached large paper clips so that when he placed the currency concoction above each ear the paper clips would also be inserted into the hair so they'd stay in place while we admired them. He moved his head from side to side. He was sitting in the desk with both legs underneath him.

This week, preparing the fall semester Georgia history syllabus, which the students sign, then becoming a contract, I'm asking them what three or four things can I do in the classroom as your Georgia history teacher this year to help you help me help you. I came to Spike.

Spike said he appreciated having study guides prior to tests; that he enjoys projects; he is delighted thoroughly and educated by going on lots of field trips; and he loves watching documentaries on the flat screen TV in the corner.

I can do that.

Spike is a one in a million billion eighth grader elf, who coats and then soaks me with his personality every day, but he's right in line with the rest of my historians on what I can do, seriously and syllabus-wise, to help him help me help him...God help *us*.

Before we went home today, in the last home room of the day, as they pack up and see me melt into an end-of-the-week giddiness and goofiness I get the impression they like, I ask Spike what else I could do to help him succeed in school and in life and help me help him help me. It's as if Spike had been waiting for the question all of his life.

Spike immediately says he'd like to have spider legs that could pop out of his back and help him crawl across the ceiling.

I ask him, giggling, actually trying to keep the giddiness going...And anything *else?*

And he'd like to have the power of invisibility. In his elf voice, Spike says, he'd like to have the power of tele-por-*ta*tion. Spike says he'd like to have a long monkey tail grow out of the end of his spine that he can whip around.

You cannot deny this child. No one, of any age, can deny Spike his time in their face and life. So we burst out laughing and point at Spike and pat him on the back.

He sort of understands. Spike thinks the way he thinks is no big deal and wonders why we find him so sensational. I guess he really doesn't mind anymore that we constantly gawk at him...in shock and awe and wonder.

It's 3:15. Lurlene screams from down the hall...LET'S GO!

Before Spike leaves for home and the first weekend of the school year, he out-of-the blue says to me with bright elf eyes and a smile...*Doh noh dah goh huh ee.*

Do...uh...*what?*

Cherokee for...Until we meet again, Spike says. Spike says he learned Cherokee over the summer. He said it wasn't a big deal. Here, he says, I'll write it down for you. It's real freaky.

Spelled in Cherokee...Do no da go hv i.

Holy God, this kid. Until Spike and me meet again. That would be early Monday morning.

I can't wait.

•

SPIKE TAKES LANGUAGE ARTS TO AN EVEN NEWER LEVEL

Spike, my teacher's pet, asked me today if they could use the phrase...bitch monkeys...a lot...when they all talked to each other.

I looked at Spike.

Spike looked at me.

Everybody went real quiet.

Spike said in his voice...Just us here in homeroom since we're all a *team* now. We'll use it here and there in our conversations with each other this year.

I kept looking at Spike with an expression I was contorting that gave the viewer the impression of wisdom, experience, age, and maturity. But I think it always makes me look dull. Maybe even stupid.

Spike said they wouldn't say bitch monkeys to anybody else around the building. Just here in homeroom. That it would just be *our* thing that *we* do.

I looked at the other eleven members of my homeroom. I saw extreme expressions of expectation and hopefulness. I got the instant impression that Spike had already worked the idea around the fellows long before afternoon homeroom. I asked Spike would they call *me*...a bitch monkey?

With great deference and respect in his voice, Spike said...Only if you want us to.

A CHICKEN IN BOTH HANDS

If I'm not continually looking for different ways to get information into the brains of students in hopes that it will stay in there forever and be used to save the world, then I'm not doing my job, even if it's a quiet Saturday morning during Labor Day weekend at the local Publix in aisle 7 when all I came in there for was some sugar coated cereal flakes and pork ribs. I also deeply enjoy a quiet but intense perusal of the toy and office supply section. I've been that way since I was a kid.

Nerdy, I admit. But who doesn't imagine all those spiral bound notebooks, one day soon, full of the correct answers and charming caricatures of their teacher's faces.

In the bottom shelf of the toy section there was a box of rubber chickens. Not the big ones that are hollow and way too creepy, but ones the size of hot dog buns—packed with some sort of foam, plucked looking, with the bumps and everything. Painted chickens...in colors of yellow, orange, and red, with a big belly and skinny chicken legs and the red claws. I held one in my hand and looked it over and squeezed it. Attached to one of the claws was a tag that read, Crazee Chicken. Made in China by a company called Ja-Ru. There's a picture of a chicken's head busting through an egg, but the chicken's head is the head of a middle-aged chicken in all the mature chicken colors, with the creepy, floppy, fleshy comb thing perked straight up. The chicken is happy and is smiling. In a word, expectant of wonderful things about to happen in eighth grade Georgia history special education.

I wondered what the security guy watching the proceedings in aisle 7 on a little TV screen might have been thinking: Middle aged man, at 10:36, in some nice golf shorts and nice loafers...Cole Haan, maybe, but well worn...the man ponders...for an unusually long time...our rubber chickens.

Middle aged man in loafers grabs another chicken, looks to the left and then to the right, and then reverently puts both chickens into his shopping cart next to the Fruit Loops.

I'm rolling away but then I glance back to see how much they cost. Less than an 8 pack of toilet paper but much more powerful. I have an idea that will change the future of education around the world and forever. At least in classroom number 1861. I think that's my internal phone number, too. But I don't know because I think calling yourself on your own phone is downright goofy.

EDUCATION IS CHANGED FOREVER

Today I instituted something awe inspiring, history making, and totally unique in the annals of addled teachers thinking up new stuff. It's the new Wiggly Plucked Chicken Award for Class Participation.

If this invention increases my student's class participation and at the same time saves the world from evil, bad manners, certain local and national TV news anchors, muffin tops, Lewis Grizzard impersonators, and lack of global harmony, I'd like to be given full credit on TV after a buffet dinner with all the world's leaders.

Successfully received by its participants? Oh, what a happy day.

Written up on the board this morning as they ran into The Cozy Room of Learning was: Introducing a New Award...The Wiggly Plucked Chicken Award for Class Participation. Good Cluck!

Some got it. Some didn't.

I wiggled the chicken above my head. Its head and neck and legs were flapping around and making sounds. I was squeezing its belly, which feels nice when you do that. I said...the chicken asks you, are you asking questions. Are you *an*swering questions? They don't have to be correct, but are you trying? The chicken politely asks, are you paying attention. The chicken asks if you're offering up discussion questions. You aren't asleep are you, the chicken is wondering.

Levon asked, while I was still wiggling the chicken above my head, if it was edible. Is the chicken edible.

No. And please do not lick, bite, or gnaw on the chicken. Don't fry it—boil, bake, broil, grill, roast it, or microwave it. Don't bar-b-que it. Don't massage it. Hugging the chicken is okay since you've earned it. But please don't kiss the chicken. They laughed like hell. With real and genuine joy.

Todd, how to we ob-*tain* the chicken?

Wonderful question. For those who pep up your class participation I'll chuck the chicken to you and you'll get to keep the wiggly plucked chicken on your desk and allow it to be your friend until someone else does better than you then I'll give the chicken to them. At the end of class, the last two people who possessed the chicken will have their ongoing class participation grade increased by three points as well as have the pleasure and the pride-inducing feeling of getting a piece of candy. Any questions about the awesomeness happening in the world right now?

Debbie said she felt like she was in first grade.

I went over to Debbie's desk and tried to poke her with the beak of the chicken. The chicken, you would suppose, is dead, but its eyes are open. Like I said, a creepy quality to doing better in class. The beak is half open. The chicken looks like it's about to scream something.

Debbie juked her head from side to side and I never could get her with it. Plus, Lurlene roams the halls all the time and looks into your door window and this would not have been a good scene for Lurlene to comprehend.

I went up to the front of the class and made another pronouncement: never question the chicken. I wiggled it one more good time, and then said it again. Never question the chicken. Don't cluck with the chicken. The chicken is always right and correct and omnipotent and plucked. On my desk in the front of the classroom I placed the chicken on top of a book: *Understanding Flannery O'Connor*.

Debbie rolled her eyes and flopped her entire upper body onto her desktop.

We accused Debbie of being glum in the face of wiggly plucked chicken happiness.

After a few minutes of education, I discovered something: when a wiggly plucked chicken is at stake, boys class-participate a whole lot more than girls. I'm pretty sure that means something mildly revolutionary.

CAFFEINE HI!

This morning, as an attention getting tactic, I thought to gargle my coffee. I took a big gulp of black coffee and tilted my head back and gargled it. I gargled it loudly.

The reason I gargled my coffee was because I had tried, ever since school began over a month ago, to get them to settle in and shut the heck up so we could start class by any number of means. Here are a few I've tried, sometimes in combinations:

- Asking them nicely to shut the heck up
- Raising my voice
- Beating the desktop with The Teaching Stick
- Sitting there silently with a dumb expression on my face
- Sitting there like a lunatic whispering things to myself

In other words, just because there's an educator in the room doesn't insure...well...*any*thing.

Benny said that's disgusting. What you're doing there.

Ramona said her mother gargles coffee.

I've met Ramona's mother and she doesn't seem like a coffee gargler, but you never know. I asked Ramona if her mother's coffee gargling got her attention.

Ramona said it gives her nightmares.

JELLY FOR GRADES

Found on my desk late today was a jar of jelly. Nora Mill Granary Georgia Moonshine Jelly, from Gilligan, and a yellow sticky note. His words:

> This if for you Todd. Cus your my faivorihc teacher.
>
> Gilligan

I'll be damned. He's already making a solid F in class and I ride him hard but with an understanding touch. I know that doesn't make sense, but you'd just have to be there. I give Gilligan all I've got, and he gives me back a jar of moonshine-flavored jelly. It's a square deal. A struggling child's affection? How oddly sweet is that?

DE SOTO KNOWS

On page 65 in the holy scripture there's a map of de Soto's route he took beginning in 1539 to look for a bunch of things he never found. It was a tragic journey, but funny for us in a way you never expect when you wake up every morning and hope to produce some intellectual stimulation to pre-teens and teenagers.

Winx thought de Soto's route looked like a llama with wings. Winx also said the route looked like a dog and he'd vote for a dog if it came to a vote. He loves dogs. Especially warm puppies, he says.

Benny said it looked like a dog, too.

I said it looked like a chicken. You all need to look at it a lot more intellectually. De Soto would want that.

Winx said it looked like Benny.

Johnny said it looked like some kind of bird.

Someone said a buzzard.

Ramona said it looked like Pegasus.

I asked Ramona what's a Pegasus.

Ramona said it's that white horse who has wings.

Okay. A horse with wings. Pegasus or not, I said I'd like for us to decide what de Soto's route looked like before we move on as I'd hate for y'all to graduate into ninth grade still wondering. Boy it sure does look like a chicken, I said one more time.

The kids voted, while I winked at a few and glared at the others. The result: Desoto's route looks like a chicken. The kids seem to really be getting it now.

DOGS CRY, TOO. THEY SURE DO

One less and I'm a mess. It's Ramona. Here she was making class time wonderful since mid-August and in an instant she's already many miles away in a girl's boarding school in the Smokies. Lurlene told all the teachers privately. The problems are not in school, but elsewhere. Sometimes what's really happening in a kid's life is what friends and teachers don't know or see.

Now I'm thinking about Ramona's mother, who we all know so well by now. She's a saint. Every interaction I've had with her this year made me feel better. I'm sure the decision was painful. Every decision you make for a child is painful in some way. Like golf: every shot pleases somebody.

I have an image of Ramona in my mind and she's smiling and being so polite and giggling and working so hard to contribute to class even if her best contribution so far is about gargling coffee. Her parents are so devoted to this child. They would do anything and everything for her...and are doing it.

I have in my desk drawer the little red dog Ramona gave me the very first day of school. Radish the Dog. A red, tan, and black Teenie Beanie. He doesn't look happy about all this either. The first day of school she ran in here and gave me

Radish the Dog and ran back out like she was embarrassed about it. Five minutes later I had her in first period. She always sat in the front row, to my left. Lurlene said if Ramona does well maybe she'll be back for our spring semester.

I hope so. I really do. Anyway...Ramona's gone on. I feel like I'm rambling and babbling here. But I feel like I deserve an unhinged moment. I just lost one of my favorites.

SOUTHERN RAIN

Principal Lurlene called all her teachers and said we had the day off. Bridges were out and so were a lot of streets, she said.

It's rained that hard for so long. I asked her what she was going to do with her free day and she said she was going to cook something. I imagine Old Burrell was going to do a lot of the eating. Anyway, they're already calling it the Great Georgia Flood. It hasn't been great for a whole lot of people.

I turned on the TV and the 81st governor of Georgia said he'd really like for everybody who doesn't need to go out to stay inside and be safe. Later, a local TV reporter interviewed one of those good ol' boys who work our roads who said we'd really appreciate it if folks would stay home and quit poking around and *gaw*kin' and let us do our *jawbs*.

I walked down a road near where I live and asked the good ol' boy who works the roads for the city if I could walk down the road and look at the bridge. He had his city truck and some orange cones and some yellow tape blocking off the road.

He said I don't care.

Some woman comes rolling up and she didn't know the roads real good and he tells her the best directions to get where she's going and she looked a little freaked out as she drove off.

The good ol' boy says to me these people come down these roads all the time and when they have to go some other way it just *bowggles* their *minds*. He threw his hands in the air.

Pays to know your area I said. I was puffing on a delicious cigar.

He said the water was bubbling up through the bridge. About three or four in the morning he said it was over the bridge but it's just right under the bridge now. He moaned we're probably going to be here all night. He looked like he needed a cold can of beer.

I walked down the road. The road crosses over a big stream that flows out of a little spring. I looked at a map a while back because I wanted to know the stream's genesis. The big stream is called Big Creek, and it's a tributary to the Chattahoochee River that eventually flows to the Gulf of Mexico. The sun was coming out finally, and mixed with the humidity I felt my neck and face begin to burn. I was thinking that detoured woman should buy a map and get to know the local scene. I told my little historians while I was teaching them a little geography one day that the moment you look at one of those maps you get from the gas station you get all intimidated and you shouldn't be. Maps are made to help you. Maps are full of information. Hell, you couldn't run a war if you didn't have maps. Cartography. It ain't for nerds. Understanding maps is James Bond cool.

You know it's been a bad rain when you see so many

dead frogs. I saw a lot of them along the side of the road. The air smells different during a flood. I got to the bridge and they had put some asphalt in the cracks in the road surface of the bridge. You could easily mush the asphalt with your shoe. I like that fresh asphalt smell. But, this was dangerous water. Orange, rushing, angry water. It was so high it altered all your memories about what the area used to look like. I go over this bridge at least four times a day. A huge, amber colored ant was walking across the bridge on top of the guard rail, going eastbound. Taking the highest road. The amber ant sparkled in the sun.

I started walking back. Next to the road and through the woods is a nice private golf course. I used to play it a lot. I walked up through the woods and onto a concrete cart path and saw another altered landscape. The fairway of the fifth hole of the course was under water, all the way from the men's tees to the green. It's a par 5. The orange water wasn't still. It was flowing, but it was strangely quiet here, on the golf course. A hawk circled overhead. I called my best friend, who I used to play golf with on this course a million times, and left him a voice mail message. I said in a somber tone, You would not believe what I'm looking at right now.

I get back up to the road block and a guy in one of those huge pick-up trucks comes rolling up. He gets told the detour deal by the city road worker. Then the guy in the pick-up truck says something I haven't heard in a long time. And you could tell the guy meant it, too. You could tell he wasn't making fun of the two rednecks standing there sweating and breathing cigar smoke by some warning cones and flapping caution tape. The guy says in a real loud southern accent, Dad *gum*…then guns his diesel-sucking monster and roars off.

The South ain't dead. It's rising and a little angry. And it's orange.

CINEMA ENEMA

Here are now five revelations learned after only five minutes into the first movie of the school year. The movie was about the glorious founding of our beloved state:

- During the showing of a movie…never, ever blurt out that that part's important to remember. They don't like it when you do that.
- During a showing of a movie, never, ever, ask them if they understand that last part.
- During the showing of a movie, never, ever ask them if they remember when we talked about that exact same stuff a few days ago.
- They like the lights turned off and the window blinds closed.
- After the movie, if you ask them questions about the movie and most of them don't have a clue what you're talking about and you offer to show the movie to them again they don't want to see the movie again.

So…revelations. One of my little historians said Savannah's a real nice place now. Forrest Gump lives there.

STRAIGHT FLUSH

A Monday is a perfect time to give some power back. I've

learned that when you make major announcements on a Monday it gives the impression that you spend all your personal time on the weekend thinking up stuff on their behalf while ignoring your personal needs and desires, and then there are always some students who don't act like they've been duped at all. Sometimes you think up this stuff while you pull into your parking space that morning.

But I've given this next one a lot of thought and I decided over the weekend that since we're really starting to cook in class discussion and some kids that haven't said a word for a month and half are starting to perk up that instead of ruining the groove, I told them, that if you have to go get a drink of water then go get a drink of water. Without raising your hand and asking...get up...and walk out...and go get a drink of water.

Petal asked...Do we ask you to go get a drink of water?

I believe I just said you could just get up and go. Walk out without making a fuss and get a drink. I scanned the room and looked at their expressions.

Some of them mushed up their lips and looked at each other. Wow.

I said I've got another one. You're not going to believe it.

No way!

I said I've decided to treat you guys sometimes like you're in college and in college when you have to go to the toilet you just get up and go to the toilet. You don't bother a professor who's on a roll by raising your arm and wiggling your hand around like crazy and asking him if you can go to the toilet. That's not what he got his p-h-*dee* for.

Jimmy Joe screamed that's right! You don't have to ask

professors. My sister's in college!

Exactly. So whatever you've gotta go do...pee or poop...poop or *pee*...then just get up and go. Enjoy.

We don't have to ask. You're *sure*.

Nope. Just go.

Wow! Thank you! *Awe*some!

You're welcome. Okay, now please get out your chapter seven study guides and ...

Four of them, at one time, Tempest, Petal, Debbie, and Sonora, bumping desks around and nearly stumbling over each other, got up and walked out.

The rest of us watched in awe.

BANANA REPUBLIC

Today in class all of a sudden Jimmy Joe asked could he go get a banana from his locker.

With a wave of my arm, as if I were granting him the most urgent request of his life, I said knock yourself out.

Jimmy Joe comes back in and waves around his healthy choice for all to see. A great source of potassium, he says, a banana.

You know, I thought, I don't know why everybody who eats a goddang banana feels compelled to say that. A great source of potassium! Hey! A Varsity double chili cheeseburger...a great source of grease! So I said...uh...Jimmy Joe...the potassium is in the banana's *skin*. You have to eat the *skin*.

Hoover yelled...Heck, *yeah!* Another urban myth foiled!

Jimmy Joe stood there, by his desk, and looked at me.

The potassium is in the *skin*, I said. Sure is.

Jimmy Joe peeled off a section of skin and started eating it.

Later today Lurlene honked at me on the speaker phone and said why don't you *peel* down here real quick and let's have a principal-teacher *chit*chat. Taste *good*...I mean...sound good?

Oh, God.

My first question of Lurlene, asked as I was walking through her doorframe, was...How in the heck did you know Jimmy Joe ate the banana peel.

Lurlene, in a pleasant, supremely measured tone, said that you don't *know* this...but *now* you do...but I slip into the printer room right next to your Cozy Room of Learning and listen through the little service window into your classroom to all the fascinating educational opportunities you offer the kids. That's how. I spy on you all the time.

I noted, with a finger in the air for emphasis, that I did stop Jimmy Joe after the first bite.

Lurlene also noted to me of the time I was substituting for Helena a couple of years back. Remember, she said, when you said to the kids that the reason Helena is out today is because she made the finals in a bass fishing tournament in Iowa?

I remember that, I said. I made it up in an instant. I was real proud of myself.

My thought *is*, still to-*day*, Lurlene said, that it would have been *much* more believable if you had said she made the finals in an archery tournament...you know...since she's the school's beloved archery coach.

I said I didn't think of that.

Lurlene said...Teacher, you have to remember that kids with autism and Asperger's disorder take everything you say literally. Eat the *peel?* Are you kidding? Helena made the finals in bass fishing tournament in Iowa? Have you lost your *mind?* They *do* not get sarcasm and wink-wink innuendo and the goofy things we say in faculty meetings.

I snapped to attention and barked...Yes, *sir!*

I know, Lurlene said, I am making myself *so* awesomely clear. I just feel it.

Lurlene had a banana on her desk. I don't know if this was staged for my behalf or if she really did have a banana on her desk because it looks pleasant and wholesome. Sometimes she has a chewed-upon apple on her desk or a salad from Wendy's in progress.

Lurlene held up the banana and pushed it toward me. She said with a mischievous squint in her eye...*Hey*, did you know a banana is a great source...of juvenile humor?

SLEEP OVER

Parent-teacher-student conferences are tomorrow and Friday. There's a vibe in the air, no doubt about it. You can feel it and if you could see the vibe it would look like swarm of locusts.

In my classes today I went around and asked each of them what they'd like for me to say to their parents. As a group they were stunned that I'd offer up even more power in the same week. They're still pretty wobbly about the recent freebie toilet offering.

What would you like me to say to your parents about you? That's a classic calling of their bluffs. I was really trying to be funny...I've got to state the facts, facts, facts tomorrow and Friday...praise and concerns, I said...but they were so stunned that no one came up with anything for a long time.

Dexter, smiling as if he had just been tossed the wiggly plucked chicken, finally said for me to tell his parents that he's still sleeping in class a lot!

He has. For the last month. I finally poured cold water down the back of his neck this week while he was dreaming about algebra. He took it like a man. He really did, waking up with everybody laughing and pointing at him. He said he was sorry. But his in-class comas are getting old and distracting to his mates who want to give Georgia history a try. Your other beloved teachers, I told him, are tired of it, too. I told Dexter, with a wink, that your parents already know. Believe me. Your parents know.

Dexter giggled for a while, but it was a nervous giggle that morphed into an expression of wide-awake silent horror. The kind of expression that convinced me of something: that when Dexter gets home this afternoon he knows he's got a whole lot of pre-conference campaigning to do.

THAT THING YOU DO. OR NOT

I'm standing at the double doors leading to the front of the building, leaning on the window with a heavy shoulder, watching the school's-out pulling up of the various chauffeurs. There's something soothing about this flow of activity. In the afternoon bright sunshine as they all go home...and Lurlene's yelling of her good-byes and of her see-you-tomorrows. She waves enthusiastically at the drivers. And then Petal walks up and says something I don't understand. She seems nervous. I ask her to say it again.

She says it again.

I said, Slow *down*.

Petal said...that she was going to stay after school...with me and where...should she wait...in here or in my...*class*room.

I said anywhere she wanted to. I told her I'm glad she's making a renewed effort. I remember how glad her parents were last week in her conference when they discovered that you could stay after school with a teacher and get insights, tips, techniques, personal attention. All in an effort to perform better in class and on the various examinations that will never end...this year or next year and for however long you want to be in school. I always thought that was understood. The asking for our time. Happily given. Usually productive.

Somebody screamed...BUSES!

The great room instantly cleared out.

It was 3:30.

I yanked open the double doors and they flew out.

In The Cozy Room of Learning I said we've got to cover some stuff quickly. I'm happy you're doing this. Instead of sitting at the desk in the front I sat down in the desk next to her.

She seemed unnerved. Petal asked if she could have another handout that explained the essay project.

Where's the one I gave you?

I lost it, she said

Petal does not say thank you much.

I asked her what were the two things she needed to be thinking about and doing for me in Georgia history right now.

The essay project and studying chapter eight.

That's right. I smiled. That's exactly right. I asked her if she was overwhelmed with eighth grade.

She said no.

I asked her if being organized was too much for her to do.

No, she said. She fiddled with her hair.

She constantly fiddles with her hair.

I told her that if and when she was ever overwhelmed or had any questions that she could come to her homeroom teacher or the teacher of the class she was worried about or to me. Any time. We're happy to help you. We all want to help you. I can't stress that enough.

Okay. *Fine.*

Under the forearm of her left arm Petal had drawn, very recently, a multi-color tattoo, with felt markers. It was pretty good. I asked her when she drew it today.

During break, she said.

Which one.

Morning. She looked out the window at the pick-up area.

I didn't look at my watch. I asked her...Is your ride here already?

No. But I have to *go.*

You just said your ride wasn't here.

I've got basketball practice.

Change of story. Petal was on the basketball team. That's

true. I knew that. I asked her...I thought we were going to work together.

Petal gathers her stuff and hustles out without saying anything.

We had spent five minutes together, doing nothing. All of a sudden I had that gawking feeling you get when the electricity goes out. Left lurching for something, maybe. I'm thinking...sometimes you don't get thanked for doing your job. I know that. But sometimes, I think, students don't know what your job really is.

SNEAKY SNAKES

We were talking about what it would be like to have a time machine that worked...and where and when we'd go.

Petal seemed to have been working up something real good. She literally squirms in her seat when she's been working something up real good. Petal?

Well, Petal said...as if she was a little angry. I'd go way back in time and look at all that *Jee*-sus stuff to see if it really happened.

Wow...good answer. No doubt, I said. That would be edifying.

See...I'd go back and see if all that stuff in the *B*ible is *true* or not. That's exactly what *I'd* do.

Okay. Great answers. This has been interesting, folks.

Then Petal asks me if I thought serpents could talk.

I said you mean *snakes.*

Yeah...do you believe snakes can *talk?*

I asked her why she asked.

Petal said she just couldn't be a student of a teacher if the teacher thought that snakes could *talk*. Petal looked at me hard...with those intense, focused, menacing green eyes and asked me if I thought *snakes*...could...*talk*.

I have never wanted to make a time machine ever in my life more than I did at that moment. What a field trip that would be. Petal and her teacher. Time riding. Myth busting. We'll take the wiggly plucked chicken with us. You know, if that's okay with her.

THE QUIZ WILL BE WAITING

Two less and I'm a mess. This time it's Felix. And this time, unlike Ramona, you could see it coming. Felix hasn't been in class for over a week and Lurlene's been hinting that he might not come back. Was on the phone with his mother the other day, she said. He won't get out of bed. He's overwhelmed with anxiety. It's not good, the poor guy. And they think he may be suicidal. I'll let everybody know.

Anyhow. What are you gonna do.

Felix would be in here right now, in The Cozy Room of Learning, taking the chapter 8 quiz. He made a 97 on the chapter 7 quiz...the best score of all my students. An examination of the life of the colonial people of Georgia. Of sixty-one questions he goofed only two. I went and told Lurlene his quiz was sitting on my desk in the front of the classroom.

Lurlene said she'd mail it to him if I wanted.

I said I'll hang on to it for when he comes back. Maybe. One day. With Ramona?

Lurlene gave me a kind look. She understands. She used to be a teacher.

WHAT DYSLEXIA LOOKS LIKE

For some time I've noticed when you give them the rest of the class off, most of them sit on the floor somewhere. I think when the pressure's off, they like to go somewhere below the teacher's eye level. That's what I think. Sometimes they don't want to go outside and play.

I'm grading tests at my desk in the back and I've got some music going. Just low enough to know there's music playing somewhere. Some others are working on their new study guides or reading a book. A couple are finishing up essays...due tomorrow. It's cloudy and drizzly outside. The moment has a nice feel but fifth period always does. They've had a demanding week, I admit. Covering one chapter in four days is a lot to ask. I do it every other week. And they've given a lot back. So they get to sit on the floor. That's what they like to do sometimes.

But I heard a question. A very personal question. It stopped me. I looked over at a twosome in the back, Herman and Albert. It was a question I had never heard a kid ask another kid: Herman asked Albert what it was like to have dyslexia.

I turned the music all the way down and sort of hid behind my computer screen. They didn't know I was listening and watching.

Albert said reading is almost impossible.

Herman asked him what he meant.

Then Albert shimmied over a little bit and pointed at a world map on the wall near them. He said do you see the word Russia here?

Yes.

Well, to me the A is way over *here* and the R is way over *there* and it's a big jumble. That's what it's like. That word does *not* look like Russia to me.

Reverently, respectfully, Herman said, *Wow*.

Albert asked Herman, What do *you* have?

Herman said all he is...is nervous all the time.

THE ATOMIC BUTTS COUNTY HEADS

They're still reading these dang essays today from behind The Lectern of Speaking because I told them to and they're still whining about it and then when they get to reading them the students seem to like being the center of attention after all.

Hap's up there going to town on his essay this morning and doing a real good job and then there's Tempest on the front row and Petal's sitting in the second row right behind Tempest and for some unknown reason Tempest turns around and engages Petal in conversation and Petal engages Tempest in conversation right back.

So these two are just going to town.

Hap's up there also going to town reading his essay.

I'm sitting at the desk in the front watching and listening to Hap...and then I'm looking at Tempest and Petal...and then I'm watching and listening to Hap...and then my attention once again turns to Tempest and Petal. For all the wrong reasons.

It would have been okay if Tempest had turned around to tell Petal to go find a fire extinguisher because her Georgia history textbook was on fire. But that just wasn't the case as far as I could tell. Tempest just wanted to talk to Petal during Hap's fine reading of his essay so she starts talking to Petal. Petal was polite enough to talk right back to Tempest. Isn't that such a great moment for Tempest and Petal in the development of what Lurlene would call a student's "social piece."

I went nuts. And when I go nuts, particular to a social situation like this, several unsociable things happen in real quick succession. Here they are:

- I yell real loudly what the heck are you doing while Hap's reading his essay.
- Then I sit up real high in my chair and say...time out...real loudly and frantically and then do the time-out sign with my hands as if the referee isn't paying attention to me and it's near the end of the Super Bowl and I think we have a chance to win.
- I watch everybody perk up real super-fast and shut up.
- I remind, real loudly, Tempest and Petal, that a fellow student is nervously doing his best to read his essay in front of a group of people and the teacher lives for these classroom moments very much.
- I look at Hap and say I'm sorry on behalf of these two atomic Butts County heads, Tempest and Petal.
- Tempest says she's not an atomic Butts County head.
- I make the atomic Butts County heads apologize to

Hap and everybody else for wasting our time.
- The atomic Butts County heads apologize to Hap.
- Then I say to Hap that he all of a sudden has the atomic power to boot anybody out of class he feels is not paying attention to the reading of his essay...especially Tempest and Petal.
- Hap smiles and asks if I am totally kidding.
- Hap asks again if I am totally kidding.
- I put my feet up on the desk; I lightly grasped the chicken; and deeply enjoyed the rest of the reading of Hap's fine essay.

TRIAL OF FEARS

I'm explaining that the easiest way to understand why and how something bad happened a long time ago is to look at it in context. Look at it from the perspective of the people of the time before and during the event. Maybe just a little afterwards, too. That can you imagine not having a feeling of owning the land where you live. You just live there and take only from the land what you need to survive. Can you imagine not having a feeling of ownership of anything, really, like the trees where you live and the streams and lakes. And even when you don't have a concept of ownership you can still be sad and mad that someone else moves you from where you live or kills you for your spot by the lake.

It was said softly, reverently, by someone...Some Indians fought back.

Yes they did, I said. I begin to preach harder. I know I'm preaching when I feel like I can't stop or don't want to stop and I physically begin to heat up. Teaching is when you stop, easily, from time to time, and open it up for questions, discussion items, or an in-class break. My own thoughts and interpretations aren't in the book. I know to start asking them to read from the textbook when it's time for me to stop and calm down.

I've got them wanting to ask questions but they don't. I've put worried expressions on their faces. They cannot conceive of this history. It's something bad that happened so long ago. More than last week.

A trail of tears? How can a trail be made of tears, someone says.

Then I get asked another question…Todd, where were *you* when the Indians got moved out?

SATAN CAN GO TO HELL!

Since the beginning of the year Spike has been pestering me about selling his soul. Not to Satan. To me.

I've been pushing him off. That's an important decision in a kid's life. I've been telling him to sell his soul to his parents. I said I bet they'd appreciate having you in their grips even tighter, but that suggestion didn't deter him.

The next couple of times Spike asked me I had some conversations with him about very strongly considering selling his soul to Satan and getting the inevitable over with. Satan, I told him, could probably offer some perquisites I couldn't…me being earthly and all. This didn't deter Spike either, as attractive as selling your thirteen year old soul to the big mischief maker should be. Anyhow, Spike was even more glued to his belief that if he sold his soul to me then that would instantly make him a better student and human being. I was deeply flattered.

So I finally told Spike I had some conditions for the sale, and if he agreed to the conditions, then he could sell his soul to me.

Of course, Spike was eager to know the conditions.

I told him that anything and everything I asked him to do...then he had to do it without huffing or puffing or rolling his eyes or whining or moaning.

Spike asked me to give him an example of what I might ask.

I said sure. How about studying the material for my class, asking good questions, and turning your essays in on time? All of your essays...*on time.*

So Spike sold his soul to me, and to commemorate the agreement I bought a five-foot long plastic skeleton in the Halloween decoration section at my local Walmart and took it home and spray painted the side of the skull and some of the joints and a little bit on both shins with red paint. You know, to resemble the blood that he'll be shedding for me while his soul was my property and he was being a better student and person.

My youngest son, Bocephus, a ten year old fifth grader, helped me paint the skeleton and knew the reason why we were painting it. Bocephus said there ain't a freakin' teacher at *his* school who would *ever* think of something like *this.*

I told Bocephus to stay hopeful.

I put the skeleton, representing Spike's sold soul to his Georgia history and homeroom teacher, in a decorative wooden box I have under a table in the corner of The Cozy Room of Learning. On the outside of the box are two, old-timey, mustachioed gentlemen looking at the flight of a golf ball one of them has just launched. Like they say, Every shot in golf pleases someone. Under the two golfing gentlemen it says, Hoylake 1928.

Perfect.

Today, I described to my guys in homeroom the new agreement between Spike and me. They were real excited. Then we decided to call the box...The Box of Sold Souls. Instantly, Clark asked me could he sell his sold to me instead of Satan and for me to go to Walmart this weekend and get another skeleton.

I gave Clark the same soul-selling conditions I gave Spike.

Clark said he really wouldn't be able to pull off most of that stuff.

For the rest of homeroom, Spike would jump up and open the lid and check on himself and tell everybody he was doing fine and then sit back down. Then he'd jump back up and check on himself ten seconds later.

As a fairly mature and responsible schoolteacher, it sure does feel wonderful to successfully motivate a student...and to deny Satan at the same time.

A TEACHER IN A HOT SEAT

No school for the teachers today. We got to go to a big teacher conference with the hopes of learning new ways to be a teacher. It was way on the other side of the state.

Now, before you think a few hundred teachers wandering

around going to different classes to help them become better teachers was real boring, let me tell you, in the class I went to, Teaching the Whole Child, the instructor held up what looked like a seat cushion and asked if anyone in the class would like to sit on a vibrating seat cushion. You know, to help keep you attentive. We use these in our school, she said.

I admit...the first thought that came into my head was not teacherly.

The blonde haired woman sitting to my right shot her hand up pretty quick and all I could think of—with this woman sitting three feet from me—was that if during the lecture she starts seeing Jesus then holy God almighty.

She's also the woman who walked into the classroom a few minutes before class started and without embarrassment announced she didn't have anything to write with and could she borrow a pen or pencil from somebody. For an instant I thought I didn't have the day off and I was back at real work. Plus, one of the instructors handed her the pen you got for free in your conference bag of goodies and it's the pen with the switches for different colors at the top: black, blue, red, and green. She holds the pen up and squeals, Do ya'll remember these kinds of pens...they're so *neat!*

I was thinking...Lady, we *all* got one. You, too, you goofy schoolteacher. Look in your bag of goodies. Now I was squirming in my seat and I didn't even *have* a sex device. So we start in on the material and there is no way I'm going to look over at her every second or so even although I want to very much but if some awesome force of nature saw to it that I could grow a third eyeball real quick on the right side of my head, well.

The class ran over by ten minutes, so this meant the woman next to me sat on a vibrating seat cushion for seventy minutes without having seen Jesus. I find that extremely gloomy and dispiriting—for her. Of course, you never know. Some women are mighty mysterious in that department I read once in a Cosmopolitan magazine in the Publix check-out line. Aisle three. The article said some women can be vacuuming the living room floor and all of a sudden see Jesus and you'd never know it.

Class dismissed. I got out of there as fast I could.

While I'm hauling it toward home my cell phone rings and it's Lurlene. I was hauling it through old Cherokee Indian territory. Lurlene wanted to know all about the day and what I learned and what good new things I might bring to the classroom tomorrow? Lurlene asked all that in a certain tone of voice that reminds you of your advanced calculus teacher who would scrape her fingernails across the blackboard to get your attention.

I asked Lurlene if she was going to, or had already, pestered all of her *other* teachers on their phones who were speeding home who had gone to the annual conference to see what good new things they'd be bringing to their classrooms tomorrow.

Nope, Lurlene said. Just *you*.

TEACHERS LOVE TO CUSS, TOO

I'm yakking about something about Georgia history and say the word hell in a sentence and I wasn't talking about heaven or hell or purgatory or anything. I actually cussed without thinking. So they go nuts about it and I just get up without saying another word and start to walk out.

They can't believe it. Somebody screams...He's kicking himself out! Throw the chicken at him!

I am kicking myself out. I really am. I walk out and close the door behind me and turn around and make a face through the window and then walk across the hall toward the benches. I'm already exhausted.

Already on one of the benches is a seventh grader named Mink who was in a lot of trouble at the first of the year...and then he calmed down for a few weeks...and now I've been getting the feeling lately that Mink's cranking it back up again for a super big end-of-days-Great Revival-apocalyptic-wrath-of-God hell raising.

He looks up at me and says he's taking a *self*-time-out.

I said good for you. A mature decision. I sat down.

Mink looks at me and then he sees ten kids gawking at me through the window of The Cozy Room of Learning door and then he looks back at me. Mink asks what the hell are *you* doing out here.

I told him I kicked myself out of class.

Mink asked if I was kidding.

I said nope. I told Mink I just said a cuss word in class and I felt like I should kick my own teacher butt out of class since I've been kicking a lot of them out lately for cussing. They've been using the s-word a lot, and very professionally, too. They're real good at it.

Mink gave me a funny look. He said he's never heard of *that* before. A teacher kicking his own ass out of class. Shit, man.

Lamely, I smiled at him.

Then we both took a deep breath and blew it out at exactly the same time.

DISCO DANCING

One day I'm time riding with Petal and we're asking Jesus some tough questions and a few days later she's exercising her freedom of screech in my direction.

When Petal freed it up this morning in the middle of a smooth chapter 9 lecture—we're talking about growth and prosperity in post-Revolutionary Georgia—she screeched that she was so tired of going through the study guides and the textbook every week because this was boring stuff and she wanted me to give them more interesting things to do to learn about growth and prosperity in Georgia and everything we've been studying and reading all year is just not at *all* interesting. Can you think of something better! Whattaya think of *that!*

Several moaned. Several always moan and cover their faces with their hands when Petal exercises her right. They know that when Petal is in a callisthenic mood that everybody suffers. Some suffer because their anxiety level rises rapidly while they have to witness an entanglement and it's sort of unbearable for them.

Others suffer because they love Petal as fellow chicks, and they wonder why she does this about every two weeks in my face, without flinching.

I'm looking at Sonora. She's about to faint.

Tempest is frozen in awe and wonder and fear. Then she

raises her hand and asks in a dry voice if she can take a self-time out.

Go. Enjoy.

Tempest runs out the door.

I suffer because I wonder if I'm doing the right and best and glorious thing as her teacher and as an adult at the moment of this precious teaching moment. But today...you know...today...I said the heck with it. I've pretty much had enough of Petal's miss prissy and massive attention-seeking-time-wasting-girlie-girl-everybody-look-at-me-I'm-so-smart-and-I'm-so-brave-because-I-jack-with-the-teacher act.

Bring it.

Let's dance.

We danced. We twirled. Petal and I spun and spat.

The disco ball exploded.

Everybody grimaced and ducked. Face in hands. Head in hands. Stop, Petal, they moaned. You'll never win this one. Please....*stop!*

She didn't stop and she won't ever win. Not when the entanglement isn't based on facts and common sense and observation and manners and respect for well-thought-out curriculum, school, classmates, and teacher.

I won. Whatever. A dancing contest.

I've never asked a student to salsa, but I will never turn down an offer and they know it.

The oxygen comes back into the building.

Petal's face is tight. She purses her lips as if she's tasting something. Something bitter.

I hope you enjoyed an honest classroom debate, everybody, where the teacher never raised his voice, never got emotional, never got tired, and always based his argument on the facts even when elbows are thrown and for however long it takes with a weird kind of love in his heart for the briefly wayward.

Hoover asks quietly, politely, breathlessly, if we can get back to the textbook.

Good idea. Chicken worthy. Hoover now has the wiggly plucked chicken.

Every minute...watch and learn, boys and girls. You, too, Petal. Especially you. Grow and prosper and learn new stuff. But let's do it all together. Okay? It's the most fun way.

WELL, WELL. A REAL RAISING OF H-E-DOUBLE HOCKEY STICKS

We come back from a week of giving thanks to not giving up.

I turn on my computer and warm up my e-mail and read fresh news from parents...of emergency orthodontics appointments this morning. He'll be in later this morning. She'll be in later this morning. Maybe. We'll have to see how she gets through this.

News of a recently departed grandmother. The family will be travelling for the next two days. Please e-mail us his assignments.

News of a recently departed and beloved family cat...so go easy on him this week. He loved that cat. He was very upset. Then two days later during the holidays he broke his arm fighting imaginary ninjas in his room. E-mail with your observations, if any. He's not had a good week. Anyway, hope everybody had a nice Thanksgiving!

And a first-person witnessing of two sunburned eighth

grade girls who visited a beach in Florida together. Petal had four Band-Aids on her face to cover up the open wounds made by too much sun...there had been some peeling open and weeping of too-fine skin. The embarrassment was palpable. Petal wouldn't look me in the eye and she normally bores right through me. Most days she'd like to choke me with both hands. It's just something a teacher knows.

I didn't say anything...ask anything...or look at her in any way differently than I normally do. I was proud of myself. Acting is a skill teachers need from time to time: to help someone else save face.

Her party animal buddy got scorched, too, and told a tale to the rest of the class, while subtlety smiling my way, of having to be zipped to the Daytona Beach emergency room for nearly sun-burning her head off.

I wouldn't have been surprised if she had winked at me.

She was still painfully red in other odd places...the red streaks on her neck looked like tattoos angrily applied. Blotches on her arms and legs. Her scalp line. On full display. But she was a good sport about it. Because you could tell that over a Thanksgiving break in sunny Florida, eighth grader Debbie Jenkins thought she had raised some hell.

THE NAKED TRUTH

I've got a real social documentarian in fifth period. It's Jimmy Joe.

Lately we've been talking about why we study history and one of the reasons is because it's fun and interesting to compare how we did things a long time ago to how we do them today. Some things have really changed, in other words. Some ain't. In the essay portion of the quiz I asked the students to pick one of the five big reasons we discussed in class and expound on it.

Here are the words of Jimmy Joe, unedited:

> **I like to study history because I like to compare the history of American ettiquite to what it is now. If some colonial person from the past went to the shopping mall in the present, they would be freaked at the poor manners and half-nakedness of teenagers.**

MARTHASVILLE MYSTERY TOUR

It's freezing outside and here I am shoving extra sock hats and gloves into a hideous bright green adidas shoulder sack just in case no one's noticed it's freezing outside and they don't have these human essentials that keep you from dying while we're on an outdoor history field trip. Some of them want more history. I'm happy to oblige. Even on a Saturday.

A few weeks ago I learned about a fellow who gives walking tours to groups on top of and under and even farther under the streets and viaducts of ancient Atlanta. The tour guide is Jeff Morrison and he's an architect and he's worked in downtown a long time and has walked a large part of it, and then he came up with the idea of this walking tour.

You have to e-mail him to sign up for it. The tour, called Unseen Underground, is only for people who really dig this kind of thing. It's out in the elements and you get to see, by default, certain human elements of the city, too. It's about a four to five mile walk, out where the railroads once merged, and still do today, but on a smaller scale, and exactly where their spewing engines stunk up a patch of the Confederacy. Thrasherville, then Terminus, this patch was once called. Then Marthasville. Atlanta.

Then Sherman's army.

I'm pulling into a Red Lobster a few miles north of Atlanta to pick up Johnny. It was asked if the teacher could pick him up near the highway and drop him off back home as it would be greatly appreciated by Johnny's parents.

No problem.

We meet up in the parking lot and Johnny's dad noted that it was noted to him by Johnny that Johnny didn't actually finish the recent final exam and even though he didn't have an exam Monday and had the day off could he come back Monday and finish it up. It would mean a lot to him to improve the 72 he scored...and to me and his mother. We know he's a slow worker.

I said he does work slowly...I know that, too...but he cares like no one else. I know he wants to be successful, I said. Here we are standing in the parking lot of a Red Lobster and it's south of 40 degrees and not expected to do better. Here we are on a Saturday where Johnny could still be asleep and upon waking could spend the day watching TV or killing zombies in video games. Instead, here is Johnny going on my field trip. Johnny's okay with me.

We're heading south and I look over at Johnny and he's slightly smiling. I figure he thinks it's pretty freaky to be flying down a highway with your teacher in his muddy truck with fake bullet hole stickers all over it who's dramatically breaking the speed limit. I asked him did he feel like puking.

He said no. He was okay.

I said with the way I drive you might start to feel like puking, but I didn't bring the trash can from The Cozy Room of Learning, so if you puke...puke out the window and spray the cars behind us, okay?

He started laughing, but he wouldn't look at me.

That's the first time I've seen him laugh in a long time. I asked him what geographical feature was it we're about to cross. I pointed over to the right. We blew by a sign that said Luther S. Colbert Memorial Bridge.

Johnny looked out over a flowing body of water.

We passed over it and down the highway a good ways.

He finally said, The Chatta...*hoo*chee.

We get to downtown and find a parking spot in a parking garage for three dollars and walk across the street to our meeting spot. A corner of Steve Polk Plaza. I'm a Georgia history teacher and I don't know who Steve Polk is and I feel slightly terrible about it. He did something to earn him a marble monument with his name on it, though, but I'll worry about Steve Polk later.

Then Dexter pulls up and his mother is driving an SUV with a dog that sort of looks like a poodle in her lap. Dexter's all excited and bundled up. Dexter's always all excited when he's not asleep. We talk and decide I can give Dexter a ride home, too. Dexter's mom zips away with her dog. I asked Dexter how much coffee he's had this morning.

Then Earl and his mom and dad show up and they're all excited about the tour, too. Earl's so bundled up he looks like an astronaut.

Then Jeff comes walking up and we all hand him twenty bucks.

All of a sudden I'm wondering where it is we'll pee.

Jeff lines us up and he stands on a little curb built around the base of a tree in the park. He tells us what we're going to see while he passes out some booklets he's made that have pictures of all the old sites we'll see...or attempt to conjure up in our minds because most of these sites have been torn down or blown up.

While he's telling us about the day ahead, a hardy-faced street woman with wild grey hair a few yards from us with a number of filled-up shopping bags lined up in a row beside her starts shouting Mother fucker! real, real loudly to no one in particular. It seems she's just angry at the air at the end of her nose.

Jeff continues his talk without pause. He didn't even look over there.

Mother fucker!

Everybody looks at each other with wide-eyes.

I'm shivering and wondering if our tour guide will tell us where we'll be able to pee.

Dexter and Earl and Johnny are smiling. They're really enjoying this. I can tell.

She screams again. Mother fucker!

Then we go underground. Or so it seems. Jeff takes us to deep and dark places under viaducts. We're actually standing on original Atlanta streets...we're actually standing a few feet away from the exact spot where the zero mile post was set in the ground to mark the end of the line...to mark where men would end the line and begin again to build rails that would open up the interior of Georgia to commerce and movement and goods and progress. The Chattahoochee River, north of us, is not navigable by boats and barges. Trains, loaded with things people need, can go anywhere. That's why Atlanta became a railroad town.

So we move on…back in time…and it feels wonderfully unnerving. Everywhere we walked I felt as if we were there to respect the dead, too. Everywhere we walked in the cold December wind we were constantly reminded of what gave birth to Atlanta: the sound of trains and their horns. Modern sounds, but rumbling and ghostly, too. Asking us, maybe, on our special Saturday field trip, to remember that a long, long time ago, right here, and right over there, and right under our feet, that people were once living and working and building and fighting and resurrecting and dying and making history for us…so mightily and so fearlessly that one day certain citizens would crave to understand it and respect it and want to steal it for ourselves.

And we're still here, in the new cycle. Resurrected. Reconstructed enough.

On the way back up the highway in my truck, rumbling toward where we all lived, Dexter and Johnny and I finally warmed up, but chattered forever about the mystifying screams we'd heard and the mystifying things we'd seen.

A PENCIL MARKS THE SPOT

Yesterday, Honoria left her Georgia history textbook, number 41, in The Cozy Room of Learning. Honoria is the smartest kid in the building. Later in the day I put it up on the

Todd Sentell

bookshelf and figured she'd discover it was lost and come back for it before she went home. The book had a fresh pencil stuck in it and I figured she'd want that, too, so I kept the pencil in there.

This morning, early, even before Lurlene or Coco the assistant principal got here; and even before the hallway lights had been turned on, Honoria quietly tapped on my door and asked me if someone had left a textbook in here yesterday.

I said...Someone?

Yes.

I said...You mean someone named Honoria?

Yes, she said softly. *Me.*

I said it's up on the shelf over there where I keep the recently orphaned.

Honoria moped over to the bookshelf and grabbed her book, and then pulled the pencil out and stuck it into the pocket of her skirt. As she was walking out she smiled at me.

I think she understood what just happened. Left-behind Georgia history textbooks are safe with me.

THE SUMMARY IS SPIKED

Today some things teachers call Damn ASPPs were due to Lurlene from all the teachers. ASPP is short for Academic and Social Progress Program. Every student has a big, orange, personal file and inside is all the academic and diagnostic information about the student from the day they began at the school, and even items from their old school.

Every teacher has to update the Damn ASPPs of the students in their homeroom and it takes about an hour to do

100

a good job on one and everybody's got about ten to twelve kids in their homeroom. That's why teachers call them Damn ASPPs. Privately, of course. Lurlene thinks we love doing these things.   •

While you're writing your summaries you know the only audience is Lurlene and the kid's teachers next year, a small but deeply interested audience.

For Lurlene, she likes to experience your powers of observation and accuracy and the woman will definitely tell you if you have not captured the kid's current essence because she knows them well, too, since so many of them spend a good bit of time in her office.

And for the teachers ahead, Spike's in particular, you write for their future...you go ahead and answer the future teacher's inevitable questions about Spike, like this:

Spike presents himself as a hyper-mannerly, alert, and socially-sensitive young man. His instant ability to make friends; his ability to easily sense the moods of others and react appropriately; and his desire to please teachers and others in authority is remarkable. His bright personality, together with his various motor tics, gives him a quirky, endearing quality, as he does not seem to be frustrated or bothered or hampered by them and in my opinion, he enjoys his tics.

Spike is obsessed with small and various objects such as toy cars, yarn, string, small rubber balls, chains, spinning tops, paper clips, and other mechanical gadgets, and he is throughout the day seen with these objects which he keeps in his pockets and instantly pulls out when he is issued

free time. Spike brings to school a new and different object each day; sometimes two or three new objects.

Spike is attentive, witty, and extremely cooperative, but he also exhibits occasional disorganization, such as remembering to bring his textbook to class or something to write with and occasionally forgets to plan for assignment deadlines. Spike is very quick to apologize for misbehaviors and perceived, or real, inadequacies in the classroom. Socially, with his peers, Spike is often seen during outdoor and indoor breaks moving from group to group, establishing some sort of interaction, and then moving to the next group. He is always immediately accepted into the group. Spike benefits from positive reinforcement and small classes. His ability to quickly remember key facts of the current topics of study in one-word or short-phrase answers in general class discussion and in pressurized, fast-paced test review games with his classmates is remarkable.

But I left something important out, on purpose, because I didn't want to scare off his future teachers and possibly make them change careers. They'll just have to experience this particular thing of Spike's on their own. I know I had to.

About twice a week or so in morning homeroom, Spike drops to the floor, pulls both ankles behind his head, locks them together, pokes his arms out to the side like airplane wings, and rocks back and forth on the bony knobs of his spine while he smiles and gladly answers our questions.

That, too, remarkable.

TOO MUCH INFORMATION

And then on a Saturday morning...you wake up, rested and refreshed, and refresh your school e-mail...and Lurlene says to all of her teachers that we've just learned that Shoshana's father has committed suicide. Just so you'll know. We'll meet about it Monday morning. Hang in there and thanks for all you do.

Then the next e-mail is a 673 word cacophony and bad grammar from a mother who's upset about her son's B+ grade. Two sentences, maybe, would have complained about the B+ just fine.

Some days, especially on a Saturday morning, who do I worry about the most? It ain't the kids.

So what do you do now? I go to Walmart and buy a new vacuum cleaner.

I come home and put the vacuum cleaner together, vacuum, and then go into the garage and hit the heavy bag. When you hit a heavy bag you don't always win, but you don't always lose, either.

THE HOMEWORK DANCE

Spike's mother caught Spike gazing for a long time at the go-go girl posters on a history web site. Spike and the rest of them are doing a history web site essay project for me. Spike's been real excited about it.

We're about one week away from the due date of our first-of-five essay assignments for the school year. This first one's about one of the five real good reasons we study history...about how interesting it is to compare places and things and people and events then and now. Five hundred or more words, please.

I've had them explore a web site called Atlanta Time Machine. It's packed with way-back-then-and-now pictures of commercial buildings, homes, street scenes, and movie and TV shows filmed in Atlanta. Five hundred words or more on your impressions of the site...why would you think someone would put so much work into the site...are these places better or worse...in your opinion.

Atlanta Time Machine is a history lover's incredible compilation of then-and-now photographs is mesmerizing. Many hundreds of them. The *now* photograph is taken from the exact same spot as the *then* photograph. The changes, or not, are remarkable.

And that special section...that special in-depth exploration of Atlanta's world-class 1950s and '60s history of being a heck of a hotbed of go-go and exotic supper clubs. And the incredible compilation of their promotional posters promoting the exotic women found in such downtown joints. In special outfits. A woman who dances with a little monkey in one of them. I sort of forgot about that section when I assigned essay one of five...until Spike's mother's e-mail arrived.

Oops. But I respect her sentiments, too. Sort of.

Seems that Spike's mother didn't think her son should be learning such things through a school project. Now we're going to have to supervise him while he's looking through the web site. She asked for my thoughts.

Fair enough, I said. Point taken. Maybe ask Spike to *not*

look at those sections while he's on the web site.

Poor Spike. He's got to be thinking that historical study introduces us to people and events...of all kinds. Right? And that if it isn't nasty...he should be able to learn something from it?

I'm hoping Spike is remembering how I've been teaching and preaching to them this way of thinking and understanding. Even as eighth graders...you can think for yourself. Don't be cynical, though. Don't judge adult behavior unless it's clearly warranted. Ask smart questions...of adults.

In this super go-go section of the site everybody has their clothes on. Poor Spike. In his confinement he's missing the history of Leb's Cartwheel Lounge poster from 1965, promoting some disc-a-go-go girls who'll be doing the swim, frug, and watusi. You can see how much these ladies love their work.

I wonder how far Spike made his way around before his research was supervised.

Kitten's Korner...with 35 kittens who dance, sing, and purr. Peachtree at Sixth Street. Plenty of parking.

Little Richard and his sensational show at the all-new Whisk a Go-Go.

Okay. Point taken, mom. This is sexy-cheesy stuff. But fascinating to know it existed in our fine community. Don't you agree?

Anyhow, seems like there will be five ladies at Carl's Club on Pine Street who won't have their shirts on...the poster sort of says. Wednesday is ladies' night, by the way.

Frank Sinatra, Jr. for one week only at the Domino.

Looks like a guy named Larry O'Brien will also be playing...a trombone.

Sockit to me!

Burlesque!

Burlesk!

Cold beer!

Discotheque dancing at the Gaslite Lounge. Congenial hour: 5:30 to 7:30

Sherrill is your daytime barmixtress at the Pink Poodle.

Phun! Gurlz! Muzic! At Bill Bentley's.

Tami Roche will be performing her fascinating dances at the Domino.

Tiny Lou at the Gypsy Room...the girl who refused to dance with Hitler.

Hellzapoppin performed in the Gypsy Room in 1953.

Johnny Morrison...half music...a half wit...at the Gypsy Room.

The Anchorage presents Primativa, featuring her original jungle fantasy...never before seen or heard by an Atlanta audience.

Gawana at the Anchorage. Chicken in the rough for $1.00.

Then maybe Spike clicked around a little more in Atlanta Time Machine, eagerly researching what before-and-after people and places and things and events to describe in his essay...and gazed at a photograph of a former governor of the fine state of Georgia running a black man out of the governor's fried chicken restaurant...with a pistol. Running a black man out of the restaurant with the kind assistance of another fellow who's got an axe handle in his moist grip.

A governor, who really didn't know better. An adult. Just like Primativa and a bunch of purring kittens and a barmixtress and their slick, smiling, shiny-suited go-go-club owners, thoroughly enjoying the Atlanta good times, profitably.

And their loyal customers, some called sex-cats. Enjoying sixteen ounce T-bones...and gyrating girls! Who dance with monkeys! While a man plays a trombone!

Adults. Adults who do these things. Not eighth graders.

Spike whispered to me in his little elf voice the next day, with his teeth bared...I know who I want to marry now.

Gawana? I figured. She seems like your type.

Spike winked at me. And Hellzapoppin, too.

HOW TO FART WITH CLASS

So you want to be an educator? Sure you do. Well then, here's a conversation you might have to have with an eighth grade boy one day. And to help educate you, here's the exact transcription of the one I had to have today...

THE SCENE: Class is over and everybody's walked out and Levon is standing by me while I'm seated at the desk in the front of the classroom. Levon has a big wad of handsome brown hair. He smiles easily and sincerely, and he's got big brown eyes with big long eyelashes. Exactly, he's as cute as a bug. Me, I've got my hair real nice and swooped back and all hair sprayed nice and hard and I have on my new black and white plaid pants with a black and white polka dot tie with black and white check fabric

cufflinks and a French blue shirt with the white contrast collar and my fancy loafers. Somebody call 911, in other words.

THE EDUCATOR: When you farted real bad in class today did you do it on purpose?

LEVON: No, sir! It just came flying *out!*

THE EDUCATOR: Okay...but you saw how it totally messed everybody up and disrupted the class and I had to ask you to go outside for a minute and it took me a while to get them back on the subject.

LEVON: Yessir!

THE EDUCATOR: Are you sick or anything? Do you have any medical issues right now that's making you fart real loud in class all the time? You know, like you've been doing all dang week.

LEVON: No sir!

THE EDUCATOR: Okay...now you know if you feel one coming on in class you know how to squeeze real hard to hold it in, right? You got to squeeze your valve better.

LEVON: Yessir!

THE EDUCATOR: Okay...and thanks for using your manners, by the way. I really appreciate it. So let's do this from now on...if you feel a good one coming on you don't even have to ask me...just get up and go into the hall and crank it out or go out the other door and crank it out while you're walking around in the grass or the driveway out there. Just cut all those bad boys loose and then come on back in and learn some Georgia history. I know you can do it.

LEVON: Yessir!

ET TOOT, TOO, ELMO?

The next day, not five minutes into class, while I'm pontificating about something to do with the fascinating history of Georgia, Levon jumps up out of his desk and runs to the door that leads outside to the sidewalk and the driveway in front of the school. He looked at me and I looked back at him and I knew exactly what was going on. I was real proud of him for remembering our cheese fire drill.

He goes out the door and it still hasn't registered with the rest of the class until he shuts the door and cuts the cheese so loud outside we can hear it in the classroom. Plus, there are windows in the door and windows along the wall and we can see his facial expression which is real distinctive to this type of hygienic activity. Plus, he's holding on to the side of the building as if he's bracing himself for an atomic bomb.

Debbie about fainted and everybody else starts laughing so hard they sucked all the air out of the zip code.

Levon comes back in not knowing we heard his barking hurricane.

I'm figuring it'll take them until college to calm down.

They finally get to taking their weekly quiz and the room is all quiet and all of a sudden Elmo takes a big block of fresh cheese and cuts it wide open.

Here's an educator's rule of thumb: no one cuts the cheese *this* loudly unless it's an accident, so now the classroom of amped-up, amped-out eighth graders on a Friday looks more like ten blind-drunk monkeys in a boxing match without a bell or a referee.

I've about had it by now so I trot to my desk in the back of the room and grab out of the bottom file drawer my can of Air Wick "Fresh Waters Aquamarina." I trot back up to the front of the classroom while they're still going goo-gaw and press the button and start moving that can right to left and left to right at their heads...and let me tell you, the white spray from this brand new, super charged-up can of room deodorant comes flying out ten feet and makes a hissing noise like a NASA space shuttle on takeoff.

Two kids jump out of their seats and onto the carpet face first as if a SWAT team just busted through the ceiling on ropes. Everybody is having a conniption fit. Debbie's into cardiac arrest by this point—she's bugging her eyes out and squeezing her neck with both hands and baring her teeth—and I swear to God if Lurlene had walked by just then and looked through the door she'd have to be carried out of the building on a stretcher. On oxygen.

This is my honors class.

DEATH OF A PRESIDENT

Down in Atlanta at the Atlanta History Center there's an

exhibit called *With Malice Toward None: The Abraham Lincoln Bicentennial Exhibition.* It ends tomorrow, a Saturday, so earlier in the week I thought to do up a little flyer to hand out to the seventh and eighth graders that said I'll be there this Saturday morning at ten anyway, so if you want to join me then I'll see you there. Parents are invited, too.

Shoshana came. She got dropped off by a friend of the family. I had already arranged to take her out to lunch after we toured the museum and take her back to the parking lot of a well known office building and meet up with her mother's friend. Shoshana's mother was still grieving and needed as much time alone as possible to form a family again. Two seventh graders showed up: Pepper and Smucker, and an eighth grader, Zippy, and Smucker's dad, who looks and acts just like Smucker.

Inside the lobby of the Atlanta History Center was a man and woman dressed up like President and Mrs. Abraham Lincoln. The president was pretty dang realistic. It was spooky, actually. Wearing the black top hat and being tall and skinny anyway, President Lincoln seemed like he was about thirteen feet tall. I went up to President Lincoln and shook his hand and said me and some of my students here...*well*, Mr. President...we're big fans.

Come to find out, these two are married in real life and it says on President Lincoln's business card he handed me that he and the first lady now reside in Nashville, Tennessee and are available for business, civic, school, church groups, and reenactments...wherever "His Story" needs to be told.

When Smucker's dad took a picture of us standing there with The Great Emancipator and his crazy wife, all I could think about is what a kick Lurlene will get out of the photograph. This is exactly the kind of photograph Lurlene e-mails to parents to show them what learning can take place even on a freezing cold Saturday morning.

Near the end of the Lincoln exhibit is the actual letter Sherman sent Lincoln that begged Lincoln to allow him to give him his Christmas present: the city of Savannah. And next to that letter is Lincoln's letter back to Sherman saying thanks. Then there's a glass case that holds the items Lincoln had in his pockets the night a good president got murdered by a scum bag.

I took Shoshana to a cool restaurant called the Buckhead Diner. When I was a kid it was a blue jean store.

Across the table Shoshana kept pushing a wad of money at me.

I wouldn't take it.

She said she doesn't eat meat or fish, so thank God there were some soups and salads for a hungry kid. She was already wolfing down the bread sticks. She got a bowl of tomato soup and a Caesar salad. After every bite she wiped her mouth with the napkin. She sits low in the seat and over in the corner real tight. Shoshana speaks in a whisper, and when I asked her to make the choice on dessert Shoshana kept whispering something just to herself and the patient waitress leaned down...then farther down...and ended up a foot from Shoshana's face.

I said after we finish I'd like to stop up the street at a cigar store I know of to get a couple of good cigars if that was okay with her.

Shoshana whispered that her father enjoyed cigars. She

said he had a lot of boxes filled with cigars in a big cabinet in the room where he died.

You hang in there, I said. I reached over and held her hand for a moment, and then let it go.

She looked at me for a long time. She didn't cry, and I thought she would. I was about to. Shoshana finally smiled.

And then we spoke of other good things—academic, historic, and culinary—over a warm brownie covered with vanilla ice cream and a spider web of chocolate syrup. A teacher and a silently grieving little girl. And two spoons.

EXAM THIS

You'd think ten kids taking a semester final exam would be a period of about an hour and half of tranquility...lightly punctuated by the sounds of freshly sharpened pencils scratching out correct answers.

I don't know what I was thinking. I was asked a few minutes into it if any questions were optional. I was asked for the millionth time if the extra credit counts against their score.

I replied that it doesn't count against your score and that's my final answer every time you've asked that question this semester. About one and a half million times.

Johnny comes in. Without a pencil. I hand him one without huffing. I'm not huffing anymore. I'm finally convinced that huffing has never, and will not ever in the future, work not one bit as a behavioral modification technique with eighth graders or anybody else for that matter.

Earlier, when I walked around The Cozy Room of

Learning, passing out the exams, I had decided to say something inspiring, but different to each one. It's not easy to think of ten witty and inspiring things...Enjoy!...Good luck!...You da man!...Over before you know it...Fight the power...Don't puke...How are ya!...My gift to you...Take your time...Love what you're doing with your hair.

Not one of them giggled.

I giggled. For quite a while. Like a lunatic, sitting at my desk, exhausted.

The telephone rang. I picked it up. No one was there.

MERRY CHRISTMAS GRAVY

This is it. The last day of the semester before we go on Christmas break for two weeks. The day already has a weird vibe to me and my only thought is that I'm too sentimental about first days and last days and memories and history. Every day we make history. I care to see it and know it and remember it and that weighs on your moods and perceptions of things and eighth graders you know real well in particular.

Coco, the good looking assistant principal, comes in and asks if I wouldn't mind having a few seventh graders sit in here with me. The girls have finished their exam already and we had them in the great room, she said, but they seem a little itchy and need someone to watch them.

The girls in the group ask if they can sit on the floor in the back of the room and play cards.

No problem.

So they go sit down in the back of the room to play cards. Like older men. Real cards. Real bickering.

After a good while I look at my watch and the clock on the computer and the clock on the wall just to make sure. Then I go over to the back wall and to The Georgia History Board of Knowing What's Going On, and write...It's Time For Christmas Break! You're Free to Go!

All the boys ran out of there as fast as they could. The girls were heavily into their card game. I said you're free to go...HOME! Enjoy!

They sprang up and waved...Bye, *Twad!*

The faculty lunch was nice. The parent volunteer association put it on in the great room in the high school building. Nice white table cloths. Candles. Envelopes with money in them for every teacher and principal and assistant principal. A fire was roaring in the fireplace. The rice and gravy brought back childhood memories of school. We ate a lot of it.

I was sitting by a teacher, Prissy, from the middle school, while I was slurping a big pile of it down. She was working on a big pile of rice and gravy, too. Prissy looked up at me and said...Doesn't rice and gravy make you feel good?

GOOBERNATORIAL RELATIONS

I got up this morning with that Monday-back-to-teaching-school-after-two-weeks-off feeling of extreme wonderment, knowing today that I'll be taking sixteen seventh and eighth grade history lovers down to the state capitol building in Atlanta for a tour.

That's formally what's on the agenda for today, and for the next two weeks we're planning to see first-hand as much dang history in Georgia as we can. We're starting a few days of what's Lurlene calls "Winter Wonderment," a real Lurlene tradition.

During the two weeks right after we get back from Christmas break kids can go to a cooking school Coco's cooked up or go to Old Burrell's sci-fi movie symposium or Mamie and Sally's science extravaganza and they can even go on a scuba diving trip to Florida.

Spike is in my group. We got to meet and talk with the governor in his ceremonial office which is crammed with all kinds of artifacts and gifts to the state. Spike asked the nice governor who all that stuff belongs to.

The governor said the people of Georgia.

Spike said since he was a resident of Georgia he'd like to take some of the stuff home with him.

The governor looked at me for some reassurance. I really couldn't give him any.

Outside, Confederate general John Gordon Brown was still on top of his horse. I gathered the kids around me and asked them if anybody knew what the various meanings of horse and rider statues meant...in regards to what the horse's legs and feet are doing. Or hooves. Fetlocks. Whatever.

Tempest said she guessed it meant that the person wasn't allergic to horses.

It was a breezy twenty-nine degrees where we were standing on our two feet. I said there are some meanings which may or may not be totally agreed on by everybody...but if the horse has one leg in the air it means the fellow, a military commander of some sort, was wounded in battle.

Some of them said, *Oh*.

If the horse has *both* front feet in the air it means the fellow was killed in battle...and if the horse has all four feet...or hooves...on the ground then that means the fellow was *not* killed in battle but that he's still real important. Isn't that interesting? Did any of y'all know that?

Spike raised his hand and asked...What if *all* four hooves are off the ground?

We hoof it down the street.

Before Christmas break I had worked the phone and found a nice lady in the Georgia Building Authority who this afternoon could get us into that little building on old Wall Street, deep and dark under a viaduct, where they keep the zero mile post on display for no one to ever see. The nice lady had us meet a worker fellow named Delmar and Delmar lets us in because he's the guy with the key. The moment we see the physical symbol for the existence of Atlanta, Spike places his wiggling ass right on the top of it.

A FOOTBALL FOR COACH RICHT

Today we went to the historic University of Georgia, and no matter how you feel about the dawgs and the dawg nation and people who live in the dawg nation and human beings who bark and snarl and hate Georgia Tech and the University of Florida...it's still one of the most ancient college campuses in America, especially the real old part.

Spike has brought along a football. The reason Spike is carrying around a football on a field trip and does not have his hands shoved in his pockets like everybody else because it's twenty-two degrees is because he wants the head football coach of the University of Georgia, a nice fellow named Mark Richt, to autograph the football if Spike happens to bump into him around campus. The old or new part. Spike asks me to make sure I say something to him if I see coach Richt walking around.

I don't have to ask Spike if he's serious. I just look deep into his eyes.

We walk through the old part of campus and then all the way down to the football stadium. The football stadium is real big and it's real empty. Coach Richt is not standing in the football field or sitting in the stands.

We ride over to a building called the Butts-Mehre Heritage Hall which is where you can look at a bunch of University of Georgia athletic memorabilia. If we were going to bump into coach Richt then the Butts-Mehre Heritage Hall would be the best bet because we all figured coach Richt's office would be in there, especially Spike. He really felt it.

We walk inside and I introduce myself to the nice lady who seems like she's in charge of greeting people. Spike immediately launches into his prepared speech about how important it is for him to see coach Richt personally…like right *now*. Like if you'd tell me where his office is I'll go on up there.

I looked at the nice woman's expression.

I looked at Spike.

I looked back at this nice woman looking at Spike. She really does have huge eyeballs.

I looked back at Spike and finally realize what a lush coating of freckles he has. That he really might be only ten inches tall. That his eyes are of an indescribable color, because he admitted to me that his eyes change color. They really do. Spike's eyes change color throughout the day...blue to green to light blue and back through his particular emotional spectrum again. The hairs of his strawberry blond buzz cut look sharp and menacing. That the tone and texture of his voice peels paint off wood surfaces and cracks blocks of north Georgia marble and your concentration. Spike pronounces every letter of every word he says and he says a lot of words throughout the busy day. But he has the manners of a butler and I know in my heart that he'll become...one day...without a doubt in my mind...the greatest salesman in the history of human civilization because he is deeply captivating to all creatures on Earth.

Except for this nice lady. She looked fairly unnerved and sweaty and ready to run somewhere...but she retorts to Spike in a firm voice that if folks want to talk with coach Richt you have to make an appointment six months to a year out.

Spike wasn't impressed. He wasn't swayed or moved. Not one bit. He said all he needed to do was run right on up there. Spike dashed toward the elevators. I had to tackle him. Right there in the university's athletic building. But the little elf didn't fumble the ball.

PANNING FOR COLD

They met the governor, sure, but all they could talk about the rest of the week was what we were going to do today. Pan for gold and grub for gems. They frantically asked...How much gold did I think they'd find? Why is gold so valuable? If they found some gold could they keep it or did they have to give some of it to the gold mine people?

We had planned on going to the site of the start of America's gold rush, Tauloneca, now called Dahlonega, in Lumpkin County. We knew it was cold all week but we didn't plan on it snowing and drizzling and freezing up Thursday night.

Lurlene called all the teachers this morning and said sleep in.

I had said to Lurlene from my warm and cozy bed, No problem...*at all!* I asked her did she think Spike would be okay, you know, mentally, with today's huge disappointment.

Lurlene said he probably went on up there anyway.

Later I called the fellow at Consolidated Mines and told him school was out today and we wouldn't be coming.

He said we'd sure like to have you come another time.

I told the fellow he could count on it. The kids were going nuts for today. They really wanted to confirm that they'd get to keep any gold they panned?

In his Lumpkin County accent he said...Thay shar *doo!*

FIELD TRIP CONFIDENTIAL

Spike didn't get to go on the week-long, overnight trip to Savannah and spots here and there in south Georgia, like where Jimmy Carter grew up. Spike was literally crawling across the ceiling and grabbing for me as some particularly happy field trippers named Boog, Percy, Elmo, Sheldon, Albert, and Hap left the building.

There was a feeling, in other words, that Spike might manage to get into a special kind of trouble called overnight field trip trouble, which can be pretty entertaining. Just a feeling. No one got in trouble on our trip. However, here's what the teacher learned:

- All the people in your dining party can easily get their nose hairs and ear hairs and eye brows singed off in a Japanese hibachi steak house in Columbus, Georgia.
- Even though they've gotten in trouble with a security guard for being loud in the museum, it's probably not a good example for a teacher to scream at them in the museum for being loud in a museum.
- If there's a gift shop in a museum, and there always are, boys will spend more time in the gift shop than they did in the museum.
- Later in the week, make sure you tell the boys that the fellow acting as a pirate in that haunted old restaurant in Savannah was really a pirate and see how they ponder over that information for the rest of the week, especially since the fellow acting like a pirate really did seem like he was one, with rotten teeth and liquor breath and everything.
- When you learn that a couple of them have not called their parents not once during the week and when they also tell you their parents have not called them not once during the week try real hard not to act like something is real, real wrong with both of those things.
- As an adult, and a teacher, you will definitely feel a little goofy hoping that there

might be some mail to Jimmy Carter in his boyhood home's mailbox. But you open the door of the mailbox anyway, and then you find yourself looking around to see if anybody saw you looking pretty goofy.

- You might consider pulling off to a hardware store and having a copy made of the rental bus key in order to keep you from totally freaking out and having a near heart attack the moment you think you've lost the only bus key.

- When you ask them to be packed and ready outside their rooms at 8 o'clock and they're packed and ready outside their rooms at 7:45 you must do all you can to ignore their irritating and smug expressions when they have successfully and totally called your bluff.

- Deeply impress the kids all week by asking site managers and museum guides questions site managers and museum guides don't know the answer to about the stuff they're telling you about.

- When Sheldon gets into that weird habit of using cuss words in his conversations and you know he really isn't doing it deliberately, don't give him a wonderful nickname, such as Cuss Master, which is the one we gave him, which then acts to encourage him even more to use profanity in his conversations for the rest of the week.

- You'll be surprised how they don't get mad when you remind them every day to please take showers or baths and to please shampoo their hair. They all know they should practice comprehensive and frequent hygiene but most of the time they're apocalyptically uninterested in doing it.

- When you get back from a week of overnight field trips and you're putting your personal stuff in your truck and there's Percy standing there watching you and you're prodding Percy to make sure he tells Lurlene that you are the most awesome teacher on Earth as well as your hero...make sure Percy's mother isn't standing behind you and you didn't know it. It's slightly embarrassing when something like that happens.

THE GETTYSBURG PROPOSITION

My most dyslexic student read these words to us this morning:

> **Four score and seven years ago our fathers brought forth on this continent a new nation, conceived in Liberty, and dedicated to the proposition that all men are created equal. Now we are engaged in a great civil war, testing whether that nation, or any nation so conceived and so dedicated, can long endure. We are met on a great battle-field of that war. We have come to dedicate a portion of that field, as a final resting place for those who here gave their lives that that nation might live. It is altogether fitting and proper that we should do this. But, in a larger sense, we cannot dedicate, we cannot consecrate, we cannot hallow this ground.**

The brave men, living and dead, who struggled here, have consecrated it, far above our poor power to add or detract. The world will little note, nor long remember what we say here, but it can never forget what they did here. It is for us the living, rather, to be dedicated here to the unfinished work which they who fought here have thus far so nobly advanced. It is rather for us to be here dedicated to the great task remaining before us—that from these honored dead we take increased devotion to that cause for which they gave the last full measure of devotion—that we here highly resolve that these dead shall not have died in vain—that this nation, under God, shall have a new birth of freedom—and that government of the people, by the people, for the people, shall not perish from the earth.

It took him over ten minutes to get through those remarkable two-hundred and sixty-eight, scurrying-around brain squirrels called words. He read each word...he repeated some words...he mispronounced a whole bunch of words, and his classmates, kindly, with understanding and patience, helped him pronounce the words correctly. It was the most beautiful reading of the Gettysburg Address I've ever heard. I chucked him the wiggly plucked chicken and we clapped for him. His happy expression at that moment shall not perish, ever, from my mind.

And because these words are so inspiring; because this speech is so wonderfully well written and so well conceived, I had another student read it out loud because she really wanted to. Montene's hand was wiggling off her wrist. Her arm was wiggling off her shoulder to get me to let her do it.

Montene read the first sentence this way:

Four score and seven years ago our fathers brought forth on this continent a new nation, conceived in Liberty, and dedicated to the prostitution that all men are created equal.

And with that, it's all pretty much equal in the only way my scholars can make it. Our special fun shall not perish from the Earth. I just know it.

REST: ASSURED

I asked Albert why he was so sleepy.

He said he went to bed late.

I asked him what was late for him.

Five.

His buddy, Herman, screamed...Five in the *mornin'!*

Albert said...*Yep.*

We all gave Albert a good look.

He looked back at everybody else. Then he said...It's no big deal.

Herman said that's really *late.*

Then I said...It's not *late*...it's *early.* Anybody see the movie Barton Fink? They said that in the movie. It's not late...it's early. Get it?

They seemed to get it.

I asked Albert what he was doing until five.

Playing video games.

Your parents okay with that? The all night part on a

school night deal? I hate to seem like a prude...but that's hard core. Five in the morning.

Albert said his parents sort of care and don't care. That they let him do what he wants as long as he doesn't give them any trouble.

Fair enough.

We asked him how much sleep he got before he had to get up and get ready for school.

Albert said five minutes.

Herman said he has to have a good night's sleep in order function the next day. Herman looked at Albert.

Albert shrugged his shoulders.

For the rest of class we all watched Albert with great interest and intensity—his head was dunking up and down, his eyelids were closing and opening, his mouth would drop open, his words made no sense, and his class participation grade was not looking so good every minute that passed— while he not so courageously fought off the overwhelming embrace of the great and universal god of sleeping in class, our good friend and leader Hypnos.

The whole scene was hilarious and mesmerizing and full of cozy classroom camaraderie...and we didn't feel sorry for Albert one bit. Come to find out, it all made him smile, and I think deep down Albert loved the attention. Even though he was asleep the whole time we gave it to him.

ERIN GO BRAGH ON YO BAD SELF

It's an early release Friday and in our Friday morning school meeting everybody seemed real chipper, except for Spike.

Lurlene starts in on the charges. They're news to me, Spike's fan club president. Come to find out, Spike has been teasing and taunting a seventh grader in math class the past couple of weeks because Spike thought the seventh grader was annoying and weird. The look on Spike's face when these facts were publicly revealed in our big group meeting was one of horror...then shame. I know. I was sitting next to him and I had to bend down and look up into Spike's face, which he was holding in his freckled hands. Just a few minutes earlier he said both sets of grandparents were coming to pick him up and take him to his favorite restaurant, and now they'd probably find out and all four of them would probably spank him. He said his grandparents had come across the ocean to see him.

I asked Spike which ocean.

He said the one nearest America.

I asked him what his favorite restaurant was.

He said I'd laugh.

I said I probably would.

Spike said...*Hoo*ters.

I didn't laugh. Hooters is an important place, Americana-wise.

Spike gets voted down by all the seventh and eighth graders and the teachers to a level of school-wide care and attention that means his homeroom teacher, me, has to spend a whole lot of time with Spike and write up a bunch of daily notes that Lurlene and even the headmaster read and then to help Spike write a letter of apology to be read to the group the next Friday morning and a whole bunch of other stuff that cuts into the homeroom teacher's newspaper reading time. Until Spike gets voted back up he has to be escorted to the bathroom by a teacher or some other kid who ain't in bad trouble at the time, either.

After the meeting, I took Spike back to The Cozy Room of Learning, closed the door, and sat down next to him in a desk.

He started tearing up, but the tears didn't drop.

I said I was disappointed to hear this new *news*.

Spike said the last thing he ever wanted to do is to disappoint me...that he'd die for the wiggly plucked chicken, too.

Then I guess your days of making fun of an annoying and weird seventh grader, I said, are long over?

He said they were.

I walked over to my desk and got a tissue and handed it to him, and right before I was about to launch into a speech about the evil of verbal bullying, someone knocked on the door. I turned around and there were two mee maws and two pee paws looking through the door, smiling and waving at their grandson, who was frantically wiping his eyes with a white tissue.

I opened the door and Spike walked into the embrace of one of his pee paws. Then they all started speaking to him. They all started speaking to him in Irish accents. Real Irish accents. I was speechless. And at that moment, after having long convinced myself that Spike was an elf, I came to the realization that Spike wasn't an elf at all, but had been a leprechaun all along.

CHICKEN THIEVES

I'm shocked that no one from the United States Department of Education has come down to observe how quickly kids with learning, emotional, and behavior disorders will increase their level of class participation by asking good questions; answering questions; offering up discussion items; generally paying attention; and not sleeping in class by having a wiggly plucked chicken the size of a hot dog bun thrown at their head when they do any of those things.

But some chicken thieves in the high school heard about how much fun we were having, so they stole the chicken.

Lurlene heard about it and said if I make a fuss about it and it gets to the headmaster that I throw a rubber chicken around the room...well...not good for her either.

I made a mild fuss about it with the extremely nerdy high school teacher who masterminded the theft.

The chicken's back. Lord I missed him.

I'm editing essays when two high schoolers come moping in with the chicken. A guy and a gal. They said they found him up in the gym bathroom, taking a piss the only way a chicken can.

Right.

Swear to God, they said.

Lame, guys. Real lame.

They asked me where the chicken goes...where is he during class and all.

I grabbed my chicken and held him to my teacher's heart.

The guy and the gal looked at each other and then at me. They looked like they didn't know if they should laugh or not.

They stood there and looked around the room, unnerved.

I could tell they also...very, very quickly...read a fine quote on the white board behind me that came out of the mouth of Petal a few days ago. It was a good one. I wrote it up there in big letters: IT REALLY HELPS WHEN YOU STUDY!

I know what the too-cool-for-school high schoolers were thinking. It was easy to tell. They were thinking I was the goofiest grown man schoolteacher they had ever seen.

I took that as a compliment.

THE LETTER IS READY

One way to get Lurlene's Irish up is to have a little bit too much fun with her ancient and consecrated school traditions.

In addition to Spike apologizing for bullying that seventh grader, he also wrote in his letter a few more things, with me as his editor. He read the rest of his letter to me:

> I will take full responsibility for my school work without whining, complaining, or arguing about it. I will complete the work to the best of my ability the day it's assigned.
>
> I will not argue with my teachers about what I think is right. Instead, I will listen to all of my teachers quietly and respectfully and will constantly work to understand that they are trying to help and educate me.
>
> Any conversation with a teacher or administrator will be done in a mature and respectful manner. With my peers, I will walk away from any potential argument; I will be positive, mannerly, and will keep inappropriate thoughts

and words and actions to myself.

This week I have had a number of productive moments performing role play exercises...I have made apologies to my teachers and to Ted...and I have realized the awesome power of manners, being positive, and listening to those who really want to help me.

I promise to you all that I will ask for help from my peers and teachers and from Lurlene and Coco when I am feeling angry and in distress. I ask for your support in my goal to be a much better community member, student, and human being.

Sincerely,

Spike

I rubbed my chin for a while, which I hoped makes me look thoughtful. And then I suggested that as Spike reads his letter to the group that we roll in some dry ice fog and then about halfway through it I crank up my patriotic music CD and play "God Bless America" on a loudspeaker of some sort...and then as Spike hits the final sentences that we have twenty Hooters waitresses come prancing in and they're kicking their white boots in the air and each one of them is holding up in each hand a platter of wings and drumsticks...mild *and* hot with ranch and blue cheese dressing...and then when Spike hits the Sincerely part...I'll release a white dove into the air and then we go nuts on the wings and drumsticks.

Spike agreed, totally, that that was a wonderful idea.

We took the letter down to Lurlene because Lurlene has to approve these special letters before a kid can read them to the crowd. She made a few edits that we didn't roll our eyes about and then I told Lurlene that Spike and I had an idea about how to present the letter...a little differently.

Lurlene loves ideas that improve her school and provide happiness to all people and she had an expression on her face that said to me she really appreciated our recent efforts and this upcoming good idea. She leaned back in her chair and professorially interlocked her hands and propped them on her belly.

I launched into the idea enthusiastically.

Lurlene's eyes got wider and wider and wider...then at the last part I thought Lurlene, sincerely, was about to faint.

I had the Hooters waitresses kicking their boots up above their heads this time and I added some flashing strobe lights there at the end. That part was new. I also continued to believe the releasing of the dove part was brilliant. A plump white dove. They have not been known to peck children's eyeballs out.

Spike was watching Lurlene closely.

I was watching Spike. I could tell Spike could tell Lurlene was not pleased.

Lurlene said...I am not pleased.

That's her favorite thing to say. I am not pleased. She can even say it without speaking. So then Spike squealed at Lurlene...But the Hooters waitresses will have on *patriotic* bikinis!

That part was new, too.

THE QUIZ REALLY WAS WAITING

Make fun of me and the chicken business and maybe how I do my hair and pretty much the way I tawk and act in general but I was right on one thing: I've had that graded test of Felix's on my desk up in the front of the classroom since October, just waiting on him for a reason that just worked like a thunder clap of glory.

I've missed him, and every day I sit there and get to see that thing of beauty. An A-plus. A big, wonderful 97 on the chapter 7 quiz, Life of the People in Colonial Georgia. And then he leaves. He was such a great kid. A great kid in class. Kind. Mannerly. He was so missed.

But he was seen today. I'm walking across campus and I see a kid in blue jeans and a t-shirt and hoodie jacket and a baseball cap playing basketball by himself on one of the goals near our parking lot. When you see some kid way out of uniform on campus it's usually somebody's brother, but it was ol' Felix, timing his visit to see his old pals when they came out of the buildings to go home. He'd be able to see them all...and they'd be glad to see him.

He calls my name first and I didn't know who he was...he'd lost weight and had a real pep in his step.

It was Felix, all decked out in what everybody's wearing these days: skateboard sneakers the size of Buicks. I asked him what he was doing.

I'm here to see my old friends!

I asked him how his mother was doing.

She's in the car over there!

I waved. I don't think she saw me.

I asked him how he was doing.

Great!

What school did he end up in.

He told me...the local public middle school.

And you're keeping up? Class and academics...okay?

They're great! I'm taking Georgia history, he said.

But I'm still your favorite teacher, right!

Right!

For some reason he takes his cap off and shows me...his shaved head.

So...Felix...you're bald now!

Shaved!

I told him I still had that chapter 7 quiz on my desk of his...and that he made a big, bad A-plus on the thing.

I did?

Sure did. I shook his hand and told him he looked great...and that I was proud of him.

We shook hands and I walked into The Cozy Room of Learning and thought for a second...I don't need that test anymore. Why would I keep it from him any longer. It's really his...and he earned it and this was the moment I guess I was waiting for. I ran back out and interrupted his basketball game again and gave him the test. See here, I said. You did great!

He looked at the test as if he really and truly couldn't believe I had saved the dang thing. For this long.

But I did. And me and Felix and the school nurse who was walking by all had a pretty good chuckle about an old quiz grade and a kid who still counts.

A CONSTANT COUNTDOWN

Three less and I'm not so much a mess on this one. It's Gilligan, who has an edge, and a certain unpredictability. But he's not going far away…he's just taking his wild thing over to another school on campus. It's the school established for seventh to twelfth graders who need to go a whole lot slower in even smaller classes with teachers who understand Gilligans on an ever deeper plane of unreality.

The reality is, and has been, that this is the best move. He'll be fine. He'll come over and see us when their Frisbee or football bonks onto our turf. Or when he comes over, smiling, sort of at a sideways angle, to talk to some of our girls. He's got the lady's man thing going on. When a recent girlfriend broke up with him he threatened to shampoo everybody's hair with his spit.

I HATE YOU FOR MAKING ME LOVE YOU

I have a phone in my classroom and it's real convenient. When kids need to go call their mother or father or nanny or chauffeur about something, they don't have to go all the way down the hall and use the phone in Lurlene and Coco's reception area.

When Lurlene wants to call me and fuss at me for something, she doesn't have to walk down the hallway. She just honks at me on my phone. She honks at me on the phone about every day.

What is not convenient is to hear kids being rude on the phone to a parent. Today I instantly started a new rule right after Hoover told me he sucked at algebra and needed to go call his mom to tell her was staying late. This was after Hoover had finished a free-form dissertation for us all about his loathing of his mother and it ended with…When she remembers to take her pills.

While Hoover was making his way over to the phone I noted to my class that the new rule I've just made up states that when one of you use the phone, we all have to shut up so we can listen to what you're saying and you have to at some point in the conversation with your mother...your choice *when*...tell her in a clear, understandable volume of voice, that you love her.

They all groaned.

Hoover acted like he didn't hear me.

Hoover dialed her number and he seemed to have reached her. He was sort of scrunched down a little bit, jibber-jabbering.

I yelled...Say it!

Hoover kept jibber-jabbing.

Say it, Hoover! Mom, I love you!

It didn't sound like he was saying it, and I knew he needed to. It's well known that Hoover and his mother have a testy relationship.

Anyway, we were real quiet and it seemed like Hoover was about to finish up so I yelled one more time...SAY IT!

Hoover finally told his mother that he loved her in a loud and weird and animal-like voice I've never heard him use, and I've known Hoover for a long time and have seen him in a number of social situations with his species peers where using his loud and weird and animal-like voice would have been perfectly fine.

We all looked at each other with wide eyes...and then we giggled and pointed at each other.

Of course, as a matter of classroom law, there ain't

nothing in the new rule about *how* loud and weird and animal-like your voice is or not.

WHOSE MOTHER IS A TOAD?

I gave them the rest of class off, which they like a lot. I'm sitting there grading tests and listening to thirteen and fourteen year olds help each other with work for other teachers, with extreme sincerity, while they have no idea the educator in the room can grade tests and spy on them at the same time while he's also listening to the Allman Brothers Band "Gold" disc two. Listen to this:

- No...no...no...solve for *k*. Dumb ass
- My elbow hurts
- If you turn it in late she'll take off seventy points
- I never knew that
- It's easy...but hard to understand. Does that make sense?
- I rush through things
- I don't ever remember getting that assignment
- That's so lame. You can do better. You're better than that
- Why is that?
- You can do this
- Lurlene won't let you freakin' do that...like...at *all*

Those are things they say to each other in the classroom,

quietly, with real kindness in their voices. It sort of thrills my heart. Then somebody grabs one of the school yearbooks and they start going through that thing:

- All the lower school kids are *mean*
- I *hate* her
- All my middle school teachers are gone
- I talked to him the other day. He told me he was dead
- She talks to me on Facebook
- He has changed *so much*
- When he came to my birthday party he tried to pull the refrigerator apart
- Everybody cool was on that bus
- Oh, look...there's memories!
- That's kind of creepy
- She was so ann*o*ying
- Her baby sister is so cute
- I *hate* him
- He's such a *queer*
- She's so nice
- Monica was so mean to me
- He like curls up in a little ball on the floor and pulls everybody's backpacks on top of him because it was thundering real loud outside
- Remember when everybody was freaking out?
- I just can't get over that...it's so *weird*
- She's the one that turned around and yelled at us that we need to stop cussing

- She looks really pretty now. She was a toad for *soooo* long
- Her mother's a toad, *too*. And she smokes like a chimney

LINCOLN STILL LIVES FOR US, TOO

I tell my scholars all the time if you don't know the answer to a multiple choice answer...don't come ask me what the answer is...*just guess*. If it's a question where you have to fill in the blank and you can't remember the answer just give it your best shot and maybe you might get one of the words right or maybe even a letter. Like I keep saying, if you don't try you never know.

Or something like that. I think I might try too hard to convince them that trying feels good.

Anyhow, today's the test on the Stealing Lincoln's Body documentary we watched. Fifty-seven questions pulled from all those fascinating facts. At the end of the documentary, we got to see his tomb as it looks today...and up above the huge marble sarcophagus a message is inscribed on the wall...the words spoken by Secretary of War Edward Stanton after Lincoln succumbed...Now he belongs to the ages.

Powerful words.

In the tomb the passage is written in all capitals, like this: NOW HE BELONGS TO THE AGES. I like that better, because it's better looking. In the test the scholars were asked what was written on Lincoln's tomb wall above the sarcophagus. You had to be paying attention to the TV screen when we were watching the documentary this week.

Of course, the answer was also on the study guide.

Anyway, they were asked on the test, What was written up there. They all responded. Most got it right.

The ones who didn't get it right got it marked as incorrect—I find myself more and more chuckling under my breath as I grade tests—but they got extra affection points for laying these four on me:

- A house divided in itself will not stand
- Once chance by another
- Here lies the man who changed times
- Whatever you are be a good one!

Well, they're all incorrect. I know it and they probably knew it, but they tried. They didn't leave the question blank. Funny, I really can't disagree with the deeper meaning of any of the four wrong answers.

QUITE A CHAPTER IN OUR HISTORY

What was it that made Georgia and other southern states so different from the North and West? The obvious answer was slavery, but there were other things as well.

So begins the reading of chapter 12. The chapter concerning a peculiar institution called slavery...by my only black student, Henry, although he likes for everybody to call him Taboo. Lurlene doesn't like it, but we call him Taboo anyway.

They probably don't go over this potentially intense scenario in teacher's school. What do you do when the black student asks—politely, with the desire to do it in his face and body language—to read the entire chapter? For the next hour and a half?

What do you do when you think he's reading it because you deeply believe he knows this is a particularly historic moment for *him*? That he knows this is a one-time chance? Depending on the circumstances. He might not be able to in high school when he takes U.S. History. He could be absent that day. Who's to say the teacher has certain views...or fears.

Exactly. You use common sense...you settle back...you listen...and then you see what happens when it's over....*Slavery had a long history in America—not just in the South. Every colony had allowed slavery, although officially the practice was banned in Georgia until 1750. Even though the Declaration of Independence proclaimed that "all men are created equal," it contained no prohibition on slaveholding. All of the 13 new states allowed the practice to continue*...and so he reads steadily, but a little too quickly.

I ask Taboo to slow down a bit, but tell him he's doing great...*Slavery is kept up entirely by those who make it profitable as a system of labor.* He doesn't wince, whine, get angry, or question it...*Blacks fought slavery in other ways, including murdering their overseers and setting fire to plantation buildings.*

We finally come to the end. The reading of chapter 12 no one will ever forget. I asked the reader why he wanted to read so badly. Why he read every bit of it.

He said it helps him learn better. Reading aloud.

Okay, I said. *Good.*

Plus, I was sleepy, Taboo said, and it kept me awake. Taboo grinned at me.

I grinned back.

Jasper said…Speaking for all the white boys, we think you ought to chuck the chicken at Taboo.

I chucked the chicken at Henry, which is never taboo.

ANUS IN UNISON

I don't have a third period, but I do have a stack of tests itching for a grade and all of a sudden Lurlene honks at me…If I would be…*so* kind…to cover Sally's class for a while. Lurlene didn't tell me why.

I didn't ask. You never ask why when Lurlene doesn't offer the reason right away so you know it's probably personal and squirmy and you know Sally would do the same for you if your reason was personal and squirmy, too.

I walk down there with The Teaching Stick—their sort of substitute teacher. There was a boatload of seventh graders just squirming to learn some life science, I could tell. I notice Sally's got today's plan all mapped out on the white board at the front of her classroom so I figure she knew something was going to get personal and squirmy earlier in the day…and that's nice to be able to plan on those things. Planning makes you feel good.

Anyway, it says to read to them out of the textbook these pages. I look at the pages in the textbook up there on her teaching desk. It was a whole bunch of business about the human digestive tract…from the mouth to the…oh, Jesus…anus…with pictures of a half cut open guy.

That's right. The anus. The ol' anus.

There is no other good word to use for this thing with sneaky seventh grade kids unless you want them to go totally crazy. Always go Latin or Greek or scientific.

I'm thinking I was going to have to say the word anus out loud with my own voice...possibly the funniest word in the English language next to chicken, duodenum, and the scientific word for hairballs...and try to keep from laughing even though I'm supposed to be an adult at this moment.

So here we go. I started in on the first part of the human digestive system and it's the tongue and the teeth and your spit glands that get it all rolling. From there it's pretty easy to follow the tube but then some smart aleck girl says what about when you *drink* something. That ain't *foooooooood.*

Whatever. After you get the food wad—which we chose as a McDonald's Big Mac combo with an orange soda—past the duodenum and down to the lower intestine and then to the rectum you tell seventh graders that the next word we're going to say you're already giggling about and poking each other over so we're just going to say it all at once on the count of three and get it out of your system (what a great pun) and we can move on maturely. So I count: one...two...*three!*...and to hear a classroom full of seventh graders saying that special word all at one time...well...it sounds like a tree full of monkeys. AYYY-NUUUSSS!

I had them do it again.

AYYY-NUUUSSS!

This highly intelligent scientific exercise was making these precious children so happy. Then I got to actually thinking: almost every day the school's admissions lady gives tours to prospective parents and they walk down the hall and peak into the various classrooms through the door and observe happy children learning wondrous things. I'm sure they would imagine their child sitting in that classroom with me as their teacher growing as a young human being learning about the human digestive tract which starts with the tongue and ends with the anus. I was thinking how memorable that moment might be for all involved if the prospective parents caught it right there on the count of three.

I also got to thinking about Lurlene. What in the heck if she snuck by right when I had my brilliant idea to get something tricky over with in the only way to get it over with...and that's to scream it. And to laugh about it, too. Laughing like a bunch of academically-engaged seventh graders should laugh...right along with their sort of substitute teacher.

THE LAME SHALL ENTER FIRST

I'm really trying to learn them about Bourbon Redeemers and Populists and poll taxes and prison reform and child labor awfulness but they're not digging it. I can tell something else is on their minds...heavily...and the beauty of what we do some days is really found after snapping the textbook shut and asking them what they really want to talk about and hearing them talk about it. So I snapped the textbook shut and asked them what the heck was going on.

Debbie said we ought to tell Sonora how much we'll miss her.

I told Sonora I'd miss her.

Debbie said you don't even know what you were going to *miss* her for.

I told Debbie and the class and Sonora what I knew a

long time ago. And added that teachers know everything...and guess what...you *still* have nothing to fear.

Debbie screeched that this rehab place Sonora is going to is like that show on TV about the world's strictest parents...and that they lock you in your room at eight-thirty and there are cameras everywhere and the food probably is awful...and there is no *way* she'll get along with the other *girls*. She's got to share some dorky room with a bunch of 'em!

I let Debbie roar on.

Petal and Tempest, Sonora's other best gal pals, chimed in, too, their teeth baring. Teenage girl sharks in chummy water.

I couldn't quite tell if this was making Sonora feel better or worse. I could never read her that well anyway. And I tried. I really tried.

Sonora...my second period Sphinx. Just like Huckleberry. Selective mutism at work. She won't talk to teachers.

It was finally time to go and Sonora hung back until everyone was gone and handed me her textbook. I told her I'd be thinking of her and to hang in there...to trust people who are trying to help you and to stay in touch.

She nodded and widened her eyes.

I stood up and patted her on the arm, and said I mean it. Take care. Hang in there. You can *do* it.

Her eyes widened even more.

Mine did, too. Because I saw fear—pure fear about a deeply uncertain future—in an eighth grader's eyes.

HISTORY CAN MAKE YOU EMOTIONAL

I'm sure Helena and Old Burrell, the language arts and English teachers, would be pleased that irony, that ephemeral thing kids have a hard time understanding, was made real today. Tell me, on the day we're studying what it means when groups organize, what are the chances that Tempest tells me that she and Petal have had it with the wiggly plucked chicken...and that it's so immature...and I should be embarrassed to have even thought it up and I'm a grown man and everything so that makes me immature, too...and that, as a matter of *fact*, there is a group of students who have started a group on Facebook called Burn The Chicken.

Right, how ironic is that...and what are the chances? Honestly, I'm not surprised one bit. I'm annoyed to no end, of course, but I'm not surprised.

Tempest, pretty worked up by this point, asks me if I want to know who's in charge of the Facebook group.

I say as smugly as I possibly can...which I'm pretty good at...Nope.

Sure you do. You *know* you want to *know*.

Nope. Could not care less. Then I ask her if she's got her homework assignment ready to show me.

Okay, then. So we start learning some more about Reconstruction and scalawags and carpet baggers and organizing and I'm thinking there ain't no way Tempest has all of a sudden started taking notes in Georgia history class. She's sitting right in front of me and I ask her with a bright and cheerful tone to my voice...Are you really taking notes? That's awesome.

Tempest says she not taking notes...that she's writing a letter.

I ask her if the letter is to the chicken...which has the effect of her, I know, wanting me to die immediately.

Petal smiles...but I don't know whose side she's on at that moment.

Tempest says the letter is to Sonora...who she misses.

I ask her to show me the letter.

Tempest rips the letter from her spiral notebook and crunches it up...and I'm figuring she's thinking the paper is my head.

After some chaos and confusion and some other things...I finally get handed the letter. I uncrunch it. I read it silently. This is definitely what you'd call ironic:

Sonora,

We are in Todd's class. I just <u>BASHED</u> the chicken! I called it a piece a shit! I pissed Todd off so Bad! He is so mad at me. I feel so good! I got debbie's phone. Her mom did want it so I gave her 50 Bucks. But it was a good deal cuz on E Bay it was like $250 usd! So I feel good about it. Petal wants me to tell you we are misriBal in Todd's class right now! This place sucks my asS! I can't wait till next year when I go to a nice normal school

Anyhow, I got a sneaky feeling...that if Sonora got the letter, even in its unfinished and unedited form, it would have made her miss us even more.

RESIDENT EVIL

A long week later, and Sonora's back. And she does talk to teachers after all.

Seems this place where she stirred for only a week wasn't necessarily for unsettled youngsters who might have a future interaction or two with law enforcement if they don't start flying straight. This joint was populated by some young folks who have already *had* interaction with law enforcement. In other words, some of them knew what it was really like to live in a jail cell.

All I had to say to Sonora was...I've heard they lay a lot of Jesus on you at that place.

Sonora said they told her that you had to go to church every day but she said they never took anybody to church not once.

I asked her about the food. I reminded her how in class a week or so ago when Tempest and Petal and Debbie were all upset about the potential quality of the cuisine...you know...during your special va-*cayyyyy*-tion. With air quotes.

Sonora said she got some nasty turkey shit and even then she ended up with just a turkey bone to eat because the other girls were pigs and ate all the meat off the bones and the house parents didn't do anything about it. Sonora said they wouldn't even tell you where any other food was...you had to look for it yourself. Sonora said she had taken some framed pictures of her family and the first night she was there her roommate grabbed them both and threw them up against the wall on the other side of the room and busted them up. She said the roommate grabbed everything she had brought...a hairbrush and some cosmetics and everything that she brought from home and threw it around the room. Sonora said her roommate grunted like an animal and had hair that stunk. Sonora said she thought she was in a living nightmare.

I said you were. I winked and tossed her the chicken. She caught it like a professional.

Tempest and Petal were real quiet. You could tell they were so glad to have Sonora back...to hell and back...that they didn't want to ruin it by flapping their yappers.

Sonora asked if she could have her old textbook back.

I said you sure can. I walked over to the shelves in the corner of the room and told her I had saved it for her. I smiled at her.

I actually think she knew I liked her and felt bad about her last few days.

There's a big row of books and her old one was the second one in from the right. I remember the bottom of the binding of her textbook was torn a little. I pulled it out and opened the front cover to reveal where she had put her name in there back in August. I held it up for everybody to see that it was hers.

Her classmates tlapped.

Sonora smiled and got up from her desk to go through all my geeky and obnoxious gyrations of getting your beloved textbook for the first or second time.

I make a big production out of it. Hand shaking. Arm waving. Humming patriotic music while I march in place. Stuff like that. It's extremely obnoxious.

Sonora endured it without huffing and puffing and rolling her eyes and making the awful expressions I remember. She didn't even try to give the chicken back. It's soft and wiggly and it has a creepy but comfortable feeling that you like and want in your life forever. It's something you talk to strangers about. Of course, I understand.

Sonora asked me if I disinfected the wiggly plucked chicken like I promised I would a long time ago.

Never lie to children.

Sonora said...*Well*, it needs disinfecting for me.

I gave her a Lysol disinfecting wipe, and she wiped the wiggly plucked chicken with the affection and care something world famous should be given.

Everybody else was watching and acting weirdly reverent as Sonora rubbed him over good. Sonora said now he's shiny like a wiggly plucked chicken *should* be—and then she took her old textbook and the chicken back to her desk and kissed it on the beak.

SO YOU WANT TO BE A SPIDER MONKEY?

Apocalyptically hyperactive Dexter was squirming in the desk I pulled next to my desk in the back of the classroom. He had come in for some after-school guidance on how to do a bit better job in his Georgia history studies.

I was listening to jazz tune *In Memory of Elizabeth Reed* by the Allman Brothers Band when it hit me. I told Dexter I knew what he should do when he grows up because of all his sensational energy and sense of fun and adventure. The heck with Georgia history.

Dexter smiled and his braces sparkled and he chirped...*What!*...like only Dexter can chirp...as if he'd been waiting a long time for someone to finally reveal his professional future to him.

I said you really ought to think about being a rock and roll star. You'd be a great one. You'd get to jump around on stage and people would cheer for you and you could play a guitar as fast and as insanely as you wanted.

Dexter's mood darkened. He said he didn't know how to *play* a guitar.

I said you could learn. People learn how to play guitars all the time. And you know a lot of these guys, after they end a concert, jump into the crowd.

Dexter said what if they don't *catch* me?

I said it would hurt a whole lot, but you'd be so amped up anyway, like a spider monkey...but when you play well and sing well and jump around on the stage real good then your fans will catch you. I promise. And then they'll carry you around way up in the air and then chuck you back up onto the stage so you can play some more songs. I watched him for a moment or two.

Dexter was really chewing on it. Then he said he believed they also get to smash their guitars on the stage, too...*right?*

Yep. Some of them smash their guitars.

Dexter chewed on that, too.

I watched him again and then I said listen to that music, man...listen to that guitar playing on this song. It's so good...making and playing music has got to be the most incredible experience, I said. I turned the volume up a little bit.

Dexter listened to that long Allman Brothers' jazz song for a long time—ears perked, like a cat on caffeine—as if the answer about what he should do when he grew up was hidden between the notes.

HISTORY CAN BE RELATIVE

I don't know how it happens even though it happens all the time but I'll be sitting at my desk in the front or at my desk in the back all alone late in the afternoon and all of a sudden I'll look over to my left or to my right and there's Clark. Standing there smiling.

Clark the seventh grader who says he can't wait for Georgia history next year. Clark has a famous and historic relative. Historic in Georgia, that is. So historic the man is written about in our textbook. There's a picture of him in there, too.

Clark wanted me to tell everyone that he's not his ancestor...that he's *Clark* and his ancestor is a totally different human *being*. That everybody's driving him crazy saying he's famous. He's not famous. His ancestor is famous. *Okay?*

I said okay, *Clark*...no problemo...I've got your back on that...and then I asked him has he ever seen the part of the textbook concerning his famous relative and his picture?

No.

I grabbed the textbook and opened it up. I showed Clark the picture of the famous man he's related to.

Clark made a small noise in his throat, as if he was suddenly moved.

I think he was. That's him, I said. You look just like him...or he looks just like *you*.

I don't think so, Clark said.

152

You look alike. It's easy to see.

Finally, Clark said...We *do* sort of look alike.

I told him...You're both smiling. *You*...are always smiling and that's much appreciated. You have a famous smile, too.

Clark reached down and touched the picture. Clark pulled his hand back and he said...I just *touched* history, didn't I?

SPIKE IN LOVE

This morning, for homeroom fun, I brought in a can of Krazy String I bought at the grocery store for the exact purpose of scaring Spike to death by shooting him with it.

I have recently come into the possession of some knowledge that he got kicked out of Mamie's fourth period science class for constantly jibber-jabbering with his new girlfriend, Farrah. This is embarrassing to me, as his homeroom teacher, since I'm sort of responsible for him. There are times when Lurlene will ask you a certain question in a certain tone of voice and with a certain expression on her face that invades your dreams...You got all your boys under control?

By the way, on the can it says, PARTY FUN! And, SHOOTS A STREAM OF COLORED FOAM! In the Caution section it says not to spray on lacquered hair and that adult supervision is recommended. This can of unknown substances under great pressure speaks to me.

During homeroom I lovingly gazed at Spike for a long moment while he sat next to me in the teacher's pet chair and told him with my whole being, through some excellent and rehearsed nonverbal communication, that everything would be okay between me and him and Lurlene if he'd wise up in Mamie's class …

He said in his squeaky voice…You got it, *boss!*

… and then I squirted the holy bejeezus out of him with my new can of Krazy String.

I had it hidden in my Georgia history textbook. And before they had walked into homeroom I had shaken it up real hard and launched a few quick bursts into the trash can to warm it up. I didn't want it to jam when the miraculous teaching moment turned up. I was surprised at how much it hissed.

Spike freaked out. I know he freaked out because he opened his eyes so wide I thought his eyeballs were going to fly out. The hissing yellow stream of whatever this stuff is made of hit him first in the right shoulder…and then I worked it up his neck for a good while…and then I unleashed Hell into his hair.

Spike was scrunching up real good as if he were covered by a bunch of snapping lobsters.

Everybody else was screaming, laughing, and basically feeling great and wonderful as the morning sunshine filled The Cozy Room of Learning.

I instantly discovered that the satisfaction you get as a teacher at around 8:25 in the morning when you squirt one of your students with a can of Krazy String in the shoulder and the neck and the hair was much greater than I expected.

In Mamie's science class today I'll bet he'll tell Farrah all about it.

CHICKEN ENVY

My speaker phone honks and it's Lurlene and she asks what I'm doing.

I said I'm talking to you. I always drop everything when you...*honk.*

How nice, she said. Listen. I need you to hide the chicken for a while. Actually, for the rest of the year and go ahead and hide the pillow it sleeps on or whatever and that stupid stand thing you hang him on sometimes. It's a real freak show.

And...uh...*why?*

Because a lot of the *chill*-ren are becoming real agitated they're not getting the chicken and this whole chicken thing is just going to get out of hand and I don't like out of hand.

I asked her...well...did she know that someone came in here and pulled its head off and I had to go to the reserve chicken? Did she know someone came in here and destroyed my property?

She said she knew that a long time ago. Old news. Just get rid of the chicken. Or whatever chickens you've got.

Now I'm starting to get agitated, too. I was thinking there might be a lot of *chill*-ren *not* getting the chicken...but there are a whole lot of them who want it and do the work to *get* it. I almost tell ol' Lurlene that I'll bet it was her who came in here and pulled its head off...but I didn't. Or I'll bet it was she. Whatever. I don't have the energy to remember pesky grammar rules right now. What I do tell her is that I've sensed the vibes and have been hiding the chicken anyway. I started doing it a few days ago.

Nice *job*, Lurlene said. Aren't *you* full of surprises.

I basked for a moment in the feeling you get when you call Lurlene's bluff. It's one of those wonderful feelings. But it's real, real rare.

Lurlene said there was something else. That she was looking at my grade book and test and assignment schedule on the computer and said we don't give *pop* quizzes...we call them *review* quizzes. So you need to change your *leen*-go.

I said that's news to me.

She said I'm telling you now...review quizzes...and then she said she went ahead and changed it for me. Review quiz.

I thought this whole conversation had an I'll-bet-a-parent-or-two-has-complained feel to it. I asked Lurlene have the *chill*-ren been complaining already about my *pop* quizzes? The quizzes are over previously-covered material. It ain't like they're pulling the answers out of the air...or guessing.

There was a long pause. A real long pause. Then Lurlene said...Ex-*cuuuuse me?*

Sometimes I forget she's in charge.

DEMOCRACY IN INACTION

You'd think the patriotic business of chapter 24, Constitutional Government, would have gotten some of the scholars to thinking about the nice things government entities do for us. Many of them are under the impression that we're a suppressed people. That we can't go out and kill somebody who deserves it and not face the consequences. Tempest said at least she'd do it when somebody had their back turned so they wouldn't have to see her coming.

Oh, boy. This isn't good.

Tempest says the health care bill takes our money and gives it to people who are too stupid and lazy to get a *job*.

An example, I say.

Tempest says that's what she's *heard*.

From who? What? What newspaper? The radio?

She doesn't know.

Petal says health care is free in England.

Okay…good…*why*? Why would it be free in England or *any*where? How does a government make it free?

Petal doesn't know. But she's sure it's free in England.

They all chime in two or three at a time about how they're suppressed and under control and that there are too many laws and rules.

Some roll their eyes. Some know better.

Some want freedom!

I ask…freedom from what? Or *for* what?

They don't know exactly. But there are a whole bunch of people, they say, who are sucking the system who need to get a job.

I hear their parents talking. Maybe. Or I hear them shout what others spout without recourse on TV talk shows.

Petal asks at what age can she leave her house and go live on her own.

I tell her.

Petal says that she's going to go live on the moon with her husband and be far away from all these damn rules.

Tempest says she's going to join her up there on the moon.

Petal doesn't seem to like the idea at first.

I calmly remind Petal and Tempest that there's no air on

the moon.

There is in the spaceship, Petal says.

Somebody moans...This is ridiculous.

I think it was Hoover. I don't think Hoover loves Petal any more. I tell them this is the most vigorous class discussion we've had in a long time. It may be a little goofy but everybody's got something to say. I could do this all day if we could keep from potentially killing each other.

Then Petal asks if there are any laws on the bottom of the ocean.

I don't say anything.

Petal all of a sudden says she's going to be president one day. She sure is. And she's going to change everything. Petal says she going to let everybody run wild.

Her classmates cheer, scream, and clap. In my direction.

ANYBODY HEAR A BANJO PLAYING?

Everybody showed up except Jasper and Taboo and off we go on the annual eighth grade two-day rafting trip.

A hippy named Murphy was the guide of our raft, number 806. In the raft was Irving, Beauregard, Claude, Benny, and Dill. We had several miles of class one-to-three Ocoee River rapids ahead of us. Since Beauregard and Benny started bickering before we nudged our raft into the water, I honestly wondered what I would do if they fell out of the raft in a few minutes and were being sucked under and they were holding their hands up out of the water for a responsible adult to reach down to save them.

Murphy, who was pretty much in charge of our lives, and

had been the ultimate professional during entrances and escapes from angry sections of the Ocoee River called Flipper, Broken Nose, and Table Saw, asked me, because I was sitting in the back of the raft near him and I was their teacher, do those two up there constantly argue. They have really been going at it, Murphy observed.

I told Murphy they constantly bicker. Yes, they do. All day. I told Murphy that those two also bickered at each other all day just this past Friday while we were on a field trip to Six Flags. I emphasized to Murphy the words, *Six Flags.* I emphasized some more words to Murphy: *Can you believe it?*

Murphy said, Dude, you must be a *payyyy*-tient man.

I allowed my awesome silence to communicate to our long-haired river guide of raft number 806 the response to his comprehensive observation.

The next day, on another river, the Nantahala, which means, "Certain type boys, God love them, will bicker incessantly," in Cherokee, Irving, Dill, Beauregard, Earl, Benny, and I were in raft number 601. Of course there was an amount of bickering. It's what they do. It's what they enjoy. They're really good at it, so now, as their teacher, I enthusiastically encourage something they're good at.

A river and sun and cigarette-seasoned local fellow named Creed was our raft guide who said after about two minutes on the river...You assholes sure do *squabble* a lot.

I looked at Creed with an expression of teacherly approval. Squabble. Bicker. Both work, but squabble's even better.

On the way back home the road show stopped in Murphy, North Carolina at a Chinese and American buffet restaurant. You could describe the buffet-style eating of over thirty eighth graders as frenzied, with a slurping and gnawing and hiccupping and chewing and licking and crunching quality to it. Then you've got the sounds Old Burrell makes while he enjoys his food.

When you could tell the restaurant employees were finally ready to get rid of us and at least break even on the ocean of Coke and Sprite and Dr. Pepper refills and cat head-sized rolls soaked in butter which were enormously popular with Huckleberry, a very Chinese waitress who was working our tables all of a sudden said something to me I couldn't decipher. Having a few manners, I politely asked her to repeat what she said...she did...and then I asked her politely to give it a try one more time. I was sitting at a table with Winx and Click and they finally lifted their heads from cramming Chinese and American food items into their sandwich holes to see what the international relations rumpus in Murphy, North Carolina was all about.

Here's what our determined Chinese waitress said to me: When you get to the *cash* register tell them you a *bus* driver and you eat for *free*.

I said I'm not a bus driver. I'm a teacher. I drive a little school bus. I drive these kids around...in a little school bus.

She waggled a finger...You no *bus driver?*

I'm looking at her, inquisitively, amusedly, with quite a bit of the two buffets in my guts and she's looking at me with my two days of gnarly-looking beard and my day-two raft trip do-rag which has red and yellow flames on it and I've got on beat-up old cowboy boots and greasy blue jeans and a moldy adidas Originals track jacket which looks like it emits a fragrance, and it does, and a social studies-type thought finally hit me: my honky ass just got profiled.

GOVERNMENT LECTURE MOAN

They all seemed to like chapter 26, State Government—The Legislature, which made my heart feel warm. They asked good questions, too. On the first day back from a long spring break we had a wonderful, vigorous discussion on how governments are organized and run, with most everybody chiming in. And then how in God's name we somehow, some way, got started talking about the movie *Black Snake Moan* I have no idea, but it wasn't me who brought it up. Although I admit once we start talking about movies I can't say I do the time-out sign.

Black Snake Moan is a sweaty movie where an old black man finds this beat-up, not-fully-clothed, redneck girl on the side of the road near his shack and attempts to redeem her by looping a heavy chain around her and attaching it to a radiator so she won't run off and then he preached a whole lot of Jesus to her. I think he plays the guitar to the girl, too, when she's not comatose on liquor or dope and the pressures of her unique life situation. Anyway, Petal knew the most about the movie and she walked us through a lot of it and we were very impressed.

Not a lot of nice people have ever seen the movie, so for educational purposes, here's a brief feel for *Black Snake Moan*...at one point in the theatrics, the old man, Lazarus, played by Samuel Jackson, says to Rae, the redneck gal, played by Christina Ricci: "I ain't gonna be moved on this.

Right or wrong, you gonna mind me. Like Jesus said, 'Imo suffa you. Imo suffa you!' Get yo ass back in my *house!*'

Then Rae screams back at Lazarus: "Or what! Or what!" Then Rae spit in his face.

Anyway, I saw the movie. I admit. It was pretty squirmy.

Then Petal said the tattoo that Rae had on her back was the tattoo she was going to get once she turned sixteen...when she was out from under the government of her parents.

Well, I'll be. So Petal really was listening to today's Georgia history lecture.

VOX POWER

I'm helping Helena out with the track meets and yesterday afternoon was the junior varsity regional championship. Elbows and knees...going as fast and as high as they can. Helena teaches language arts across the hall from me. She's the school's track coach.

At the track meets I use the school's track and field team official megaphone so everybody can know real well how high and how fast their child went. You put that thing up to your lips and squeeze that trigger and blast out words that crackle like lightening.

I thought to bring it to class today. I thought to use it in class. By talking into it. The megaphone.

And now I'd like to offer up to my friends in the teaching business that the greatest tool for teaching eighth graders Georgia history is available at Radio Shack. It's the AmpliVox S602M 25W Piezo megaphone with a detachable mic. The model number is S602M and the catalog number is 55025884.

There's also a switch you may accidentally push (three or four good times) that makes the megaphone produce an extremely loud siren sound. Let's make that: siren brain-melting *blast*. I cannot tell you how loud this siren brain-melting blast is, but if you wanted to get the attention of some kids in China while you were teaching Georgia history in the United States then this is the switch you'd push on the AmpliVox S602M 25W Piezo megaphone with a detachable mic.

Georgia history spoken through a megaphone. The genius of it boggles the mind.

By the way, the greatest teaching tool on Earth for inattentive school kids costs only $109.99. It's worth every single nickel. Their extremely attentive expressions today were worth priceless Confederate bills.

LAWFUL THINKING AT THE LAST SECOND

A popular question from the scholars during chapter 28 this week, State Government—The Judicial Branch, is always...Do you think I'll ever have to go to prison?

That's fair. It's a real-world question to the real world information we're learning in a chapter whose key words and phrases are plaintiff, defendant, criminal case, prosecution, felony, capital felony, misdemeanor, jury, superior court, trail jury, grand jury, indictment, and the word that gets them all hot and bothered the most: juveniles. Something about the word...juveniles...sets them off. That's been quite a revelation, and makes me think that when they're hanging out with each other over the weekends that they talk about how much they're watched by their parents or the police and the delinquency of the kids they know down the street who've gotten in some serious trouble.

But it gets us talking and that's good. It gets them talking about when their mother got pulled over for speeding...or when she went through that stop sign and got caught. But what scares me is that some of them wonder why people have to obey laws. They ask why they're so oppressed and regulated and controlled?

Petal asks in a dark tone...Why are there laws in the *first* place?

I give them the simplest and most powerful and easiest-to-understand answer: in hopes of attempting to keep billions of people from killing each other.

In a tone of voice, as if she was defeated, Petal said...I guess you're right.

YOU GET AN "A" FOR SELF ADVOCACY, HOWEVER

I got a Sunday afternoon e-mail from Tempest who was miffed about her performance on Friday's quiz. Seems she discovered over the weekend on the computer grading system that she made a blazing 49 on it and she's not pleased and she begs her case thusly by e-mail:

> **Todd,**
>
> **Due to my 49 on your last quize, I now have a D in your calss. I made a 49 on the quize because i did not study, due to other home work and quizes. I thought I would do better on it, but, I did not.**

I was wondering if thair is any way that I could retake the quize on Friday or Wednesday, in lunch and learn. Thank you, and I will see you tom.

Tempest

No problem. I let Tempest take it again. This time she made a 52.

BUTTER ME UP ANYTIME

Every two weeks or so Lurlene will bring me some food. I don't try to figure it out anymore. I take it and thank her quite a bit and eat it and it's always good. Today was some bodacious blueberry pie. Later in the day Old Burrell comes into The Cozy Room of Learning and bellows with a finger wagging in the air...*I saw her put four sticks of butter in the dang thang!*

CAPITAL PUNISHMENT

I had to get up real dang early this morning for a real adventurous reason: assistant principal Coco and I took Hap, Fatima, Boog, Hoover, Jimmy Joe, Frank, Elmo, Beauregard, and Claude to our nation's capital on a jet airplane and back for a one-day field trip.

Waking up real early was extremely annoying because an extremely chirpy local radio personality said it's early in the morning but also the middle of the night and ain't that a crazy thang...as if he's pleased with this information.

I wondered who'd be late to the airport and was surprised

to find out it was me.

The kids zipped through the National Museum of American History as if the floor of one of the most popular Smithsonian Institute's museums was a hot grill.

On the steps of the National Air and Space Museum, while Claude and Beauregard and I were eating various lunch food items obtained from a foreign street vendor, while the rest of the group was across Jefferson Drive, sitting in the grass of the National Mall eating expensive nation's capital cheeseburgers obtained from an overpriced cheeseburger joint run by some college guys, a local con man named Bernard walked up to us and attempted to have us believe that he was a former Marine.

Bernard also attempted to have us believe that he loved his country and that hard times had recently fallen on him, and then Bernard handed Beauregard a card, which he asked Beauregard to open as well as to read out loud the message inside the card that Bernard had written. Our friend Bernard didn't know that Beauregard is possibly the most dyslexic eighth grader in the United States of America as well as our nation's territories. Beauregard, being the super good sport that he is, though, started in on the message.

After about ten seconds, I believe Bernard wondered what the hell he had gotten himself into, so he snatched the card back from Beauregard and got to the point of our meeting which was Bernard asking me for some money.

I told Bernard, politely, that I didn't like being put on the spot.

Bernard said he understood and then he complimented me on the way I was dressed and asked me, very cordially, if we were on a field trip.

I told Bernard that after we finished having our lunch that we were going into the National Air and Space Museum. I nodded up that way.

Claude was enjoying a soft pretzel and a cup of lemon sherbet and a Coke for lunch. Beauregard was now eating his package of Skittles and drinking a Coke.

Bernard said it's a wonderful museum and he hoped we'd have a good time in our nation's capital...and then Bernard darted off and started in on a group of teenage girls ten feet away from us who seemed like they were either from Tennessee or Kentucky or Alabama or Mississippi or South Carolina. I know their teacher was Mrs. Philpot because after a moment or two with Bernard they started frantically looking around for Mrs. Philpot and then they started screaming real loudly for Mrs. Philpot.

Claude patted me on the back and said I sure did handle *that* guy.

We learned it costs $18 per person to get into the International Spy Museum and per person we were eleven. This particular bit of information was not involved in the budget planning of our one-day field trip to the nation's capital, so Coco calls Lurlene back home to ask if it's okay that we spend nearly two hundred unanticipated school dollars. All the kids were watching Coco's expression very carefully while she was talking on the phone to Lurlene, and then they screamed and yelled and jumped up and down at the reason and understanding Lurlene displayed from back down in Georgia.

Then Coco asks if I happen to have a credit card with me.

As you move through the International Spy Museum displays, you begin to feel a super high level of creepiness all over your body. The final thing that struck me is that in order to be super sneaky you are definitely going to have to stick, from time to time, in the service of your country, various items up your rear end.

Back home, as I flopped my weary body into my truck in the airport parking lot my weary mind turned to wondering wearily what mischief might have occurred at school today. I had told my mid-afternoon study hall bunch yesterday that Lurlene, for tomorrow, was bringing in America's most infamous and most unreasonable substitute teacher, Mrs. Hulga Warthog, to watch over you during study hall while I'm gone to Washington, D.C. with some other kids.

Spike had instantly perked up and asked if Hulga had a *wart*.

I said she did, actually. And the thing was bright red and the size of a *golf* ball. And then I added...And the wart *moves around*.

Spike was extremely excited.

ECUMENICALLY YOURS

Lord have mercy Lurlene means well, but I got her goat pretty good this morning. And why was the getting of her goat too easy? Was she not thinking? Lurlene's one of the most perceptive and intelligent people on the planet. Heck, she hired *me*.

Anyway, here we are during the week leading up to Friday, Good Friday, and Easter Sunday and Lurlene sends us all an e-mail saying if any of you have huge assignments due this week or tests that you might have to give our Catholic students some extra time because of their worship schedules and whatnot.

Now you're telling us? When huge assignment due dates and test days were announced weeks ago...to all students of all faiths, or not? Some kids don't worship nothing except when school lets out.

I had to take a deep breath on this one...and then compose my e-mail retort with respect, but with a little finger waggling, too. What an opportunity to help Lurlene see it my way!

I typed away. Then I spell checked. Added a couple of nice verbs and nouns. Looked to see if I had too many adjectives. Spell checked again. Mumbled it out loud to myself. That sort of thing.

Then I hit SEND.

All day. Never heard back.

I think I won this one. That's always my guess...that she got the point and didn't want to get into a cheesy debate by e-mail. And the woman will debate all day until you get that e-mail from her that says...*stop*. Anyway, today, I think I won.

But really, no one can convince me that the choice of religion and what you spiritually believe is a not hugely personal decision...and why should it, or would it, effect the time you spend educating yourself. Lurlene, what if my Baptist, Presbyterian, atheist, Confucionist, Rastafarian, Taoist, Wiccan, Xbox 360ians, Mormon, Anglican, Air Softians, or Hindu students object, too...and ask to be let out of assignments and tests this week? What do you suggest I do? Honor their requests, too?

Sorry. Forgot the Methodists. And the Unitarian Universalists. And the Body of Christ Church International U.S.A.-North. Norths. Northists. I really don't know because I really don't care. We're all supposed to be equally nice to each other.

THE GREAT UNFURLING

Vexillology is the scholarly study of flags. It sure is.

And ever since I was a kid I've loved looking at flags in books and wondering what the colors symbolize and why they put a bird there and a cross over there and whatnot.

You may say that's so impressive to be a kid and interested in vexillology but I'd say back to you that I was also just as interested in shooting passing cars and the flesh of my friends with my BB gun.

I've been promoting the deep joy of vexillology to them for a couple of weeks and how much they'll really enjoy something new and kind of fun, too. Come to find out, I noticed at the beginning of vexillology week that their attention level is way up and their ears are perked up like BBs are whizzing by. Maybe they just had to get through the end of summer and then the blazingly beautiful fall season and through the chill of our grey winter and well into spring before they felt settled and ready and available for learning.

Today, Old Burrell, my colleague from across the hall, caught wind of the eminent vexillology lecture action for the week because the kids were real unnerved by the prospect of it and were talking it up around the building and holding each other in comforting embraces, and Old Burrell asked me what the heck vexer-lowlowgee meant.

Shocked, stunned, amazed, I told Old Burrell, as if I was talking to a dangerous person, that vexillology was the scholarly study...of flags.

Old Burrell said that should be good for the kids. Vexer-lowlowgee.

I believe he burped a little while he was reading some quiz or test or assignment instructions he just grabbed from the printer. I backed away slowly.

Anyway, I started in on the scholarly study of flags today with a passion in my tone and spirit and soul and an unfurling of all kinds of flags I've collected in my days on Earth and a look-see at flag books I've collected and then I think it hit them that I might, too, be dangerous.

I told them what they'll need to know for the infamous vexillology examination while they gazed, and became dazed, at my eminent vexillology handout:

- What are the two main things flags do?
- Graphic elements in flags usually do what? The word starts with an "s."
- The earliest known cloth flags were thought to have come from where?
- There are how many recognized countries in the world?
- What's the name of the dude or chick who carries a flag?
- What do you think is the ratio of our national flag?
- What's the ratio of a square flag?

- When was the last time the United States flag was changed?
- Can you burn the United States flag and not get in trouble?
- What's the protocol for when and how you should burn the United States flag?
- Why did the United States flag go through so many changes?
- If I leave the United States flag up during the night, then I should do what to it?
- The study of flags is called what?

Oh, man. They were truly freaked out. Then, when they discovered there was still a lot of class time left and I had no intention of dropping dead or being snatched up by winged monkeys, we continued with basic flag types:

- What's the name of a flag that has a strip of color that runs along the outer edge of the flag?
- Two bands of color either horizontal or vertical?
- Three bands of different colors either horizontal or vertical?
- A field divided into four different quarters?
- A center cross that divides the field?
- A cross that divides the field where the vertical is to the left of center?
- An X-shaped cross?
- A complete cross surrounded by the field where the arms are equal?

- A triangle of any size or shape?
- A narrow band that acts as a border between two colors?
- A zigzag edge like the teeth on a saw?
- What's the name of the type of flag...the flag itself...that's triangular? (a trick question...I had to)
- What's the name of the most famous pirate flag?
- What type of animal does the word "pennon" come from?

And they think they're going to get away from me before we talk about flag and flag pole parts? Oh, ye gods, I think not:

- So anyway, what's the ornamental knob on top of the flagstaff called?
- What's another name for the pole?
- What's the round mechanical device called that allows the flag to pulled up and down?
- The rope or cord used to raise the flag is called what?
- The metal ring used to secure the clip to the flag is called what?
- The inner, lower left portion of the flag nearest the flag pole is called what?
- The top quarter of the flag nearest the flag pole is called what?
- What's the outer part of the flag called?
- An emblem in the center of the flag is called what?

- The background area of the flag? What the heck's is that thing called?
- What's another name for the background area of a flag?
- What's the name of your favorite teacher?

I asked them in an obnoxiously excited voice...Is vexillology righteous, or *what!*

Herman, who was now sweating and sporting a couple of crimson cheeks, said, very breathlessly, as he took his glasses off and before I think he expected to lose consciousness: Boy, *Todd*, we sure do have a lot to learn about vexi-*llow*-lowgy!

What I think the breathless Herman really wanted to say was, Boy, *Todd*, speaking for everyone, we sure do hate your greasy guts and wish you'd drop dead immediately and go to Hell!

I told Herman I'd be here all week.

THE GREAT DEFACING

For reasons of vigorous seeking of fun I've allowed them during the infamous vexillology week the opportunity to deface my picture on the cover of the infamous vexillology examination packet and hand it in without the fear of an honor council investigation. If you're a teacher of vexillology of hormonal teenagers and children and you're thin-skinned you're in the wrong racket.

My picture is a color photograph I pasted on there and I'm smiling like a maniac and I'm wearing a coat and tie and my hair looks pretty good and they get to mark it up.

They have to take the examination first...then they get to spend what time remains on getting me back for educating them so well. There isn't a penalty...I don't get all huffy...and I don't criticize their drawing skills. I tell them I like the attention, good or bad, but they can't be nasty, use cuss words, or draw something sexual. I pronounce the word sexual like this...*secks-shull*. I don't believe they know what I just said even though they're from the South, too.

Anyway, here are their near-the-end-of-school feelings expressed through the world-changing power of adolescent humor, imagination, and the humbling nature of vexillology:

- Many students have drawn the intersection of a sniper scope's reticule between my eyes.
- A snake has crawled through my brain and its head is poking out one ear and the tail is coming out the other ear.
- I have a chicken on each shoulder and both chickens are evil chickens.
- Round, black sunglasses with loop ear rings.
- My arms, in several cases, have been extended and hands and fingers have been added and I'm enthusiastically hanging birds with both hands...or if I'm hanging a bird with just one hand the other hand is choking the chicken and the chicken is dripping rivers of blood.
- Other images drawn on the page: Georgia history tests in angry campfires; severed

heads with the mouths still screaming and the eyes still wide open (particularly creepy); space aliens choking the chicken; I have a lot of underarm hair poking from out of my suit jacket; a drawing of a feisty group of leprechauns who are alleged by my vexillologists to live up my butt; and many notations on various places on the sheet of the numbers 666.

- Various messages are extended to me from my vexillologists in word balloons or in headlines, for example: You pick your nose when no one is looking!...Nice mullet plugs!...Seek knowledge now!...If you pretend to like me I'll give you an A!...Flags are awesome!...Hail the chicken!...Cluck the chicken!...Get over your hair!...Are you ready to stand tall before the man?

Most told the truth about who their favorite teacher was. And for the question about what type of animal does the word pennon come from...well...it surely ain't a pig or a raccoon.

It's a bird, but not a chicken.

They're listening, though, and remembering some of what I've said and what they've read and discussed, and that makes me happy. I've said to them since August: Don't ever leave a multiple choice question or a fill-in-the blank answer...*blank*. You might get it right. Use your imagination.

But I've never told them that their imaginations—right or wrong or somewhere in between or in outer space—might make a weary teacher live for another day of academic mischief. I've never told them that, because I'll bet they already know it.

They're giggling at me.

And I'm laughing so hard I'm about to pass out at my desk in the back—while I'm grading their infamous examinations and reviewing their evil artwork.

They're kindly asking if they did an outstanding job defacing their teacher.

They sure clucking did.

VEXILLOLOGY DOESN'T BLOW AFTER ALL!

They have said to me that they'll never look at a flag the same way again. They have said to me that now they'll pay more attention to what a flag might communicate, represent, and symbolize.

I'm tearing up. I really am.

They have also said to me that since they have a better feel for what a well-designed flag looks like then they'll speak up and tell anybody who'll listen when they see any flag anywhere and at any time about the elements of the flag that could be changed and made more balanced and logical and communicative.

It's what vexillologists do.

Flags are eagerly presented from the front of the room. Snap says the red on his flag represents him getting better at baseball because he's been trying hard. The picture of him used as a charge in the canton is of him in the dugout during a baseball game.

Montene says the crucifix represents her love of Jesus.

Spike says the picture of the nose on his flag represents

his concern for his mother who wants to get a nose job. Spike says the meaning of a hammer about to smash his alarm clock glaring the hideous time of 6:30 in the morning should be pretty obvious.

Hap's flag represents a place he'd like to live in and rule called Haptopia.

Beauregard didn't have a name for a new world represented by his funky flag, but Beauregard says it would be more of a kingdom and he'd be the ruler of the kingdom.

Albert had a near perfect flag. Elegant and simple, the way professional vexillologists like a flag. Albert had drawn a heart and inside the heart symbol it said Brandi + Albert. As simple as that.

We asked Albert if he loved Brandi, who goes to another school.

He said he did.

I asked Albert if Brandi loved him back.

Albert said he was pretty sure she did.

I asked Albert if wanted to keep his flag.

Albert said yes and he wasn't embarrassed one bit as he carried it back to his desk.

Click's bi-color flag was elegant and simple, too. Click didn't have to, but he wrote his explanation out so when he presented his flag to us he would remember all the details and get them right. I'd say he did present it right, on deeper levels of vexillology than he might possibly realize. In Click's words:

My flag of choice for this assignment is a two banded horizontal bi-color design. The ratio of my flag is roughly 1:2 because my flag is of a

rectangular shape. On my flag I have the colors yellow and green and together they represent my active lifestyle. Green represents my love of the outdoors along with my lifetime wilderness experience and practice of survival skills. The main purpose that my flag serves is that the flag I have come up with represents the things in my life that I enjoy being a part of and experiencing for a lifetime to come. The way I decided my flag to be positioned is yellow for the top color because that is the part of me that I think means the most, and on the bottom I have green for my secondary love for adventure. Yellow symbolizes my friendly, peaceful approach to people and who I respect and care for.

Click, outstanding job, you vexillologist human being 14 year old wacky kid who I have always liked a lot. I'll offer to you what I think might be the greatest sign of respect and appreciation for a flag and what it represents, communicates, and symbolizes...your flag, Click...and that's saluting it. I salute your flag and I salute you and Albert, too, my real good vexillologists.

KID CITIZENS ROCK

So after eighth graders finish the textbook and a week of vexillology blows their minds...what's the next logical and brain-numbing subject to entertain them with!

Exactly...citizenship!

I thought I might have to call an ambulance for about fifteen of them.

First, we came up with what we thought was a great

definition of citizenship as it related to 14 and 15 year olds...folks who aren't driving three thousand pound death machines around yet. I told them their comfy world will change real quickly when the state patrolman leans into your driver's-side window for the first time. That arguing with him before he opens his mouth, unlike how you treat your teachers from time to time, will be a super big and memorable moment for you. Enjoy!

I think I have their attention.

Here's our comfy definition of what a good citizen is: A good citizen obeys the laws, has respect for his country, and attempts to meet the community's expectations.

Good stuff. We decided that community means the whole world since some of their parents are real rich and get to travel to foreign countries, like on cruises through the Bahamas.

Next, we all worked real hard to come up with a bunch of characteristics of what makes a good 14 or 15 year old citizen. Here's what we came up with:

- Don't litter
- Don't loiter
- Don't trespass
- Take care of your pets and be responsible for their behavior
- Do the safe thing
- Report crime and the suspicious or dangerous behavior of other people
- Respect others' property
- Don't vandalize

- Obey pedestrian laws
- Obey cycling laws
- Learn and understand all laws
- Don't cuss in public
- Don't shoplift or steal anything that's not yours
- Recycle when you can
- No PDA

Could there be a whole lot more? Sure. But I don't want to overwhelm them and they don't want to overwhelm themselves because they know this list and the definition of citizenship is actually the test. In other words, the test is them regurgitating the list and the definition from memory. The real test will come when they actually use a few of these on their own.

Petal says she'll never have any fun now. *Never.*

I said you will, and it's called college.

POW! NOW GET OUT OF HERE

This afternoon I watched a bunch of happy kids...ours...and a bunch of kids from a school for the deaf, too, run and jump and throw things. Debbie included. It's her first time on a track team. Running as fast as she can in the one hundred, two hundred, and four hundred meters and winning last place every time...with her dad watching and cheering and her Georgia history teacher, too...*First call...Girls' four hundred meter dash...Second call...Boys' sixteen hundred meter run...Y'all need to be standing right here at the orange cones...Right now!...*I was announcing results loudly enough into a megaphone where everybody could surely hear a special pride in my voice when I say the name of a girl who's trying her best at something new, participating with a good attitude...who shoots straight up, not forward, when the starter's gun goes *Pow!*

A LOOK-SEE. MAYBE NOT FOR ME

There was a knock on the door and a seventh grader was touring around some kid the seventh grader said was maybe going to be an eighth grader around here next year and can he show him The Cozy Room of Learning.

The wide-eyed potential victim was named Dupont, we learned, and Dupont might have been about two feet tall but he seemed pretty sure of himself. We all welcomed Dupont and when he came into the room everybody wanted me to show their new friend Dupont The Teaching Stick and The Globe of Happiness and the wiggly plucked chicken. In other words, all the things they've been making fun of for most of their eighth grade career. Now, go figure, they were giddy with support and inspiration for everything that's ever occurred within The Cozy Room of Learning, which had been wonderful and fun and had changed their lives. I'm fairly sure of it.

Somebody screamed...Are you a knowledge seeker, Doo-*pont!*

Poor old Dupont, I could tell—profoundly and immediately—looked as if he had walked into a camp meeting of howler monkeys who were feeling very territorial at that moment and had been drinking a lot of beer. Every eye was on him. They were all leaning toward him. They all had grins on their faces that were—profoundly and immediately—a little blood thirsty.

I tried to break the ice. I asked Dupont if he liked...vexillology!

Dupont said he didn't know what that was.

I told Dupont we'd learn him some vexillology! No worries! Then I asked Dupont if he liked Georgia history!

Dupont said he didn't know yet. He was from Long Island.

A howler monkey screamed...Do you like getting chickens chucked at your *head!*

Proudly, decisively, with his chin up, Dupont told the class that chickens make him extremely nervous.

We laughed at DuPont. Not with him...at him...because he wasn't laughing along with us. He was one fearless little dude. I cannot fathom why Dupont would have said that to these chicken addicts. Man, could you feel the room getting humid. I scooted over real quick and opened the door for our visitors so they could get to safety.

Dupont and his tour guide scooted on out real fast.

I yelled after Dupont...Have a good summer! See you in August...maybe!

Then Spike summed up the event pretty nicely from my new Sella Mortis, the chair of death...my nice living room chair I brought from home wherein only the teacher's pet sits. Spike said in a lofty tone of voice, as only a trusted teacher's pet can deliver without reprisal, that if *Doo*-pont comes back here *next* year I'll be surprised as *hell.* Spike looked up at me and winked.

SIGNS OF STRESS

One of my brightest, sweetest, and most inquisitive students, who possesses a whole lot of maturity for her age and a whole lot of academics on her mind, started to get up from her desk...to go get a drink of water...or maybe to go use the restroom. But she didn't make it but one step. Honoria passed out and dropped onto the floor with a thud.

It's something you see...and you don't register what has actually happened for a too-long time. I wondered why Honoria would do something so goofy. My greatest academic achiever.

We finally rushed to her.

The school nurse delivered her back to The Cozy Room of Learning a while later. She told us Honoria's going to be okay.

We cooed over her. I let them have the rest of class off.

Honoria said her brain got full and it went wild and quit.

It sure did, Honoria, and we saw it. We hope to God we never have to see it ever again. You there on the floor. When you woke up you started crying. You were so embarrassed, but everybody understood.

Honoria said quietly, starting to cry again...I love every one of y'all *so much*.

DEAD RECKONING

They've all been pestering Lurlene and Coco to go on more field trips, especially field trips that didn't cost much as the pesterers noted that if field trips didn't cost much that their parents were okay with that, too.

Lurlene asked me...Mind taking a wad of them one day to a place that will scare them out of wanting to go on more field trips?

In the Oakland Cemetery visitor's center, Clark asked the nice volunteer fellow where he could find his great-great-grandfather and the nice fellow gave Clark a map and showed him where he was resting. Clark said thank you and walked out to the porch with the map and the fellow came trotting out there and told Clark...uh, young man...that the maps cost four dollars.

The rest of the group went on ahead to the Confederate soldier section. Clark and I went to pay our respects to Clark's great-great-grandfather. On the way, Clark placed a golf ball on the gravesite of Bob Jones.

When we found Clark's great-great-great grandfather, Clark asked if he could call his father to tell him where he was standing at that very moment.

Give him a holler, I said.

After Clark talked to his father he asked me what he should do next. How do you...like...honor somebody in a grave?

I told Clark to just stand and gaze at his great-great-grandfather's headstone and his great-great grandmother's, too, and just be silent and calm and think about how important family relationships are. Just gaze and think. That's what you do.

Clark's great-great-grandparents died a long, long time before Clark was born. Clark still seemed like he was going to cry. But he didn't.

As we walked back toward the buses in the cold wind, I could tell Clark was moved. He takes deep breaths and blows them out when something heavy is on his mind and has a hard time forming words at first. I put my arm around his shoulder. I told him he did a good thing today, and that it had been a great pleasure to be with him.

On the way back up the highway we came to the only toll booth in the historic state of Georgia. I started reaching into my coat pocket where I had put some toll booth money earlier in the morning.

Clark tapped me on my right shoulder. He held out his palm. He had two quarters in it.

I thanked him and told him I had it covered.

Clark insisted that he pay our toll. It was something he really wanted to do today. He said he'd been planning it.

I took the two quarters from Clark, and told him he was a mighty good citizen, too, just like his great-great-grandfather, a long-ago governor of Georgia—a state he helped make a better place, too.

BATHROBE HUMOR

During the exam period, which started Tuesday and lasts until next Tuesday, you don't have to come to school on the day your free period has an exam.

The school wants you to call it your planning period, but you're actually free to leave the campus on a regular day and do whatever you want during your planning period so I call it a free period. Say free period around Lurlene and she goes nuts. She'll say you're supposed to be in there planning for what's coming. I always say I've already done that because I have. This usually leaves the woman speechless, and that's always a big moment in the history of American education.

So guess what today is? Exactly. My free period. I don't have a third period. I didn't get out of my nasty bathrobe until ___ o'clock in the dang ___.

Free to do what, though, I have no idea. You go four hundred miles an hour for almost ten months so it's hard to slow it down and think about your own strange and embarrassing desires for too long. But do something healthy, maybe, like a long jog, followed up by weight lifting and some time with the heavy bag? Or something nutritious, like a long afternoon nap?

I performed one of the four aforementioned items and then I watched a DVD that new substitute teacher, Charla, who looks like Tammy Wynette, had given me a few days ago with a sticky note stuck to it that said, in her curly-girly letters, that there were people in this movie like people in our families. Charla is very, very much from Tennessee. She must get a hillbilly vibe from me.

Anyway, the movie is called *Sordid Lives*, and it's about a bunch of loveable and eccentric people with necks that are sun burned. The movie's tag line is: A Black Comedy About White Trash.

In one scene an old woman named Sissy is hovering over the stiff corpse of her sister while the smiling corpse is lying in a coffin. Her sister's got a dead mink or a ferret wrapped around her neck. Sissy had already walked into the empty church smoking a cigarette and she says to her freshly dead sister as she's waving smoke out of the way with her hand...Heyyyy! I guess you don't mind if I *smoke*. It just wasn't the right time to quit with you dyin' and *all*. I only lasted for three *days*. I failed again, but after five husbands what *else* is new?

There I am, late in the afternoon during my all-day free period, in my nasty bathrobe, laughing at the TV screen all by myself. I felt like a lunatic and it felt damn wonderful.

HUCKLEBERRY FINALLY HAS SOMETHING TO SAY

Giving them a free look-see of the actual spring semester exam last week as a study guide—blank, no answers—was a real tension easer.

And today, the moment I plopped the real thing on their desks this morning and said *Enjoy!* they went right to scratching out the answers as fast as humanly possible and some unusual suspects were the first to turn it in for some good grades.

Huckleberry was the second student to toss it at me. I asked Huckleberry how he would think I'd look upon a student who pays attention and recognizes certain opportunities, such as having the actual exam ahead of time and being able to fill it out with researched and correct answers so he'd make a great grade on the actual final exam?

Huckleberry didn't say anything for a few long moments.

I said the word I'm looking for starts with an *f*.

Huckleberry says, from his own larynx: Uh, freakishly?

Favorably...is the word I'm looking for. Your beloved teacher, I said, would look upon that *favorably*.

Huckleberry looked unmoved, so I changed the subject to

a one that evokes happiness in school kids. I asked Huckleberry what he was doing this summer.

He said his mother was going to kick his ass around the house. Huckleberry said his mother said he was going to have to make his own food and wash his own clothes and mow the grass.

I tried not to show my shock that Huckleberry actually spoke some words out loud in class from his own larynx. Finally. After almost ten months. I gave Huckleberry a teacherly look and asked, What's wrong with *that?*

Huckleberry said something else in class, from his own larynx, but it was unrepeatable. One of the words started with an *f*, too.

WHAT'S A SCHOOL'S-OVER TEACHER'S WORKDAY ANYWAY?

It might have been the last day of school yesterday for the *chill*-ren, but it ain't for us. Today and tomorrow are what's called teacher work days and all I can do is sit slumped and sad and exhausted as I look over The Cozy Room of Happiness and think of what all went on in here since...God knows. I honestly cannot believe how fast school years go by.

I could tell you who's got to go to summer school, but summer school isn't a punishment. It's redemptive. It's a fair and reasonable and quick second chance. Anyhow, there are quite a few who'll be redeemed starting in a couple of weeks.

But I'll give you a revelation. I've got some energy left. A revelation at the end of another school year from a teacher of kids with learning, emotional, and behavior disorders. My revelation...my belief is this: I think teachers are the most important people in the world. When someone asks me what I do, I cannot tell you how proud I am to say, I'm a schoolteacher.

No one is ever not impressed. Not with me...no. But with the deeper feelings and powerful memories the word schoolteacher evokes.

DO NO DA GO HV I

And on the very last day of being at school before the teachers get to take two and a half months off and finally get our dry cleaning caught up, I'm thinking of my deepest belief about school and children and teachers and teaching and what it all really means.

I deeply believe children are the most-*most* important people in the world. They are, and always will be, and always have been. That's what it means.

I remember exactly when I learned it. It was many years ago, at 8 o' clock in the morning, when Principal Pam and her dog Bluto opened a classroom door for me...a guy who wanted to become a teacher. A guy who wasn't afraid to try something new. And here I am, in two months I'll start over at another school for kids who wouldn't last two days at this school.

I have lost my teacher's mind.

PART 3

JUST BEFORE A WAR WITH SOME ESKIMOS

"Friends," he said, "the time has come. The time we've all been waiting for this evening. Jesus said suffer the little children to come unto Him and forbid them not and maybe it was because He knew that it would be the little children that would call others to Him, maybe He knew, friends, maybe He hadda hunch."

—Flannery O'Connor, *The Violent Bear It Away*

What was the sensible thing to do?

—William Golding, *Lord of the Flies*

I LOVE A student who's persistent. I love to see a student, no matter how hard something gets, who keeps trying anyway, every day, and who does it with a great attitude. I love it when students smile while persisting. Sometimes they bark out a few awful cuss words and a few awful cuss phrases, sometimes accompanied with salacious body gestures, but that's okay—because you know it's the passion for accomplishment speaking. I love it when a persistent student finally accomplishes a life-consuming goal...and finally and successfully punts an orange basketball way up above us where it sticks between a steel beam and the gym ceiling, ripping yet another huge hole in the plastic sheeting.

Lamar, a pudgy but country-strong sixteen-year-old with a Beatles mop haircut, was so excited. He'd been trying to lodge a basketball in the ceiling for weeks.

And this isn't even our gym. It belongs to a church. So do the toilets and the spooky, spider-nest of a kitchen and the former Sunday school classrooms, each with a wooden, hand-made lectern.

Every morning, from 8 to 8:30, at my new school, around thirty tuition payers, from first to twelfth grade, are allowed to annihilate something that isn't theirs. They kick soccer balls into the walls. They zing footballs and soccer balls and basketballs and volleyballs at the gym ceiling. The plastic sheeting *pops*. They throw tennis balls at each other's heads as hard as they can. They knock over the huge plastic trash cans. They scream at nothing and anything. They cry. They twirl around on the dusty gym floor in fetal positions. They chase and intentionally trip each other...while the school's "Chief Feel Good Officer," a trained and tame chimpanzee kept in a cage during the day in the headmistress' office, chatters and squeals and screeches and yawns and farts and burps. Students with untold numbers of sensory disorders have to cover their ears. It is a deafening, surreal scene. The chimpanzee has a human, female name.

For thirty minutes of each school day morning, this is the way we begin, and then we line up, shut up, and pledge allegiance to the flag of the United States of America.

I call this thirty minutes of early morning migraine-making cacophony "Lord of the Flies." There was a book, and two movies, which I know were not movies—they were documentaries.

The same two old men from the church walk in and look at us for a long time. One is wearing overalls. I think I know what they're thinking, and it's probably not Christian. They shuffle away to unclog our toilets again. Clothes don't flush. Neither do magazines. They were here yesterday. And last Friday.

I teach, and a few weeks in I realize I'm not as mentally prepared as I need to be for my new place of employment and my charges. So I park the truck and ride my motorcycle to work in heavy street traffic. It's a death wish and an early-morning mind sharpener that affirms you are alive. My left thumb lives on the horn button. The cat lady I see every morning with the "Purr More Hiss Less" bumper sticker does not like for me to reside in her blind spot. She almost ran me into a Starbucks one morning. Into an oncoming yellow school bus on another. My big back tire leaves fifteen-foot skid marks on a Georgia state highway. I seem to always get behind a fellow in a Chevy Blazer whose tag reads BOBB. Bobb's flicked-out cigarettes bound back along the asphalt toward me, and leap up at the last second and *tick* off my helmet. I arrive to school fully revved.

My textbooks are twelve years old, donated from schools all over town. President Clinton has not yet appeared in my civics book.

While I was being interviewed, I was asked if I'd be

willing to take on the slow learners in the high school...could I teach them civics and language arts and vocabulary and literature and art appreciation without any academic expectations whatsoever...and before I could answer I'd been hired to do it.

So I place my right hand over my heart and start pledging. Lamar, too. Our school mascot shambles over and holds my left hand. Lamar was so jealous.

TEACH THIS

On the first day of school I asked my students how they learn the best and what they're good at. It was a question more for me, I said, but would eventually be good for you, too. You know, once we get to work.

A few of them huffed and dropped their heads on their desks. That's the power of the phrase...*get to work.*

I had a yellow legal pad out and a pen ready to write. One of the nicest things you can do for someone is to shut up and listen to them...and even write down what they say while they're watching you.

They were watching. I got the impression no one had ever asked them those questions.

Fabio said he loves vampires. Nesbit said he's good at sleeping late. Brainerd said he wanted me to quit talking so fast.

I made the time-out sign with my hands and said...Oh-*kay.* Why don't we start all over again.

BLACK IS THE NEW GREEN

I don't have a real classroom yet because they're still clearing out a classroom for me across the hall from Mr. Warbird's and Miss Velvet's classrooms. My future classroom is crammed with a bunch of Mr. Squirm's science junk.

Mr. Warbird teaches math and history and Miss Velvet teaches sociology, and some other subjects I'm not quite sure about yet. Mr. Squirm is the science teacher at this school. He won't stop talking once he starts talking even when you interrupt him several times. To find this out on my own was a real life moment.

The door of my future classroom opens only three feet. You reach a hand over to the light switch on the right. Suddenly...old, student-made Styrofoam globes of Mars and other unknown planets. Desks. Chairs. All kinds of filing cabinets. Boxes of beakers. Busted-up lecterns. A plastic jug of crawfish soaking in something. A plastic jug of grasshoppers soaking in something else.

Most of ceiling tiles are missing and pink wads of insulation are dangling into the room. Looking up through the holes you can see the roof of the school. When it rains it's loud in there.

It's loud anyway where I teach. For now I've got a corner of the commons room—with a huge, three-thousand pound wood desk for me and some tables for two for the students in front of a real blackboard that's really black and I've got orange chalk. When class breaks they're all in there running around and banging things and laughing and talking and chasing each other.

But during class everybody knows not to run and scream as they walk across the room to go to the bathroom or get a drink of water.

Precious, the school's secretary came up to my corner classroom this morning and said she needed to take my picture for my employee ID badge.

I said okay, and stopped the process of education immediately for some students who seemed grateful. I stood up in front of my black blackboard, on which I had scrawled a whole bunch of life-changing information in orange chalk such as: Your weekly writing assignment is due Friday!

A little later when Precious came back up here to give me my new employee ID badge she said check it out.

I checked it out. My blackboard came out green and the writing in orange chalk was yellow. Freaky, I said.

I *know*, Precious said. I *know*. She looked like she wanted a hug.

I asked Precious when I needed to wear this thing and for what occasions.

Precious said she really didn't know.

Precious works just part-time, so that makes sense. She performed half of her job.

DIEGO ENJOYS SCHOOL ACTIVITIES

Even though they're held on Friday afternoons after school, I like faculty meetings. It's satisfying to share ideas and chitchat with like-minded people after an intense and exhausting week of sharing ideas and chitchatting with wild-minded adolescents and young people.

Of particular note on today's agenda was the news of a lower school student named Diego. Diego, we were told by his teacher, Miss Manhater, has been for the last couple of weeks locking himself in the school's activity room and masturbating. Diego locks both doors, she said, and masturbates in there.

To my surprise, no one started laughing or pointing at each other.

It was then calmly explained to us by Miss Manhater that she's going to meet with Diego and his parents next week to explain that at his age it's okay to masturbate all you want, but not at school.

And then we passed around a pan of brownies.

THE CHEESEBURGER TEST ANXIETY LECTURE

When I announced today that next week we'd have our first test in civics class over section 1 and 2 in the workbook Biff started whining and thumping on his desk with both hands.

Then I handed out the study guide and said with a wink or two that the study guide would be very, very, very much like the test, and after we all worked through the study guide together then they'd probably do real well on the test.

This wink-wink-nudge-nudge information did not make Biff stop whining and thumping.

I asked Biff to stop whining and thumping anyway. He was also rolling his eyes around as if his pupils were chasing something. All this was making Fabio, Lucy, Nesbit, and Brainerd uneasy. I told Biff so. I told Biff it's okay to be nervous about tests, but if you let me help get you ready for the test then you'll be fine. I promise. Trust me, I said. I sat down in the front of the class and let Biff go on for a few more moments.

In addition to Biff whining and thumping and eye rolling about the test, he also told us that he was a failure at tests and a failure in life.

Nesbit was sitting there with a bloody tissue he kept pressing on some sore or wound or something on his bloody bottom lip. I thought about vomiting but I was on a roll.

Then I made a huge teaching mistake. I kept talking. I asked Biff, politely again, that he wasn't a failure and to please quit whining and maybe he could meet with me after class and we could...go over some strategies that would ease his mind?

Biff said no way.

Then I really went nuts and said I'd like to give you my quick cheeseburger lecture.

Biff paused for a moment.

I said you know what a cheeseburger is, right?

Biff said he did. That he likes cheeseburgers.

Okay, then. So if I gave you an assignment, and everybody else, to describe to me, even in writing, what a cheeseburger was like, then you could probably do it real easy. You could tell me what the buns look like and that the hamburger is made of ground beef and whatnot and what color mustard is.

Yeah.

So what that tells me is that you *can* memorize things. You just have to get real familiar with it and becoming real familiar with something requires some diligent work and study and that means you have to work hard and spend time doing it and maybe sacrifice something else for it like playing video games or sitting on a couch and staring at something for long periods of time while snacking. So anyway, that's my infamous cheeseburger lecture I said.

Right then, Biff jumped up, rumbled out of the classroom and into the commons room where he kicked one of the couches several times real good and dropped enormous cuss bombs at the couch while he was kicking it.

I walked up behind Biff and asked him to try to calm down.

Biff said why don't I go fuck a cheeseburger.

I told Biff there was no way I'd do that to a cheeseburger as that would be particularly unholy. I said it was probably illegal, too.

Tonight I had to calm his parents down, too, by e-mail. They said I called Biff a whiner. I said I told him...he *was* whining. You are whining, Biff, I had said calmly, and it's not a good look for you.

A few e-mail exchanges later, Biff parents thanked me for what I was doing for their son. His mother said I was changing lives!

I went to bed thinking this was still going to get worse. The infamous cheeseburger lecture usually has a long-term, unappetizing quality.

SMELL YA LATER

I was teaching my civics class some good stuff about the Great Wall of China and I heard Miss Velvet across the hall scream at somebody in her class...If you have to fart like that...leave the *rooooom!*

I started laughing. While I was laughing I was looking at my students to see if they heard her, but they didn't. I guess they really were interested in how long it took to build the Great Wall of China. Which was a pretty long dang time.

Then Miss Velvet yelled...Simeon, I'm almost *done* with you to-*day!*

I looked at my watch. It was only 8:45.

IT GOT WORSE

Right after I handed out the 18 question test on section 1 and 2 from our workbook, which was full of geography questions, Biff jumped up again and said he refused to take the test and then he rumbled out of the classroom and into the commons room where instead of kicking the couch he sat down on it.

When I came back into the classroom Nesbit said he wasn't going to take the test either and instead of rumbling out of the classroom Nesbit stayed in his seat and started shaking.

Lucy, Brainerd, and Fabio were wide-eyed.

Nesbit was shaking so badly I asked him to come out into the hallway with me so he wouldn't freak out his classmates any more. Out in the hallway Nesbit literally started frothing at the mouth, and in addition to shaking, he started sweating, too.

Just a few feet away, Miss Velvet had heard the rumpus and she came out to see what was going on. She's known Nesbit for a couple of years, so she said for me to go back into my classroom and that she'd talk to him and maybe walk him to today's counselor.

There are three ladies who alternate days of the week where they come in and help kids like Nesbit from all over the building who are having a rough day. Two ladies have PhDs and one lady is still working on hers. They stay real busy. They saddle up to teachers later in the day and ask...So what happened today with...? You know, tell me *your* version of events.

Nesbit never came back to class, and he never came back to class for the rest of the week. That's basically my version of the worst of the events. I miss him.

IT GETS BETTER

I had a third student decide to seek attention. Monk does not like to do classwork and he definitely does not like to do homework, even if a homework assignment is to bring one word, and a comment about its etymology, to class tomorrow to talk about with your pals and your favorite teacher.

Classwork gets Monk to squirming and twisting around in his seat, and the mention of homework will get Monk to not doing any more classwork while he's squirming and twisting around in his seat so he doesn't have to look at you anymore.

This has been going on for some time.

I have met with his mother. I have had a number of lively e-mail exchanges with her. I met with her a second time. She always says she's about to go over the edge. She makes a hand gesture when she says it, and it looks like she's squeezing a grape between her fingers.

I keep educating, though. Monk keeps twitching and squirming. The day before a vocabulary test I pull my ultimate teacher trick and give Monk a copy of the test. Just Monk. The actual copy of the test. Fifteen vocabulary words we've been working on for two weeks. Just match the words with the definitions on the next page. The actual test.

I get an e-mail from Monk's mother that night, at 11:18. I just wanted to let you know, she says, that Monk is not ready to take the test tomorrow. I appreciate your understanding in this matter.

All of a sudden I'm told that Monk will no longer be coming to second period language arts class, and instead, he'll sit in the commons room during that time using the time as a private study hall, while you keep an eye on him.

I met with his mother a third time. She says she's about to go over the edge. She squeezed the grape again. I told her she's already told me that. I patted her on the arm and told her to take care. Then I had to walk away. Before I turned the corner, I turned and saw her already cornering Miss Velvet, squeezing her grape.

I am convinced that Monk's mom is secretly and smugly grateful for not having to do as much of Monk's homework anymore. One class less. She's making progress. I am also convinced that strong mothers create strong young men and that crazy mothers drive their sons crazy and make them crazy and everybody else crazy, too.

At least her late-at-night e-mails stopped. When late at night you hear that familiar beep of a newly arrived message…you wonder how much more cooked-up momma drama you can take.

LEARNING MOMENT

Sometimes they sneak up on you, too. Learning moments.

The school needed some inflation needles for our beat-up soccer balls and footballs and basketballs and I bought some last night and brought them in.

I'd been throwing the football with Red the past couple of days in the gym before the day started and we'd been throwing a dull football. Red catches pretty well and he can throw it long, but they usually go way over my head and bounce into the boy's bathroom or clank around under the water fountain.

In the equipment room this morning I was going to screw one of the new needles into the hand pump but Red wanted to do it. I let him. No big deal. A teacher and an athletic student in the sports room fiddling with equipment. Manly stuff. A couple of real warriors.

Red had a hard time grasping the needle and he couldn't get it screwed in. He fumbled with the pump with his other hand. He dropped everything on a table and tried again. He made odd, frustrated noises in his throat.

I offered again to do it.

Red tried again. His hands didn't seem to be connected to his arms. Or to his brain. I felt for him. Sometimes you have to watch what would make most people turn away.

I offered to do it again. He gave me the pump and the needle and ran out. A minute or two later we were throwing a firm football back and forth, just like I promised him we'd do the morning before.

Todd Sentell

THE ANGRY CHIHUAHUA NAMED PEANUT

Runners run. Swimmers swim. Philosophers think about things. And writers write. So every week, in hopes of my language arts students becoming better writers, they get a writing assignment on Monday that's due Thursday. One hundred words minimum. Typed. I tell them I'll edit it for you as many times as you hand your draft to me before Thursday but not on Thursday. Take me up on this offer and you'll surely receive an A. Maybe an A-plus.

The first week of school they got to write about anything they wanted to, and then I started cooking up fascinating writing topics that thrilled me but irritated them. Some think the entire idea of getting a weekly writing assignment is not fun in any way.

Most of the time I let them get started on it in class. One thing about these kids: they do not like homework. It's not a battle with most of them. It's a dinner table apocalypse of the End of Days variety.

This week the assignment was to write a fictional story about a talking Chihuahua who goes to Six Flags Over Georgia. What would he do? What would the Chihuahua say? What kind of hilarious madcap mischief would a dang Chihuahua get into at your favorite teacher's favorite childhood haunt?

Brainerd gave me his first draft by the end of class on Monday. He's a quick typist. He has a fine imagination, Brainerd, but it requires that I scratch my head a lot as I read his work:

The Talking Chihuahua Named Peanut

The talking dog gos to six flags the other day and says to the manager I want to work at six flags you faggot and the manager says okey you talking dog.The dog was wearing a red leather jacket with is name tag that says peanut and Im working at six flags baby.A guy comes up to him and says you are not human.Of course Im not human im a freaken Chihuahua now to you want to ride this fraken thing or not and then he says whatever. At the bummer cars he was taking a break he got on to the bummer cars to see if it was working but he went to fast and crashed in front of the rear he was driveing everywhere running over people and the manager says what are you doing you stupid dog and the dog says I cant stop this thing the he says haveint you tried the brake he said oh right he puts his foot on the pedal and he stops then peanut says wow this thing was freaken fast then the managers face turned red then he says you stupid dog you wreaked the whole park then he says I can fix that. The end

Now that's some stream of consciousness writing. Chihuahua style.

ROUGH DAY

Today was one of those days that leave me, and them, staring at nothing, exhausted. Today I feel that most of my students in my classes will not go to college and will end up living with their parents for the rest of their lives. Some parents will probably be okay with that and some won't. Some of my kids will be okay with that, too.

They have been inattentive, uninterested. Grabbing for any answer, no matter how odd or way, way off. Some have shut down. Some have slept through what I thought were riveting lectures on riveting topics.

One student in particular, who rose above the waves of the usual slosh of disinterest, despite my cajoling to take school and life and relationships a bit more seriously, has me feeling that he will somehow graduate from this school and after the graduation ceremony he will be treated to a nice lunch at a nice restaurant and then go directly home to be placed under the stairs.

For some it won't be what college they go to, it'll be what federal prison. For others, they'll just disappear into civilization and they will find friends and find work and be okay. I don't know if they'll be happy, but they'll probably be okay.

We'll try again tomorrow.

WORDLY CONCERNS

Words are powerful things. They're sometimes like bullets on a page of paper. Without words, all we'd do, I guess, is draw, wave our arms around, spit, and grunt.

In first period language arts class today, we read, going around, one at a time, the new fifteen words at the beginning of lesson 4. *Punctilious* landed on Lucy. She asked...Is that OCD?

I was struck silent for a moment. Struck impressed. She's so sneaky smart. Lucy has obsessive compulsive disorder. I said, Not really. God. Sort of. Read the definition.

Lucy said...Careful of and attentive to details, especially ones relating to good manners and behavior. Punctilious.

In class, sitting at her desk, when Lucy speaks to you in her always-quiet voice, she puts her right elbow on the desk and then presses the four fingers together. Then she moves her thumb underneath her fingers and it all looks like a duck beak. Lucy doesn't move the fingers like a beak when she talks, but she told me one time after I asked her why she does that...It helps me communicate better.

Lucy also constantly picks at the skin on her arms and pulls out her arm hair and picks at the skin on her ankles and picks the hairs off of her ankles, too. All the teachers let her do it for a while and then ask her to stop. She stops without complaining, but then she starts up again when you're looking the other way. She pays attention while she picks, but sometime you can catch her lost in that world and she can't find where the going-around-the-class reading had ended with Brainerd or Fabio.

Miss Velvet, her homeroom teacher and advisor by default, says Lucy's mother is oblivious to her daughter's disorders. That's hard to believe, but it could be true. As a teacher you get to know the parents real well, too, by default.

Lucy had come to class today with the hairs of her right arm shaved off. Her left arm still had hairs. No one other than Lucy's mother would have shaved the arm. I'm pretty sure. Maybe Lucy's mother is oblivious to everything else that puts her in this school.

Now we're quietly working on our own in the vocabulary workbook, except Lucy. She's hunkered down over her left arm. I don't say anything. I get up and walk around and look out a window and actually whistle a little bit and then sneak up behind Lucy to discover that in the duck beak she had hidden a pair of tweezers.

Punctilious.

FREE MONEY

Fall semester parent-teacher conferences are coming up. They're optional for the parents but not for the teachers. I teach eleven students. Some of them in two different classes, so that puts me with five students I teach only once during the day. I get to teach and cajole and bark at and preach at Brainerd, Fabio, and Lucy twice a day. I'm sure they love it, too.

I have one parent-teacher conference scheduled. It's with Peetie's mother. So today, a few days out, I asked Peetie, with the most sincerity I could muster, what he'd like for me to tell his mother.

Peetie said...I don't knooooooow. To be fair, Peetie moaned it. That's the way he talks when he's under any kind of pressure, self-imposed or otherwise or perceived.

I told him I was serious. Really, what *good things* would you like for me to tell her?

He moaned again. I don't *knooooooow*.

I asked him one more time. Then I told him this is your chance. That I was wide open to ideas.

Kells said...*Dang*, Peetie. I really think he's serious.

WHAT IF

What if there was a school where students were advanced to the next grade based only on their emotional and social maturity and intelligence? Even if a kid's a genius. Even if he performs at the highest academic level, or beyond, he can't go to the next grade until he quits whining, moaning, screaming, shutting down, shouting, pounding his desk with his hand, rolling his eyes, huffing, and breaking things.

Or all ten in one class period.

The first thing you begin to notice about a person you meet for the first time is not how rich they are or how educated they are. The first thing you notice is if the person has any manners. Guys, despite your challenges, you're capable of learning and using manners.

I tell my students this genius information every day. And when they huff about it, we role play until they pound their desks.

A TOTAL BUG OUT

If you were a television reporter with nothing better to do than to go up to people on the street and ask dumb rednecks on the street their opinions on monumental world events such as…"Do you think a little seventy pound kid could thoroughly disrupt and discombobulate a P.E. class where kids were actually encouraged to scream and yell and run and jump around?"…I would pretty much guarantee you the dumb rednecks and any other sensible people would say, But you're not talking about a kid named *Bugs*.

Coach Hank asked me to substitute this week in his P.E. class for reasons unknown to me other than Coach Hank knows I don't have a class when he teaches P.E. to Bugs and the rest of his pals.

Before the class I went out to my truck and got my coach's whistle. In small independent schools a teacher has to sometimes wear many hats.

It's hard to put into words how Bugs can disrupt a P.E. class in a huge gym with large amounts of elbow room, and even if I had filmed the event you still wouldn't believe it. I was constantly blowing the whistle at Bugs. He really must love sharp, loud noises. I know I did.

Anyhow, later in the day I was so messed up by the monumental world event that I asked one of Bugs' teachers if the school had Bugs on a behavior-modification plan.

She looked at me with a goofy expression on her face as if I were crazy. Then she said...He's okay when he's interested in the subject.

I looked back at her with my goofiest expression.

I have a thought, now. Disband the Army, Navy, Coast Guard, Marines, and Air Force and just send Bugs to areas of conflict around the world. Just Bugs, and let him do his thing. There will be peace on Earth. And then we can charge great sums for the rental of Bugs to other countries. That is my thought.

On Friday all the kids in the school went on the annual one-day rafting trip to North Carolina. I was asked to stay back and help Miss Velvet with the non-outdoorsy types. Miss Velvet doesn't like to fall out of rafts into cold river water. After they all bugged out I saw that somebody had left on the table in the lobby of the school a list of the mind and behavior-altering drugs the students take. I was pretty sure this list should have made the rafting trip, too. It's got a drug dispensing schedule on it that I'm sure would be real helpful to everyone's enjoyment, or not, of the school rafting trip.

I looked down the list of students. There are some mighty powerful drugs at work in most of them. Sometimes two drugs. I got to Bugs.

Next to his name was just one item: VITAMINS.

ARE MUSTACHIOED MEN ALLOWED IN THIS ESTABLISHMENT?

Clutch is growing a mustache. So is another guy who I don't have in class.

In class today I asked Clutch how he thinks it's looking. He reached up and rubbed his finger along what are just a few wisps of real whiskers to sprout one day. The prototypes, say.

Clutch smiled, but didn't say anything. He hardly ever says anything, but he smiles just fine.

Kells said...It's looking good, *Clutch!*

I asked Clutch if he and Hamlet, the other guy, were currently involved in a mustache-growing contest.

Clutch shook his head no.

Later in the day, in the commons room, Hamlet was sitting in a chair between classes doing absolutely nothing, and when I saw Clutch walk by I got the two together and made sure they knew starting today that they were in a mustache-growing contest with Mr. Sentell as the judge. Hamlet never says much either, but he did manage this: My mother says I have to shave it off.

Like Clutch, Hamlet grinds through the day without words and complaint. But he's got a few good wisps growing, too, and he knows it and he's proud of himself. You can tell. When something's deeply personal, Aspy kids can show some real emotion. Some real joy, too.

Clutch stood there and smiled at Hamlet. Hamlet smiled back.

A BIT TOOTISH, ARE WE?

Miss Velvet marched into my classroom today out of breath and asked if I had any room spray because she's really had it with them farting all the time in her class.

I thought for a moment...What advice do you give a fellow teacher whose students know they can constantly get away, every day, with farting the moment they walk into her class? Obtain a flame thrower? A Taser?

I think they've won, and once they've won around here there's not much you can do to come back. I told Miss Velvet I didn't have any room spray...I reached into my teacher's drawer of snacks and headache pills and chewing gum...and pulled out my can of Old Spice "After Hours" body spray.

Miss Velvet said...So yours fart, too?

Nope, I said. I don't allow farting in my classes. I just like the way this stuff makes the air smells. Super sexy. I tossed her the can.

Miss Velvet huffed out.

I guess I just gave her the advice she needed.

THE MAGIC WORD

I subbed for Coach Hank again today, but this time it was a different P.E. class that didn't include Bugs. But I was ready for him. I had my whistle even though it really doesn't work on Bugs and I deep down know it.

It's loud, that's for sure. It gets my attention when I blow it, but after a while what you really need is a howitzer. Or just say the word...homework.

Homework. Tonight's homework. Let's just make the rest of that section of the workbook...*home*work.

I blew my whistle in P.E. today in honor or Bugs and Coach Hank, but in civics class I know now I'll never need a whistle to get their attention. I hardly ever give out homework, but today I did. Just a thinking question. Bring what you think is the answer to school in your head tomorrow and when class starts and I tell you to give me your answer to the question...you may yell the answer at me.

So here's how Lucy, sleepy Brainerd, Biff and Fabio reacted to my unholy utterance today:

- Fabio looked as if I told him his dog got run over. Then he started rubbing his big head of hair, wildly, with both hands as if he were searching for a snake in there.
- Biff instantly dropped his head and made an audible huffing noise.
- Brainerd grimaced, and then kept his grimace going pretty wildly for some time while staring at me. He looked as if he was hoping I was about to say...Just kidding.

- Lucy, for maybe the first time this semester, really looked me in the eye. She took her glasses off, leaned toward me, and widened her eyes as if I had announced it was time for an eyeball inspection.

Homework. I thought about asking what monumental activities ten seconds of thinking might destroy at home, although you could think of the answer while you drive home and then it would be called carwork, but didn't. They were freaked out enough.

TABOO WRITING

We've been working pretty hard on thirty new words from our Wordly Wise workbook, and today on the test, after the frantic matching up of words, I asked them to take six of any of the thirty words and use the word in a complete sentence. Lucy really does like music. But I think she might like the personalities who make the music even more:

1. Taboo from the Black Eyed Peas had to <u>recuperate</u> because he got a shot that made him feel fragile.
2. The Black Eyed Peas <u>meanders</u> from place to when they're on tour.
3. One of the medicines Taboo was taking <u>exhorted</u> him not to not take it with alcohol.
4. Taboo's grandmother sometimes <u>dote</u> on him.
5. After a accident that broke his tailbone, Taboo had to stay <u>sedentary</u> for 3 months.
6. Taboo was <u>lamenting</u> because his girlfriend left him.

I Googled Taboo of the Black Eyed Peas. Seems like an okay guy. That's what Lucy says, too. And she'll yell at you if don't agree with her.

RAISED EYEBROWS

A little kid came up to me this morning during Lord of the Flies and said how happy he was that his eyebrows grew back. He stood there and smiled at me and worked his eyebrows around. Today was casual day, too. Instead of the school uniform, the kids can wear about anything they want on casual day every other Friday. This fellow was wearing a green t-shirt and there were pictures of stereo speakers on the front. Just stereo speakers. Nothing else. Weird. Who thinks t-shirts up?

Anyway, I hardly ever see this kid. I don't even know his name, but he picked me out this morning of all the teachers and other kids to tell me the good news about his eyebrows growing back so I won't overthink it. I asked him...had he been sick?

No.

Shaved them off himself...while partying massively?

No.

I looked deep into his eyes and could tell he was making it up as he went along. And then, the best and only response I could think of, I delivered. I shook his hand and said...Congratulations.

The kid said...For *what?*

ROLLING ADMISSIONS. ALL OVER US

Lamar is a new student, just admitted after we've been at it for several weeks, and he's been placed in two of my classes. Since his first day with us a few days ago, he's been showing me and the rest of his new classmates how to raise a highly purified form of hell.

This morning I got an e-mail about Lamar. It was a message to Lamar's teachers from Headmistress Lynyrd Skynyrd:

> **Monique called this morning and wanted you all to know that Lamar was detoxed over the long weekend of all medications. She would appreciate it if you would provide her feedback on his behavior so she can keep his doctor informed. Her observation at home is that he was much less agitated but she is not sure how things will go at school after the short break.**

What great timing: things are not going well for Lamar at school after the short break.

At all.

In any way.

Here's what I didn't e-mail to his mother, even though it's my honest testament, forged by being in the same zip code with him every day.

Lamar also has a new and dangerous-looking hairdo I can't quit looking at.

Anyway, here goes my attempt to calm myself down:

Monique,

I'm so happy to have Lamar as a new student in two of my classes, but I think he's confused! School is for <u>making</u> friends!

I'd have to say that Brainerd won't be Lamar's fan club president any time soon. Brainerd is one sensitive dude—just mention the word "homework" and see some real spider walking up walls and across ceilings—but I have to side with Brainerd on this one: I guess if Lamar had singled me out on his very first day of school and insisted on flicking his wiggling green tongue at me all day, even in class and at lunch, that I'd be deeply unnerved, too, and wondering if there was a God. I should tell you that Lamar's tongue is so green and the wiggling and flicking is so vigorous and persistent and enthusiastic that I won't be surprised if Brainerd brings a pair of pliers to school and pulls Lamar's tongue out of his head and then shows his own tongue to Lamar before Brainerd stomps the tongue to death.

You know those magician guys who spin dinner plates and put them up on sticks while they toss tissues up in the air with both hands and sort of juggle the tissues while they ride a unicycle while other people in leotards jump onto their heads? Exactly. Guess which one of those Lamar likes to do in civics class? Exactly. I had to kick him out of class so I could hide the box of tissues from him because he was making everybody else so dizzy and mesmerized they almost puked.

My fault for getting all worked up when it looks like Lamar says "fuck" under his breath all day. You don't have to be a professional lip reader to catch the awesome power of that one. Lamar says he's saying "fine" but I know better. So, what the fuck! Fine, I'll give Lamar the benefit of the doubt!

Call me sensitive, too, but I did take it personally when Lamar didn't have anything to write with the other day, and after I gave him a brand new pencil to use he instantly and angrily crushed the tip of the pencil into his desk as if he were trying to kill the desk. I casually noted to Lamar that he'd probably need the pencil...for the rest of his classes? No? Maybe? Lamar looked at me as if I were stupid and said he'll sharpen it later...duh. Makes sense to me.

Had any kid he bullied in the other schools he's gotten kicked out of ever punched him in the nose or tried to strangle him to death with their bare hands?

Would you like to know what he says about you and your ex-husband and some weird cousin of his who he says is also his uncle?

Maybe I should tell you he gets kicked out of class...out of both of my classes...every ten to fifteen minutes. I'm doing all I can to keep him in class, which is my noble goal as a teacher who cares, but I hate to think about the money the other student's parents are wasting because Lamar won't let me do my job which means the other students aren't getting the expensive education their parents are paying for. I can just imagine what the other students are telling their parents about this new guy at school named Lamar. If the e-mails and meeting requests to Headmistress Lynyrd Skynyrd about this new kid Lamar aren't already flying around I'll be real surprised.

Anyhow, I imagine you're overwhelmed, too, but I promise I won't give up on him here at school. Every once in a while he does us all a huge favor: he'll ask if he can take a time-out...he scoots right on out the door and then we never see him again for huge chunks of the rest of the day. He usually ends up with one of the school counselors, and he says he really loves those ladies and that they have some great talks. Of course, the school counselors don't get treated by Lamar like we do. I wonder how they'd handle it if they received an all-day dose of in-your-face disrespect and defiance of even one of my simplest class rules, such as, "Lamar, Please don't make ear-exploding jungle animal noises every time you yawn."

Hang in there. Of course, there are other places for guys like Lamar, but they're called emergency rooms, county jails, and federal prisons.

I'll give Lamar some credit. Hey, Lord God in heaven have mercy on all of us, right? He's got some real quaint charm, and he lays some of it on me from time to time. I always get amused when Lamar asks me a question...and then when I give him the answer to the question he argues about the answer. And then when I tell him I've got another answer that he might like even better he interrupts me with another question...another question so far off-topic that there's no measuring device known to human civilization that can determine how far he is from Planet School.

I'll chalk something else up to quaint charm as opposed to giving in to thinking that Lamar is possessed by multiple demons or outer space aliens. A lot of times he'll be freaked about something and I'll give him some wonderful advice and some great guidance which I know to him looks like more work. Anyway, after I'm finished pretty much pointing him in the direction of the beautiful light, which usually takes me a couple of minutes, he'll mumble under his breath..."Whatever" or "Fuck that." Like I said...super quaint!

Well, in closing, in language arts class, we've been reading and interpreting and enjoying J.D. Salinger stories while Lamar flicks and wiggles his tongue at Brainerd and constantly taps Lucy on her arm while she's concentrating real hard on pulling her arm and leg hairs out with a pair of tweezers. Lamar really is good at making Lucy not like him. In civics class, I'm fairly sure the students have been fascinated with my passionate lectures on how to read road maps. Dang, why would Lamar want to get kicked out of class while we're having so much fun?

I wimped out. I e-mailed Lamar's mom and told her that Lamar said he'd straighten right up if he had a stress ball to squeeze. I said to please have him bring one to school if he has one, and if he doesn't, please purchase one this evening. Thank you!

THE RIVER OF PANE

A long time ago, a Christ-haunted writer, Flannery O'Connor, wrote a Christ-haunted story called "The River" about a little boy named Harry Ashfield whose party animal parents find him a new babysitter who takes him to hear a hick preacher at an orange river. The new babysitter isn't some hot, high school cheerleader who's pretty good with kids and needs money. The new babysitter, Mrs. Connin, is a cynical, critical, speckled-skin, night-shift working, Jesus freak task-master whose own children have no manners.

At the end of the story, Harry drowns himself in the river, gladly.

Before Bevel drowns himself in the river, several other fascinating things happen: Harry personally changes his name to "Bevel;" Bevel, upon being introduced to Mrs. Connin's three sons, immediately gets bullied by them; Bevel gets run over by a pig and cries about it for five minutes; Bevel steals a picture book about Jesus from Mrs. Connin; Bevel gets baptized in the orange river by a preacher whose name is also Bevel; and early the next morning Bevel rides the street trolley out of town all by himself with no problem at all while his parents sleep off their hangovers after the previous evening's sex orgy. Then, later that morning, after his trolley ride, Bevel drowns himself in the river...while the local gas station owner, who has a purple tumor hanging off the side of his head, chases after Bevel in the river with a huge peppermint stick.

Flannery O'Connor is my favorite writer of all time.

On Wednesday and Thursday of this week, I read the story to my literature fanatics in second period language arts class. They loved it. And then, today, I read some questions to them about the story and they answered them on paper. There were seventeen questions in all and one asked them if they thought Bevel was smart or stupid. Another question asked them...As it refers to Mrs. Connin, what do you think "skeleton" means? The last question was this: On the deepest level, what do you think the story is about? Kells wrote:

I think this story is about a boy. A boy that thinks he can find happiness in the river. The happiness about not being around drunks and smokers.

Clutch wrote:

Bevel was trying to Baptize himself in the river so that all his Pane was gone. Which was to stop his Parents from having Partys and getting Drunk.

Good for Kells and Clutch. I didn't mark their answers as wrong. We all figured that Bevel was a whole lot happier now, too, floating in a river that probably led to the beach. Red and Peetie weren't convinced Bevel was dead. When you think about it, the story really never said so.

Next week we're going to read another Flannery O'Connor story, "Revelation." On the best level it's a story about a nasty fat girl who's smart in school who beans a smug fat woman in the head with a huge book called *Human Development* while they're both sitting in a waiting room, waiting on the same doctor. Leading up to this revelation takes up almost half of the story. Honestly, why would we want to read any further?

POWERFUL WRITING

Kells told me today, in front of everybody in second period

language arts class, without embarrassment, that when his mother read my report card comments she cried.

He's a good kid, and I've never worried too much about him. And I think he's improving every week: socially, academically, and creatively.

I think what that means is that Kells was probably a pretty hard case not too long ago.

FUN WITH HAIR

Yesterday, in a serious tone of voice, I asked Clutch if he was growing his mustache on school time.

Clutch looked off into the distance as if the map of the United States on the wall of my classroom held the answer.

I asked him again...increasing my tone of voice to a level of comic obnoxiousness never before seen in American education. *Clutch*, you're not growing your *mus*tache on *school time...are* you?

I deeply believed that Clutch does not understand zany humor. Missouri, I guess, urged him to say ... *Yes*.

Today, as second period was ending, Peetie said I'd like to pay Clutch a compliment.

I thought, This should be interesting...as in all my years I've never had a student pay another student a compliment.

Peetie said I'd like to thank Clutch for not allowing his mustache to disrupt class.

In about three seconds everybody got it. We laughed so loudly Mr. Warbird across the hall opened his door to see what the rumpus was about. Then Peetie said...And I could *hear* the damn thing growing, too.

CHOICE COMMUNICATIONS

What dang teacher says having to keep up with e-mails is a hassle? My heart beats when I mash the refresh button, and then imagine, in a moment of insanity, what I really want to write back:

> **E-mail from Brainerd's mother**
> **Brainerds papers fell out of his binder this morning on the way to school. They were behind the seat. I didn't see them till i got home. Just thought id let ya know. Thanks**

Good to hear from you! After your son discovered all the work he'd produced this week in class wasn't in his binder the poor chap nearly had a nervous breakdown. I sprayed him with a hose to get him to come off the ceiling and when that didn't work I lit the tip of a rolled-up newspaper and smoked him down! Anyhow, he frantically redid everything in class from the entire week. Now he has *two* sets of papers!

> **E-mail from Fabio's father**
> **Could you please give Fabio a bit more time to work on his writing assignment? He says that microsoft word was not working on many of the computers at school today and due to things we have planned over the next couple of days we are not going to be around the house or computer much. Thanks.**

Gosh, dad. Sorry the extracurricular activities you force on your son are disrupting his education. Pardon me, but *no*. He's known about the super easy assignment for three days.

E-mail from Fabio's father

He said something about being lectured about taking responsibility and not being able to get a word in edge-wise. Perhaps, he misunderstood something. I don't know. I get so many mixed up versions of things. Thanks though.

He's exactly right. He got lectured today by me because he needed it and he was also constantly interrupting me while I was lecturing. You want some, too, in the pick-up line today? I'll be happy to come by your window. Now start giving your son some tough love. Start being a father, will ya? And please stop e-mailing me!

E-mail from a calm mother

Thanks very much for your attention to the many details. Trying to rush through assignments has been an issue with him for almost as long as he's been in school. I think his anxiety builds to the point that he just has to relieve it, even if it means not doing the assignment as thoroughly as he should. He's told me that he appreciates how you help him, even when it makes his life momentarily tougher!

You're welcome. I really enjoy teaching your son. He's a good kid because he's got good parents.

E-mail from our admissions lady

Teachers: I just received another e-mail from Gordon's mom. She said she will try to make the conference even though she may be sleepy.

What? Does Gordon's mom play video games all day and all night, too?

E-mail from Lucy's mother
having a hard time getting her up will update.

Mom, no problem! Just do what my dad did to me when I wouldn't get out of bed on school day mornings: yank all the covers and sheets off the bed and carry them out of the room.

E-mail from Avi's mother
I'm keeping Avi home from school today. He went to New York over the weekend for his new cousin's Bris and they didn't get back until really late last night. He's exhausted and that's a recipe for disaster with him.

Jesus, how's his poor cousin?

E-mail from Brainerd's mother
Can you make sure you write in brainerd agenda that he has to finish his draft? Brainerd might tell me otherwise. thanks

I'll guarantee you he'll tell you otherwise.

E-mail from Larry's mother
We had to put our dog down late yesterday and we have had him 16+ years. Larry may be a bit fragile today.

Larry, welcome to world of pet ownership and one of the toughest moments in life. Hurry up and get another dog.

E-mail from Fabio's father
He keeps telling me he did it in class. Thanks

He really did do it in class. Sometimes you have to believe him, but *when* to believe him I really couldn't say.

E-mail from Fabio's father
Fabio is now saying something to the effect that he was told today that he does not have to re-test because of some other test you are focusing on now. Is this so, or is he mistaking the fact that you are letting him decide if/when with the idea that he doesn't have to re-take it. Please let me know. Thanks.

That wacky Fabio! What a master of confusion your son has become! I don't know what he's talking about, either, and I'm the dang teacher!

E-mail from Fabio's father
Fabio never brought home material to study for such a test (a study guide, book, outlines on chapters to cover, or worksheets). Or he didn't tell me about it if he did.

Lord have mercy! If Fabio would have brought home his study guide, his book, outlines on chapters to read over, and worksheets...you definitely would have known it!

E-mail from our admissions lady
Teachers: Juanita called this morning saying that Toby will not be in today. He was out of control and was taking him to the doctor.

After you spanked him with a wet two-by-four, I hope. I know Toby, and that would really get his privileged, self-absorbed, smug, entitled, defiant, rude, disrespectful attention.

WHAT A GUY!

Mr. Warbird teaches Georgia history and when he leaves his door open I can hear him from across the hall.

It's hilarious to hear someone else teach something you taught for years. I asked Mr. Warbird, who also teaches math and finance and public speaking, if he's ever taught Georgia history before.

He had not.

A little bit of what we are and what we stand for and where we're from comes out in teachers, I guess. Mr. Warbird is a Yankee from Philly. From across the hall I listened to this carpetbagger scream: Oglethorpe...now *this* guy. Oh, yeah...and To-mo-*chi*-chi...now *this* guy!

And on and on. In his Yankee squawk.

TEACH LIKE YOUR HAIR'S POSSESSED

When we were in the gym this afternoon getting them out to their rides by screaming their name real loud, a new teacher from the Other Side of the Building edged up to me. We casually yak in the morning Lord of the Flies, too, but today her yak was urgent.

Her name is Miss Kentucky. She's from Kentucky. Miss

Kentucky has an enormous wad of red hair and freckles and a pug nose and she's maybe four feet tall. Her ancestors surely spoke with Irish accents, but she speaks like an angelic hillbilly. She told me one time that her accent ain't as bad as some of her relatives and people she knows from where she grew up.

Miss Kentucky said she felt bad about something. She named off all of the kids in her last class. The person who assembled that class must have been out of their mind. One of the students in the class was Bugs. Really, after hearing the roll I thought what the class really needs is Miss Kentucky and three experienced prison guards posing as parent helpers to assist her.

Anyway, Miss Kentucky said she barked—very extremely gutturally—at them and that she felt bad about it.

I asked her to give me an example.

Miss Kentucky gurgled some words from out of her throat while she gawked open her blue eyes and shook her head which made her wad of hair shiver as if had been electrified. The whole deal was moderately horrific. Miss Kentucky said they had about worn her out and that it sort of felt good to holler at them.

I said in a complimentary tone...that's your Satan voice. Every teacher should have a Satan voice on standby to use when the time is right. Your Satan voice, I explained, comes from deep down and it's so scary that it should even scare you if you do it right. And it should scare them, too, but kids always end up liking it and asking you to do it all the time. At least, I said, that's been my experience.

PLEASE REMEMBER TO FLUSH!

Somebody doo-dooed in the lower school boy's bathroom urinal.

THE HUMAN ANIMAL

I think I'm learning more about some of my students through their weekly writing assignments. I observe everything they say and do, but when they give it back to me in writing I always pause, read, and then ponder.

So if you were an animal this week, what animal would you be and where would you live and what lifestyle would you lead?

> The animal I want to be is a Tyrannosaurus Rex because I sometimes feel like one. I sometimes like to eat meat and I sometimes have a bad temper. I would live in the woods of North America or Asia. In the morning, I would go for a walk in the woods, looking for something to eat. If I see humans coming toward me, I would quickly find a place to hide. I wouldn't talk to the forest animals because I am shy. But I would sometimes ask them a question or two. This is the life I would lead if I was a Tyrannosaurus Rex.

That Lucy. Picking an animal who's extinct, but distinctly her. Fabio was a vampire.

LOOKS LIKE BASKETBALL

Imagine the sound of fourteen fourth to seventh grade boys dribbling thirteen basketballs as vigorously and loudly and courageously as they can. But then there was one little boy didn't have a basketball to dribble. We ran out.

I got asked by Headmistress Lynyrd Skynyrd if I would be Coach Hank's assistant basketball coach of the lower school boys. A few weeks of practice on Monday and Wednesdays and only five games, she said.

I said okay, while I was imagining it would turn out to be exactly what happened today at our first practice. Screaming. Arm flapping. Whining. Moaning. Two laps. Stretching. Wandering off. Lamar not paying attention, even when a whistle is blown, and my whistle and Coach Hank's whistle is loud. Eddie not wanting to stand in line next to Eldrick because Eldrick is mean to him.

Some kid comes walking up in the middle of one of our drills. I ask him if he's on the basketball team.

He says he thinks so.

I asked him if his mother or father filled out the sign-up sheet and gave it to Coach Hank this week. That's what sort of does it.

He didn't know.

I asked him might he have been the person to pull it out of his backpack and give to Coach Hank.

Nope.

I went back to assistant coaching the basketball team. A moment later I looked around to see if the kid who thought he was on the basketball team was hanging around. I never saw him again.

One little kid who I had seen around the building had a mole on his upper lip a few days ago and today he didn't. I asked him what happened to his mole. He said he cut it off this weekend with a razor blade.

Coach Hank has been coaching sports for a long time. While they were working through the dribbling drill—which looked like broken pistons of an engine that won't turn off— he nudged up to me and asked me what the heck we should do next with these guys. I was flattered. Coach Hank was as wide-eyed as me.

BORED MEETING

On Thursdays the school orders pizza for all the kids so they don't have to bring a lunch or buy a lunch. We eat at the eight tables I set up every day in the gym. They get a couple of slices of cheese pizza or pepperoni pizza. They cut in front of each other in line because they love Thursday pizza day so much. Bugs is the worst. And he's also the best at getting caught.

While pizza was being eaten without much chewing, the school was also having a board meeting just on the other side of the gym wall. I figured they could hear the commotion.

I wondered, while I was hoping to get a slice of pizza, too, why wouldn't the board members of the school, who work to support these kids, come out and have the lunch portion of their lunch meeting with us?

Bugs is a whole lot more interesting than spreadsheets and gourmet tuna croissants.

QUIET DEMOCRACY

The state of Georgia law requires you to vote at the precinct where you are registered. If you are unsure you are at the correct precinct, please see a poll official. Authority: Rules of the State Election Board

Today was election day and the school handed the gym over to a bunch of nice old ladies and some ballot booths. So instead of Lord of the Flies all the kids had to go right to their homerooms.

From a walkway above the gym, I watched a whole lot of people come in and vote for Sunday liquor sales and other things, and my only patriotic thought was...what if we unleashed the kids and let these nice old ladies and the people who take the time to vote their wishes mix it up with the kids and basketballs and the footballs and the Hula hoops and the elbows and knees and arms and legs.

There would be screaming and crying and bickering and meltdowns to go with all that, too. I wondered what these local citizens might think.

Of course I know what they'd think.

WRITING UP A STORM

This week's writing assignment was to write up a story, pretending you're a cashier at a grocery store, where you interact with three customers of the personality of your choice—nuts, smelly, cranky, annoying, whacked out, whatever. I wasn't shocked at what got turned in. The cashiers at my grocery store seem dangerous, too.

Clutch, who has selective mutism as well as that mustache that's still growing on school time, turned in the most remarkable story of my students. Notice I said Clutch *has* selective mutism and not *suffers* from selective mutism because I'll tell you he's not suffering from it one bit. I think he's fine not saying a thing in class unless he has to.

Anyhow, Clutch wrote a story called "Storm Over Nevada" where he was a cashier at a grocery store in a town in Nevada about to get hit with a huge storm that was predicted to wipe the town off the globe. People were really buying a lot of beer tonight, Clutch noted in his story.

The Clutch-like cashier in the story was named Durk Sanders. Let that sink in...Clutch is calling himself Durk Sanders. This is a name a script writer would give a guy who dispatches the North Korean army with just a Bowie knife.

When I read the story out loud to the rest of the class and got to the character name of Durk Sanders, given to himself by the mild-mannered Clutch, the fellows thought very highly of Clutch's literary coolness. Come to find out, Durk was a high school student, just like Clutch.

Durk's first customer was an old lady who rolled up with a cart full of cat food. Durk's second customer was a body builder who rolled up a cart full of protein powder and a pack of Marlboro Lites. Durk's third customer was a girl who went to his high school who Durk really didn't know. Durk, however, had always thought she was plain smoking hot, but was too timid to ever say anything to her.

Being a cashier at the grocery store, Durk mused, forced him to talk to people. Durk started talking to the girl. Her name was Linda Clark. Durk never said what she was buying, just that she asked him what he was doing after work...and since an apocalyptic storm was coming this way why not they get to know each other better in the waning hours of human existence.

As I read Clutch's story and got to this electrifying point in the tale, Kells, Peetie, and Red were hooting and hollering in honor of Clutch.

Clutch was smiling, but not with his teeth. He smiles a lot, but never wide enough to show his teeth, which are covered with braces. His glasses are as thick as bricks. His face is covered with red, angry pimples. Clutch also has a speech impediment.

Here's the last sentence of Clutch's story...When my shift was over, I walked to the parking lot to find Linda waiting for me. She was leaning against a light pole. It was storming finally, but the real storm was about to begin.

Kells, Peetie, Red, and their teacher hooted and hollered some more. We all looked at Clutch...Durk...and asked our secretly cool friend the obvious question: What the hell's gotten into you?

POINT SHEET JUST SHOOT ME NOW

This morning, instead of having to go to first period, Miss Velvet got all the high school kids to sit still and shut up while she held a big meeting in the commons room about the new point sheets.

They listened pretty well, too, because the announcement was about how the point sheet you carry around with you all day that the teachers mark up was now re-formatted and rethought to better provide a weekly award system for your good behavior. Miss Velvet said it was basically time for all of y'all to stop singing badly, name calling, bickering, chirping, squeaking, whistling, touching each other, hitting each other, licking each other, making fun of each other, constantly speaking in bad Australian accents, telling the same joke over and over and over, and anything else that annoys and irritates and angers all human beings in the building while wasting our time.

There was some shifting and murmuring. Then Mr. Warbird made a few comments, and as he spoke his voice got louder and louder as he went through the list of annoying things again. Then he said that the lower school kids really look up to you...so start flying straight!

Coach Hank yelled next and his volume switch shorted out, too. Coach Hank also said, while he was making it up as he went along, that the lower school kids really look *up* to you....*so*...uh....*cool* it!

Then Headmistress Lynyrd Skynyrd walks in and starts dispensing her thoughts about the new point sheet...and certain hands start raising. Over the next ten minutes, Simeon the farter, and his good buddy, the king of teenage defiance of America, Abraham, insulted and interrupted Headmistress Lynyrd Skynyrd with a level of calm, experienced, professional precision and determination not to be believed.

These mind-manipulation artists specializing in teachers, school administrators, coaches, school counselors, their psychiatrists, parents, and grandparents, would ask Headmistress Lynyrd Skynyrd a question and when Headmistress Lynyrd Skynyrd was answering the question

Simeon or Abraham would blurt out another question, this time without raising their hand. They performed this technique several times between them. I was in awe. My mouth really did fall open.

Headmistress Lynyrd Skynyrd was visibly knocked off of her stump. Red faced, she stuttered and stumbled and repeated herself. At one point she waggled a finger. At another point she was so flustered that she told them if they had a better idea then to...put it in writing...and get it to her! Headmistress Lynyrd Skynyrd started for the door.

By then, three kids were lying on the floor. A number of them were thumbing their electronic devices with calm, experienced, professional precision and determination, which is not allowed during serious school time.

Lamar, whose volume switch was shorted-out at birth, wondered loudly aloud from his prone position on the floor at the hustling Headmistress Lynyrd Skynyrd, HOW MUCH LONGER!...*he takes a deep breath*...WAS THIS MEETING!...*he takes another deep breath*...GOING TO LAST!

Just fifteen minutes later, in second period, Abraham got kicked out of Spanish class by Miss Kentucky because he was manipulating her mind, too. His earlier sparring session with Headmistress Lynyrd Skynyrd, won by him by a unanimous decision of the teacher judges, left him still riled up, and when he got kicked out of class he proceeded in the direction of the school's front door after turning over three tables in the commons room, and then busted out of the front door and continued at a good pace on up the driveway, and then Abraham ran down Verdant Boulevard a good two to three hundred yards while Mr. Warbird ran after him in his teacher clothes. Right down Verdant Boulevard, which runs by a synagogue, a Methodist church, a Presbyterian church, an Episcopalian church, a drug rehab center, and a neighborhood of townhouses from the low $900s. Glenda Spandex is your on-site agent!

When Abraham moped back into the building, Headmistress Lynyrd Skynyrd suspended him for the rest of the month. Come to find out, Abraham arrived at school that morning already apocalyptically agitated and ready for war because over the weekend he felt he had received, in his opinion, a bad haircut.

During mid-morning snack time, Miss Kentucky was sipping from a mug while I slurped down a jelly-dripping PB&J. I had made a fat ham sandwich for lunch. We were sitting at a table in the commons room while the high schoolers were singing badly, calling each other creative names, bickering, chirping, hair pulling, whistling, touching each other, hitting each other, licking each other, making fun of each other, constantly speaking in bad Australian accents, and telling the same joke over and over and over.

I whispered to Miss Kentucky that the only successful result of our big meeting this morning was that Headmistress Lynyrd Skynyrd got a good ten minute taste of what we have to put up with every minute all day long, all week, every month all month, and then we get angry e-mails from parents at eleven 'o clock at night...and we never storm out of the room in a huff!

Miss Kentucky smiled a satisfied smile, took a sip of her steaming Ty-phoo tea, and said with grin...Delicious.

IF YOU CAN, PLAY. IF YOU CAN'T, WING IT ANYWAY

It's real easy to get a bus full of middle school kids even more freaked out on the way to their big basketball game. All you have to do is point out the Krispy Kreme store that's on the same street as the recreation center where you're about to get slaughtered by the other school. The sign screams in red neon: HOT DOUGHNUTS NOW. DRIVE THRU. Point out the Krispy Kreme doughnut store to the kids enthusiastically, but keep driving. That's the trick.

The name of the other school we played was Champions Experiential Academy. They sure were. At halftime they were leading 22 to 4, but we were more interesting to watch.

One of our players, who had sawed off his facial mole with a razor blade the other day, on his way down court to set up on offense, would often stop by to get a drink of water...during the actual playing of the game. We coached him out of the habit by screaming at him and shoving him back onto the court in a way that looked like, from the parent's perspective across the court, the kindly administering of hugely encouraging words with an affectionate pat or two on the back. You have to practice the coaching technique and hope the parents can't read your lips. Another time he dropped by during the game and said he was having a heart attack. I told him having a heart attack would most likely get him out of homework...so play hard.

Only one of our kids, Ferrari, was going back to school with me and Coach Hank in the bus after the game, so I got his attention during halftime and told him that if he kept playing like he was, which was a peculiar style of basketball probably never before seen in this part of the county, that he could eat all the Krispy Kreme doughnuts he wanted after the game.

Ferrari screamed...Oh, my God! I don't have any money!

I pulled out my money clip, wiggled it, and by God the bill showing on top was a fresh twenty. Upon this beautiful teaching moment...that the underpaid teacher-coach would be buying a lot of doughnuts and allowing him to eat as many as he wanted...Ferrari began jumping up and down. When he jumps into the air, he pulls his legs up underneath him where his knees poke out east and west. While he's in the air he flaps both hands as if they're covered with angry ants. Maybe scorpions. I watched Ferrari jump up and down quite a few times. That loud buzzer used by the scoreboard operator finally stunned him still.

Ferrari is thirteen years old and has the mind of a mischievous pixie who's constantly being electrocuted at all his joints. His body seems to be made of wiggly rubber hoses. Ferrari is the most hyperactive kid, mentally and physically, on all continents of the world and more than any kid who might also be sailing around on any of the oceans and seas, too. I've always liked him. He's the only kid in the school who eats yellow mustard. I brought in a special bottle one day just for him and I hide it in the school kitchen. I don't have him in class but Ferrari says I'm his favorite teacher anyway. I think bribing kids with yellow mustard is fine because it works.

For our team, in the first half, Ferrari had been the guy who always seemed to get a hold of the ball to take it down on offense. He steals it from his own teammates he loves basketball so much. And that was okay with me and Coach Hank because Ferrari knows how to dribble and run real fast at the same time.

But Ferrari, we learned, on the very first play of the game, would put it up, high altitude B-52 bomb style, with both hands, the moment he crossed mid-court. The crowd loved the kid. Me, too. Ferrari makes everything interesting. Everything. But he hadn't hit one yet from his personal launching pad between mid-court and the apex of the three-point line...and he was really trying. Even when he outraced the other team and could have laid it up with time to spare Ferrari would stop and pop.

His bombs, with not much spin, would *clank* off the rim or *boing* off the backboard, and one time the ball bounced way up and got stuck between the backboard and the contraption that connects the goal to the tin roof. A guy from the recreation center had to come over there with a bamboo pole to poke it out.

So I told Ferrari to keep it up in the second half. You know...doughnuts.

He did.

We lost big, though, to a coed team of super special kids just like us, 33 to 9, but the real highlight of the game was when Ferrari finally and correctly calculated barometric pressure, wind, distance, the curvature of the earth, axis tilt, seasonal anomalies, El Nino, the Jet Stream, and his excitement for a promise of unlimited doughnuts with the coach's money. Statistically, Ferrari was 1 for 16, but universally, he was the crowd favorite. When Ferrari finally helped the cause with three big points, everybody in the stands jumped up and down and went nuts, too. The moment was preceded by near silent, mouth-open marveling as the orange bomb floated toward the golden ring.

Whoosh!

I listened to the sweet roar of bi-partisan parents going nuts for a kid's momentous moment in time during a lopsided basketball game for kids who really don't care about the final score. The apples don't drop far from their trees. Sometimes they drop just right.

At the Krispy Kreme I handed Coach Hank the twenty and said to Ferrari to go nuts. You earned it. I juked open the squeaky bus doors.

Ferrari leaped out of the bus from the top step to the asphalt parking lot and screamed back at Coach Hank as he ran akimbo across a busy parking lot...Are you going nuts, *too!*

Waving the twenty around in his hand, Coach Hank smiled at me and said...You're cool with this, right? Spend it *all?*

I said go nuts. We *all* deserve it.

NERVOUS NEIGHBORS

As a teacher who personally seeks knowledge on my own time, it's the oddest thing to read the community newspaper and find out that the school where you work doesn't even have a permit, what's called a special-use permit, that allows you to do what you're already doing: teaching kids and being a school. It's our business, the teachers, but not our business to do anything about it.

I muttered my odd news discovery to Miss Kentucky.

She said...You're *kidding*.

I e-mailed Miss Kentucky the link to the article...and then I read the best part over again myself:

> **District 5 City Councilwoman Debi Marlboro said..."We promised people one thing. We promised people a different type of city, a city that was going to be free of patronism, free of politics, free of favoritism and free of political micromanagement." Marlboro also blasted the neighbors of the school who described a situation in which a special-needs student "escaped" the school. "You owe the school an apology. These are children. These are not hardened criminals," Marlboro said. City council members approved the school's special-use permit 5-0.**

Could Abraham turn into a hardened criminal one day? Maybe. I think the other day might have been a test run.

USE YOUR INSIDE VOICE

Miss Kentucky mainly teaches the little kids on the other side of the building, but comes over to help us out from time to time, and she tells me she has to tell them they don't have to stop reading aloud at every period. Just keep reading until I tell you to stop. She says, lovingly, in that sweet voice of hers, that she has to tell them to turn pages. Miss Kentucky giggles...They act like they need permission to do everything.

When I'm across the hall from her classroom in the copy room, I can hear the syrup flowing. She calls them sweetheart and darling and sweetie and baby and honey. She says it calms them down and calms her down and makes her feel sweet herself.

I've seen her in action in the fog of war in the computer lab, too, with a mix of my older kids fighting for seats with fourth graders. I let them fight it out. Live and learn. First come first squirm. But then there's calm, sweet, Miss Kentucky, refereeing for the other side. She always wins.

But when she comes over to our side of the building to teach a bunch of hard core and hardwired makers of mischief she forgets to change her tune. This week in Lord of the Flies she told me she always forgets to flip the switch...that walking into the dump of the commons room should be her trigger. Or getting run over. Or both.

She teaches Spanish in the extra classroom next to mine and when I hear her call Abraham or Dalrymple or Morris sweetheart or darling or sweetie or baby or honey I cringe. They aren't real close to any of those things.

When she says sweetheart it takes her several seconds to say the word in that Kentucky accent of hers....*sweet-haaaaaaart.* Every day she has to ask them to stop farting, too, just like Miss Velvet. Miss Kentucky asks them in Kentucky English so there won't be any confusion...Darlin', please stop your *far-tin'...oh-kaaaaay?* It's juss not *niiiiiiiiice.* And it *smay-*yullllls.

Today I heard a fellow tell her to start treating them like *real* men and to stop talking in that hideous bunny rabbit voice.

TEACH LIKE YOUR HAIR'S ABOUT TO BE FIRED

I got it. Now I know why Mr. Warbird screams louder, yells

louder, pounds the white board louder, and pounds his lectern louder. Now I know why he calls them some pretty good names. He also likes to karate kick his door closed. It's loud as hell when he does it.

I got it. He don't care. He's teaching and guiding and instructing from the gut.

A couple of weeks ago in the faculty meeting Mr. Warbird announced to everybody that his wife, a big muckity-muck with a big accounting firm, is being transferred to New York city. Like, this coming weekend. But, Mr. Warbird screamed, he was going to hang on and leave at the end of the school year!

We screamed and yelled. Right. Sure. Stay until the end of the year.

I caught him in the parking lot later. Right. Sure, I said. You're not staying until the end of the year.

He said he'd catch a plane one weekend and she'd catch a plane the next weekend and so forth and so on. He admitted they had already bought a house outside the city.

I asked him where.

Outside the city.

Mr. Warbird said he didn't want to seem like a snob. A house in Westchester County, he said.

I told Mr. Warbird he couldn't snob me. I'm too much of a dumb hick to tell.

So now he really yells and screams and pounds things and calls them creative names. He can side kick an innocent classroom door shut like Chuck Norris. I wish I could teach like I don't care if I get fired. Some days, though, I think that's the best way to do it.

PUBLIC TWEAKING

Mr. Warbird teaches a public speaking class in the afternoons and today he left his classroom door open and I got to hear some speeches. I guess it was for a grade. One guy would come up and stand behind Mr. Warbird's lectern and speak and then they'd clap and holler and then the next guy would come up and deliver his speech. It didn't take me long to figure out the controversial topic: Do you think cloning an animal or a human should be legal?

It also didn't take long for me to figure out that none of them understood that a clone would develop from a few molecules or whatever and grow and learn at a regular pace, like a human or animal baby. They all thought their clone would pop out of a test tube or some machine at some nuclear, government-run cloning institute as a sixteen or seventeen year old dude ready to rock and roll. In other words, they all thought that their clone would be extremely helpful in doing their homework and chores and even in coming to school on their behalf...sort of as a twin.

One guy, the farter named Simeon, said in his speech, in his loud and squeaky voice, that cloning was stupid and a waste of time. Simeon said that if you were a human clone of yourself walking around town you wouldn't be unique at all.

SEX FOR FOOD

I had to hand out cheeseburgers and chips in the kitchen today during lunch. A local caterer brings the food and we heat it up and hand it out. If you want lunch it costs five dollars. Sometimes we get spaghetti. It's real good.

A huge, nine foot tall woman with hair like a bale of briars, who came in to substitute for Miss Manhater, walked in and asked if she could have a cheeseburger and a bag of chips.

I said sure. Welcome aboard, by the way.

She reached into her cavernous cleavage and pulled out a wad of money. I gave it to her for free.

BUYING PROTECTION

Today is the last day of the semester before we go on Christmas break and Brainerd's mom gave me a "Teacher's Guardian Travel Angel Visor Clip" as a gift.

I pondered it for a while. I pondered the last four months. I decided to keep it in the classroom.

COFFEE JOLT...WITH CREAM AND MONEY

Biff's mom tracked me down and gave me a little gift bag that had a comical picture on it of Santa Clause screaming Ho! Ho! Ho!

After she walked away I dug through the red tissue paper to find a Starbucks cardboard envelope. I figured that a Starbucks gift card was in the envelope. When I saw she had written $110 on the amount line I really got to thinking about how much she thinks I've helped Biff in civics class this semester because he started off by running out of the classroom on tests days to find furniture objects to kick in the commons room while he whined and cussed and now he's all prepared for tests and seems to like them a lot. Heck, he ended up with a final fall semester grade of 101.

On my way home today I ran into by my local Starbucks with all that delicious money. Even a small cup of regular coffee costs a lot. Don't get me started on the fancy mugs and the bug-eyed folks staring into something electronic.

Anyway, I decided to overindulge in my recent teaching success so I grabbed a bag of Kenya (juicy acidity; currant), Organic Yukon Blend (hearty; well-rounded), and Christmas Blend (spicy, sweet & perfect when we're together). I thought about getting some of those expensive, pre-made sandwiches with cheese wedges, but I remembered I had some curled-up sliced ham in a package, yellow mustard, and loaf bread at home already.

They grind all that coffee up for you, too...for free.

When the girl at the cash register, Malicia, told me the price for all that coffee I didn't even blink. It's fun and easy and effortless to spend other people's money. I handed her the card.

Malicia did some zippy-looking things with the card, then she said...Forty-two ninety-eight.

I said I don't understand. You know, just take it off the card.

She said you owe some more.

I said I still don't understand.

She said the card had only ten dollars on it.

With a mild, pleading tone in my voice I said...I just got that card from Biff's mom not thirty minutes ago. I'm his civics teacher. She wrote one hundred and ten on the gift card part. She wrote Merry Christmas, too. I swear to *God*.

It's out in my truck. Do you want me to go get it?

Malicia, with a mildly uneasy look on her face, glanced around the store, like she was all of a sudden dealing with a merry lunatic. I glanced at the people in the line behind me. Them, too.

DIVINE THIS

Like I said a while back, I don't mind faculty meetings because you get to giggle and talk about the wild stuff the students and their parents do and a lot of times Headmistress Lynyrd Skynyrd will pass out paychecks.

Today we're back from Christmas break on what's called a "teacher workday." We aren't working. We're sitting in a dang meeting and the big topic is pretty much Headmistress Lynyrd Skynyrd reminding all the teachers that we have four counselors with advanced degrees and boatloads of experience who come in all week on rotating schedules to help us out with the hard cases. She said we really don't mind too much that you send them to me all the time when you kick them out of class, you know, but now please send them to a counselor *first*.

All the counselors started talking about all the things they do and all the things they say when a kid mopes into their office. One of them said she sort of gets mad that they don't have enough time to resolve the issue or just calm them down. She said that she apologizes for sometimes sending them back to us madder and more freaked out than when the whole business started.

Honey, I'm thinking, we don't have much time either to

get stuff fixed. Maybe if each class lasted...three months.

One counselor said there ain't no magic words sometimes...that all they can do is provide a comfortable and soothing place to hang out and talk if they want to and if they don't want to talk that's okay, too. Remember, we've assembled a sand box in our counselor's room and they can play in there!

I thought I'd offer up some humanity, so I raised my hand and thanked the ladies for being available and for all they do. It does feel good to see them hunkered down with a kid being crushed under the tremendous emotions caused by four algebra problems for homework.

Then, all of a sudden, the old gal of the counseling staff, Morgana, jumped up and said she'd like to show us all something that's really been working for her and the kids she sees. I hoped Morgana was talking about how she and the other ladies had discovered the secret to eliminating the most dreaded threat to world happiness: teenage defiance. I instantly sat up in my chair and adopted a note-taking posture, just like the finest teacher's pet. Then I looked around the conference room to see if Headmistress Lynyrd Skynyrd had us some doughnuts and some coffee and orange juice. I looked around a little harder. I started chewing on my pencil eraser.

Morgana pulled out of her satchel parts of two coat hangers she had cut into what look like "Ls." She had slipped some drinking straws on the handle of both coat hangers. Morgana said these two things may look like old-timey divining rods, but they're not used for finding water...I use them with the kids to show them how much energy they produce.

Don't need magic for that. I looked around the room. I was the only teacher or school administrator not making a goofy face.

Morgana asked Coach Hank to stand up and move away from her about ten feet. Morgana pointed the energy things at Coach Hank...and they moved.

I about dropped an egg.

The energy things ended up pointing way starboard and way port. I looked around the room again. My colleagues were struck dumb. I mean that in a couple of ways.

Morgana asked Coach Hank to walk toward her slowly...and for everybody to watch what happens.

The end of Morgana's energy things started coming back together.

I really just about dropped an egg. An ostrich egg. The biggest bird egg there is.

Morgana said see how Coach Hank's energy is like a bubble and how as you get closer to somebody you can feel their energy get all around your *own* energy space!

I didn't know whether to walk out or phone in my credit card number. Maybe magic Morgana could conjure us up some coffee and some dang doughnuts.

STICKER SHOCK

I was eating an apple. I was making a lot of noise while I was eating the apple, while the fellows in second period were walking in, because the apples in the grocery store I bought over the weekend are an especially super crispy type of apple—Fuji apples.

I now know that when I bite into a Fuji apple and chew the hunk of apple I just bit off and then when I gnaw on the apple and lick its juices from off of the skin of the apple and from off of my hand and my fingers from a standing and welcoming position from behind my lectern, I know that this is an arresting scene to Red, Kells, Clutch, and Peetie.

Normally, when they come into the room they try to write witty things on the chalkboard or Kells may still have Peetie in a headlock from the last class. Today they all sat down right away and shut up and quietly stared at me while I made eating noises.

Kells asked me had I ever just gone ahead and eaten the little oval sticker labels they stick on apples these days.

Maybe, I mumbled.

Kells asked if the label was still on the apple I was eating.

I looked. Yes, I mumbled. The sticker, not as big as a quarter but not as small as a nickel, had a bar code on it, the number 4131, the abbreviation USA, and the word FUJI. I was impressed. I held the apple up in the air to show them the label. Then I ate it.

Kells, Red, Clutch, and Peetie were not that impressed.

I thought it was an endearing moment.

Kells said his brother eats the labels off of apples all the time, and that's why he goes to this school, too.

JUST THROWIN' IT OUT THERE

On the morning of a casual dress Friday, where Lamar was wearing a t-shirt that said on the front, "Micah 6:8," and on the back of the t-shirt, "Do justice, love mercy, walk humbly," he also brought in a printed-out page off of Amazon which included photographs of three throwing knives his mother ordered for him the night before.

After knowing and teaching Lamar, it's a chilling moment when something like this happens. But even if he had shown me a picture of a basket of warm beagle puppies his mother bought him I still would have been chilled. I got to thinking...everything Lamar does has a chilling effect. He perhaps would have eaten the warm puppies.

I took the page from Lamar and gazed at it. These aren't elegant knives the butler places by your plate while you're chowing down with the Queen of England. These things look menacing. These things look like they'd slip between a couple of ribs and into your heart or liver real easy. I asked Lamar was he planning to bring them to school?

Lamar said brightly...Would you like me to?

NAILED IT

Anytime scientists poll teachers on what makes them so happy to perform the most dangerous work on Earth, I think the scientists are always amazed that being paid a butt load more money is not at the top of the list. What's at the top of the list of any profession is being recognized by your superiors for the good job you do.

I think that crazy notion goes for students, too, especially when they're trying to figure out the wacky meanings of the short stories of J.D. Salinger, especially a story he published way back in the last millennium, "Just Before the War with the Eskimos."

When I asked Clutch what he thinks is the real reason Ginnie and Selena bicker like a couple of crows...he got the answer right. I tossed a beautifully wrapped piece of Godiva chocolate at his head. I've never seen him smile so wide, but I had to look away when he started gnawing on it.

When I asked Peetie why he thinks Eric reached into his bathroom trash can to pull back out a dang razor blade...well...Peetie pretty much got it right. He got a Godiva chocolate thrown at his head, too.

I had nine chocolates left, and the class discussion deliciousness that teachers dream about went on for so long all the chocolates got eaten. I scrambled around in a couple of drawers for more food. I found a paper clip and a nail.

Clutch answered correctly the question of why do you think Franklin seems like such a dandy. Clutch caught the paper clip I lobbed at him and observed it in his hand, with wide open-eyed delight, as if it were his first Varsity chili dog with onions.

Then came Kells. About why do you think Selena kept that dead chicken for so long, he told us what he thought. It wasn't correct. It was way far from correct, but he tried and he had been listening hard all week and I appreciate that. I tossed the heavy, four inch-long nail at him.

Kells missed it.

The nail clanked around on the top of his desk and then it fell onto the floor. Kells juked out of his desk after it. A dang *nail*. You would have thought he was chasing after a winning Powerball ticket.

FIELD TRIPPIN'

In civics class I offered up the idea of going on a field trip sometime this semester and they got all excited about it when they found out that I would only plan a field trip that lasted all day and that they wouldn't have to go to any other classes.

Then they got back in a funky mood when I explained that when you go on a field trip you should go around the next day to all of the teachers of the classes you missed and see what work they need you to catch up on from the day before...from the day you went on a fun field trip.

I proposed that a good civics class-related field trip might entail an excursion to the state capitol or to a Civil War site. Maybe we could get a tour of the federal prison, I said.

Lamar had a funny expression on his face.

I thought I'd go crazy and interact with him. You don't like to go on excursions, do you, I asked.

I don't like excursions.

I'm sorry.

The *word* excursion, Lamar said fairly loudly.

What's wrong with the *word*?

Every time you say it I think of the word ex*cre*tions.

No kidding.

Lamar said I think of all of our excretions and all of the nasty excretions of animals, too, when you say the word ex*cur*sion.

Everybody laughed. Me, too. I told Lamar and the rest of the class that I personally like to go on field trips and I like to use the word...ex-*kurrrzions*...because I have in my mind all of us in hiking boots and khaki safari pants and safari jackets with rakish safari hats going crazy learning new things. On my...ex-*kurrrzions*...I said, I always work real hard to find the very best place to stop for lunch and maybe even a cool place to stop for a unique snack or whatnot before we head back to campus. I gave Lamar a hard look...ex-*kurrrzions*. I'm the teacher who knows how to have fun on *field* trips.

Lamar said I bet you look stupid in a safari hat.

GRANDPARENT TRAP

In parent-teacher conferences, even when their child has all A's, you never know if you may get scorched by a parent for something you haven't thought of. And I've been in some conferences where they last about ten minutes because everything's going well and everybody's happy, but the parent came anyway because what they mostly want to talk about is how grateful they are to you and the other teachers for:

- Changing his life for the better
- Teaching him manners
- Teaching him discipline
- Making him take a bath finally
- Encouraging him
- Building his confidence
- Teaching him how to raise his hand in class and not be embarrassed
- Showing him that all this ain't a game
- He never could shoot a basketball before he met you

I had a mother tell me one time that she just loves those new words you're teaching him! Actually, she said, he's driving us crazy saying them all the time in those goofy sentences you make up for them! I like those parent-teacher conferences the best. As opposed to today's, where a mother, and later, a grandmother came into the room with a certain teacher's failings in mind.

Me. My failings.

Lucy's mother sat down and asked in a bothered voice who of you was Mr. Sentell.

I smiled and raised my hand. Hello! Good to meet you!

She asked me...Now what classes do you teach Lucy?

I didn't know what to say. I sat there with a dumb look on my face. The other teachers, too. Not that I didn't know what classes Lucy was in...it hadn't occurred to me yet that Lucy's mom...might be...well...not paying attention to her daughter's education.

I told her what classes I teach Lucy.

Lucy's mother tapped a finger on a piece of paper she brought with her. It looked like a print-out of her grades. Lucy's mother shouted...How can you give her these grades!

I didn't know what to say. I sat there with a dumb look on my face. The other teachers, too. Uh...I said...she *earned* those grades. I said that's the result of her effort, despite my constant encouragement.

The mother shouted...This is not *her!*

I sat up in my seat a bit more. My heart started to pound. I'm being shouted at by another adult. Why waste time trying to figure this out, I thought. She's crazy. And this is the parent-teacher conference you hear about...in a nightmare.

And then Lucy's grandmother appeared at the door. She was breathing hard and sweating. She looked like she was about to have a heart attack...or drop to the floor...it wasn't pretty. She had to climb two flights of stairs and walk across the commons room, she said. She wobbled over to a seat next to her daughter. And then she shouted...Which one of you is Mr. Sentell!

Hello!

The grandmother grabbed the sheet from her daughter. Her hands were shaking. She yelled at me, too...You don't know her! You don't understand that she's better than this!

Calmly, I said, I have an idea. I said I'll be happy to write up a plan, just for Lucy, since I know her very well now and understand her goals and interests and academic and social personality about how she can easily raise her grades. How about that?

The grandmother shouted ...Fine!

And your best e-mail address?

Lucy's mother said she had a bunch of them...but that she was really too busy to check them.

I looked around at my colleagues just to make sure I wasn't the one who was crazy. I thought Mrs. Yinyang was going to faint. Miss Velvet's face was turning maroon. And then someone said...Why don't we talk about how Lucy's doing in *science* class. She just *loves* science.

I got that plan all written up and sent it to the e-mail address the school had for Lucy's mother. It was a dang good plan. I never got a thank you from Lucy's mother or her grandmother. I *am* the one who's crazy, because I honestly thought I would get a response...just a simple thank you.

Lucy's grades went up, though. Lucy gets all the credit for those, too.

RIGHT BACK ATCHA! GET SOME!

Now things are even! Somebody doo-dooed early this morning in the high school boy's urinal.

FISH STORY

Lamar's back! I have no idea why, of course, but Headmistress Lynyrd Skynyrd suspended him. Go figure.

Anyhow, he's been gone a few days and I found out that he couldn't come back until he had seen a psychiatrist, so I guess he saw a psychiatrist and here he pops into first period, yelling, in an English accent...Hello, *goov*-nah!

It's casual dress Friday, and Lamar's wearing a green t-shirt that says in white lettering: Lamar's my name! Fishing's my game!

Now I'm wondering how the psychiatrist is doing. While I'm contemplating any and all deeper meaning of his t-shirt message, Lamar yells again...Hello, *goov*-nah!

I yell back what the heck is the deeper meaning of your t-shirt? Are you a fisherman, Lamar, of catfish...bass...the occasional bream? I don't think Lamar can tell I'm mildly terrified of him and hope, through the use of humor, to keep him from his mission, I'm sure, at least for a few moments, to become the Antichrist. Starting in my first period language arts class.

Lamar said he likes a bream and a bass and a catfish, but

he said that his most remarkable fishing experience was when he once caught a flounder.

A flounder?

Lamar said that the flounder he yanked into the boat flew up and bit him. Lamar showed me the scar on his hand. Lamar said flounders are weird fish. Flat fish. And they'll bite you.

I nodded at Lamar and mushed my lips.

Lamar flopped into his desk and seemed tremendously happy about being back.

This realization unnerved me, and made me think about anything I could accomplish professionally today. They'll make you a great sub at the Publix down the street.

WHAT ELSE WOULD HE ENJOY DOING?

Lamar was barking at Mr. Warbird and Mr. Warbird was barking right back. Here I am trying to grade Brainerd's essay and I can't help but be transformed by the across-the-hall debate between these illustrious academians. I was also gnawing on a submarine sandwich.

Lamar asked Mr. Warbird why do you always *yell* at me?

Mr. Warbird said because you're always *interrupting* me...and *ruining* a thing I call my teacher's *mo!*

Lamar yelled no I'm *not!*

Mr. Warbird yelled yes...yes, you *are!*

No, I'm *not!*

You just *did!* If you worked for me, Lamar, you'd be *fired!*

I looked up from my essay and my delicious submarine sandwich which was dripping oil and vinegar on Brainerd's essay that had no periods at the ends of his sentences and watched Mr. Warbird lean over the top of his lectern and eyeball Lamar real good. Mr. Warbird said in his low, just-you-and-me Satan voice...I really don't *need* this *job*. Know what I *mean?*

I never heard Lamar utter another word.

PROGRESS GETS HIJACKED BY A TEACHER

I wish I could have talked to Lamar's parents before they got all squirmy and made him, but having a parent-teacher conference this morning works okay, too.

Come to find out, Lamar's mother doesn't have asps for hair, fangs for teeth, claws for hands, hooves for feet, or yellow eyes. She pretty much gave us the lowdown, in the calmest and most articulate tones, on Lamar from birth to today. She wasn't Jerry Springer material at all. She was about as far away from being on the Jerry Springer Show as Margaret Thatcher. Anyhow, after her remarks, I took in a deep breath and thanked whatever god Lamar worships for getting him this far. I don't know why Lamar's dad wasn't there. Maybe he was home hiding in his gun safe.

Once Mr. Squirm the science teacher butted in there was no subtle, or even obvious, gesture we made that would make him shut up, so we ended the meeting with Mr. Squirm still talking as we all stood up and walked out of Mr. Warbird's classroom. I was one of three other teachers ready to talk to Lamar's mother and start a plan to help Lamar get better and be happier. We never had a chance. Plus, Mr. Squirm's got a weird voice and he wears dumb shoes.

While Mr. Squirm was walking away...through the commons room in his dumb shoes...telling Lamar's mother how long he's been teaching and how he's working so diligently to apply all of his incredible knowledge of behavior and emotion management into the head of Lamar, Mr. Warbird said Mr. Squirm sure does know how to highjack a parent-teacher conference so nothing really gets done, doesn't he?

Miss Velvet said he sure does.

Mrs. Yinyang said he sure does.

I said he sure as hell does.

Then we went to our classrooms and started our day, without having gotten anything done in the important last hour of our lives. Good manners ain't science, rocket or otherwise.

BIG BOILING ZITS

Lamar finally brought in a stress ball. I have to give him credit. I asked him did Mr. Squirm urge him to do it or did he think to bring one in himself?

Lamar said Mr. Warbird gave him one of his. Come to find out, Lamar said, the *fine* bastard's got a drawer *full* of them.

Oh.

Anyhow, in civics class, after Lamar wasn't spewing out any correct or near-correct answers about how the government works, he slammed both hands onto his desk and announced to the rest of his unnerved classmates that he was now going to get out his stress ball. Lamar reached into his enormous backpack and got out his stress ball. Lamar started squeezing his stress ball.

The doomed stress ball was the size of a tennis ball and it was the color of the sky on a real pretty day in Bermuda where it's real pretty every day. But when Lamar squeezed the stress ball a part of it would bulge out between his fingers and the color of the part bulging out turned from a pretty Bermuda sky color to the color of brown toilet water. The bulging part looked like an enormous, inflamed pimple and this development began to excite Lamar. It seemed as if the stress ball was filled with some sort of liquid, too, and as Lamar was relieving his stress the ball made some significantly creepy liquid-like noises.

I have never been more mesmerized in my life as I watched Lamar work his stress out. I closed my civics workbook shut. Like a schoolmarm, Lucy was frantically tapping a pencil on her desk for Lamar to stop...significantly creepy liquid-like noises...Brainerd was scrunching his face up as if he had just eaten something rotten or sour, or both...significantly creepy liquid-like noises...Biff was turning red and was a couple of seconds away from running out of the classroom...significantly creepy liquid-like noises...Nesbit was sitting next to Lamar and Nesbit was staring at me with wide, haunted eyes, asking me, with all the powers of his telepathy, if it would be okay with me if he put both hands around Lamar's neck and relieved his own stress by squeezing...significantly creepy liquid-like noises. Fabio hardly ever comes to school, so he was really missing some fun today.

Then a thought hit me. I told Lamar that...you know...the

pimple-looking thing emerging from your stress ball...the way you're so professionally making it pulsate over and over and over and over while we're trying to learn how the government works...significantly creepy liquid-like noises...reminds me of the huge and nasty boils and carbuncles that emerged on Lieutenant Muldoon's face, a character played by veteran actor Bruce Willis in the movie *Planet Terror*, as Lieutenant Muldoon was succumbing to the horrible inevitability of the bio-nerve gas, just before Lieutenant Muldoon's swollen and hideous head exploded all over the place.

Lamar said he had not yet seen the movie *Planet Terror*...and then asked if we could watch it in class one day.

I thought of wanting to be in Bermuda at that moment real bad. I knew a place by a rock on a beach.

Telepathically, while I was on the beach in Bermuda, Lamar shouted...*Well*, are you going to go *get* the movie so we can *watch* it in *class!*

Significantly creepy liquid-like noises.

Watch it in class, Lamar? Brother, we're living it right now.

VIRGINIAS ON MY MIND

Around here, everybody deals with their case of the Mondays in their own peculiar way. I think the best way is to pretend Monday is a Friday state of mind and get through the awful first day of the work week that way. Act real happy. Giggle at anything. Be so publicly perky as to be hated by all other human beings, fellow teachers and students alike.

Nesbit, in my civics class, always has a case of the

Mondays. For the rest of the week he's okay, but Monday horrifies him. Here's how I know: every Monday he sits there, steel rod straight, with clenched teeth and a tight jaw and wide eyes, not moving, sort of frozen, as if space aliens are rubbing has spine up and down with north Atlantic Ocean icebergs.

Today, a damn Monday, Nesbit had a bad case of the Mondays. Before we got started mooking around in section 19 of our beloved civics workbook I adjusted my face to appear pleasant, and I asked him...Nesbit, do you have a bad case of the Mondays?

Through his clenched teeth and tight jaw, Nesbit said...*Yes.*

I asked Nesbit that if he started reading the beginning of the section out loud would that ease his horror of the reality that he was at school on a Monday morning in my civics class with me engaging him in a teacherly way?

Nesbit giggled a little bit, still through clenched teeth, and began reading out loud. Section 19 is about the history of the Bill of Rights. As Nesbit was reading, he got to the word "Virginia" while he was still nervously getting over his case of the Mondays and he pronounced to me and Fabio and Biff and Lucy and Brainerd and Lamar the word "Virginia" like this...ver-*ji*-nia.

Lamar screamed OH MY GOD! very loudly.

I admit, I broke character and laughed pretty much like a donkey. After composing myself, I calmly asked Nesbit to keep reading, but by now he was pretty well unhinged because there were a lot of upcoming Virginias in the text and Nesbit was sitting next to Lamar. Just having Lamar in the room is enough to give you a case of the Mondays on an early-release Friday. When Nesbit got to the next "Virginia" he was really nervous and he really slaughtered it and it came out...vah-*ji*-na. So did the next one, and the next one. Vagina. Vagina. Vagina.

Lamar screamed again...OH, MY GOD! And then he added...MAKE HIM STOP!

Nesbit loves to read out loud in class so that's why, I'm fairly sure, he kept going. Reading out loud helps your class participation grade, too. Plus, Nesbit is a healthy teenage boy and I'll bet virginias are more on his mind than the fascinating constitutional nuances of the Bill of Rights of the United States of America.

I urged Lamar to run out to the commons room and take deep breaths and do back flips out there, which he did, and then I asked Biff to read for a while, which Biff did, pronouncing the rest of the virginias correctly...to our mild disappointment.

I love Mondays so much.

GOD PLEASE HELP US, TOO

The reason I use any boy's bathroom in the building is because I like to constantly test my will to live. Barely alive, I came walking out of another horrible bathroom experience to find Lamar standing at my classroom door with that school counselor who challenged our sense of logic and reality with her shirt hanger energy rods at that beginning-of-the-semester-teacher-workday-no-doughnuts-and-coffee waste of time.

We were in a break between classes and I asked what was happening. Come to find out, the counselor found Lamar without the use of her divining rods and needed to take him back to her office to talk to him about something he did way back yesterday.

I asked what he did.

Neither one of them would tell me, but I'll bet it was an alluring moment in American education. I also got to thinking that Lamar's probably been up to a whole lot more since yesterday. It takes a lot to keep up with him. The counselor ought to just sit in every class with him. That's where the action is.

All of a sudden Lamar handed me a rectangle piece of card paper. I could tell there was some writing on the other side. I asked him if he wanted me to read it now.

Lamar said he sure did.

I asked the counselor if she knew what the card...note...business was all about.

She said she had no idea. They both started walking away. Lamar started giggling.

It was Lamar's business card. His own business card. Now this is truly alluring...when Lamar's not causing others to question life on Earth, he's a real handy helper. In the middle of the card was an oval, and inside the oval it said, "LAMAR'S HELPING HANDS." On the bottom, left-hand side of the card was Lamar's name and his cell phone number. On the bottom, right-hand side of the card was this: "Need Any Help...Just Give Me A Call!"

I looked at Lamar, dumbly, with my mouth hung open, and then looked back at the card. In the middle of the oval was a comic book-like image of a lawnmower with bright eyes and a toothy smile. In the lawnmower's hand...a rake, a hoe, and a shovel. Exhaust fumes were blowing out of the lawnmower's rear end.

I looked at Lamar being led away by a school counselor to go get coddled for something he did yesterday. Old news. Another waste of time. He's already planning ahead.

Lamar screamed back at me...Hey! I'll come by your trailer this afternoon and blow the hell out of your leaves!

AND THE TRUMPET WILL SOUND

The Education of Lamar is becoming a daily hit parade. I can't wait to get to school and I can't wait to leave.

Today in my first period I had them studying for tomorrow's vocabulary test. It was nice and quiet, which spooked me, so I asked them if they'd like for me to play some music, quietly, while they studied.

Everybody said yes except Lucy.

Sorry Lucy. I said all I've got in the laptop is the Allman Brothers Band...Stand Back: The Anthology disc one. Cool?

I thought Lamar was going to leap across the room. He screamed...I've got some music! Can we play it!

Why a vision of Marilyn Manson came into my head spooked me deeper. I said sure...what is it? Marilyn Manson?

Lamar said, with wild eyes, that it was a Louis *Arm*strong CD.

I said, as emotionless as I could possibly stand it...You're *kid*ding. I thought about Lamar...Louis Armstrong...his twistiness and unending surprises. His unpredictability. He really is as unpredictable as a squirrel juking around in the middle of a busy street. They typically don't get run over.

Lamar handed me the CD and I started playing it. Our first selection was "Nobody Knows the Trouble I've Seen." Lamar sat there and stared at me, while smiling, instead of studying his thirty new vocabulary words.

I asked him...why a guy like *him...you* know...would have a Louis Armstrong CD.

Lamar said he likes to hear trumpets play.

I asked Lamar if he played the trumpet.

Lamar said no.

I stared at Lamar for a long moment, trying to figure out what just happened. I couldn't figure it out, so I thought to give him a piece of candy. What the heck. It seemed sort of like he might have just done something good. I opened my desk drawer and discovered I didn't have any more candy. I told Lamar so, and then I said all I have is *this*...I reached into my mouth and pulled out the wad of my chewing gum and held it out. Lamar's expression, for a millionth of a second, showed me he strongly considered taking it.

THIS IS MAYBE KNOT GOOD

About fifteen seconds into today's vocabulary test Lamar slammed his pencil on his desk and announced that he was giving up because he couldn't remember any of the words he studied real hard last night.

I urged Lamar, in my most encouraging voice, to give it one more try.

As a grade for the test, Lamar asked if I would use the

mock quiz his mother made for him last night on some Internet computer program. He said he made a good grade on it.

I said no, but still with a teacherly tone of encouragement. I almost made myself gag.

Lamar asked me if he could use my phone to call his mother and maybe she could fax the quiz to me to prove that he did a quiz already.

I said no, but thanks for the offer. Plus, there's not a fax machine in here. I waved both arms around.

Lamar started to rip the test up until he saw the look on my face.

Then he asked me if he could draw his feelings.

I gave him a new look this time that basically emoted...What the heck. Draw your feelings.

Lamar took out a piece of paper and began to draw his feelings. After he finished, Lamar gave me the piece of paper. The result of Lamar drawing his feelings was a picture of a helicopter-looking contraption floating above the ground. On the nose of the helicopter was a nozzle which was sucking up students and placing them into the helicopter's "Punishment Rooms." There were twelve Punishment Rooms. Lamar had labeled the helicopter's blades "Punishment Blades." In the bottom, right-hand corner of the paper was what looked like a porpoise with an urgent expression on its face and it was swimming in some waves. Lamar had labeled that uplifting scene "Random Dolfin."

I asked Lamar what was the meaning of the random dolfin (misspelling his) on a feelings drawing of students being sucked into helicopter punishment rooms.

Lamar said he just likes dolfins and since they all look alike, like Chinese people, he figured it was a random one.

I went back to fiddling around on my computer while the rest of them were still taking the vocabulary test. A few moments later I looked at Lamar. He had snuck into his backpack and now he was looking at me through a pair of binoculars. I asked Lamar why he was looking at me through a pair of binoculars, you know, when we were six feet away from each other.

Lamar said that he was looking at me so closely that he could see what I was thinking.

I asked Lamar to look real close and tell me what I was thinking.

He said to probably put the binoculars away.

I went back to fiddling around on my computer. A few moments later I looked at Lamar again.

Lamar had curled his tongue up and was poking it out of his mouth. And then he asked me how small I could make my tongue.

I curled my tongue up and poked it out.

Lamar was extremely complimentary.

Earlier that day Lamar came up to me during Lord of the Flies and gave me a trinket he said he made just for me last night. Hanging off of a metallic blue carabiner was a white rope and it was intertwined to form an odd shape. The closest thing to nature I could come up with was the shape of a walrus without hind flippers.

Lamar saw the gratitude and innocent fascination on my face, and said it was a "Dragonskin." He asked me to keep it with me for the rest of my life.

I asked him was it for keeping demons away from me.

Lamar said yes...except for him.

As Lamar was poking his tongue at me, I pulled the trinket out of my pocket and wiggled it at him. Lamar was right. It didn't work on him.

SOME BUGS HAVE LONG TONGUES

The science teacher, Mr. Squirm, is really trying to pass a kidney stone or lately he's having fun doping himself up on pain pills. I have my suspicions. I like the way he mopes around all hunched over. That's a nice touch.

What this means is I have to substitute his science classes because one of those things is keeping him from coming to school...a lot. That also means I have to have a productive human interaction with Bugs in fourth period. Mr. Squirm teaches the lower school kids, too.

In science class, Bugs really enjoys learning about science. He's classroom smart. Bugs also enjoys picking his nose and eating his boogers, while comfortably sitting there next to the window with the spring sun washing over him. There he is, picking and eating. Like a pecking chicken. Pick, eat, enjoy. Pick, eat, enjoy. Pick, eat, enjoy.

Bugs doesn't mind if you stare at him while he's picking his nose. I believe he sees his nastiness as a point of pride. Then, I learned through first-person observation (staring), when Bugs has harvested all of the boogers contained in both nostrils, he'll take a finger and swab out what's left and lick that up.

I found Bugs' determination admirable, and told him so.

During class he was also answering a whole bunch of science questions correctly so I felt balanced. We were talking about the parts of plants. Stamen, pistil, ovary...that sort of thing.

We came to the end of class and I asked Bugs what it was like to be able to eat all those boogers and to lick up all that slimy snot without gagging.

Bugs said he wasn't finished.

I asked him what could possibly be left, unless he was going after his ear wax.

Bugs poked out his pointy-looking tongue...and then he poked it out some more...and then the tip of it slid right up into his right nostril. Bugs has a really long tongue.

It's a science class. Of course. There are jars of formaldehyde with creepy things inside, floating around. Plastic torsos with the guts hanging out. In a box there are bugs stuck through with pins. And then there's Bugs. Science says he's participating in attention-seeking negative behavior. As a substitute teacher in a science class, I say Bugs really enjoys eating boogers. It's as simple as that.

HOT FOR TEACHER

Very early on the morning of the day a new substitute teacher came in for a trial run, I found Mr. Warbird alone in his classroom with a moist face, a pale face, and shaking hands. He was also sort of talking to himself, too.

I asked Mr. Warbird what was wrong and he told me something that you tell only another teacher who won't laugh at you while you also have a moist face, a pale face, shaking hands, while you sort of talk to yourself. Mr. Warbird told me that the kids were driving him crazy...seriously driving him totally crazy...and that he didn't know if he could take it anymore. He ran down a list of their names, which was pretty much everybody.

It was very early on a Monday morning of a week where we didn't get out early on Friday. A week of no field trips. A full and solid week of action. The kind of week that feels like an anvil is resting on your forehead by Tuesday mid-morning snack time.

I told Mr. Warbird what another teacher tells another teacher after the usual business he just told me. I said: Just try not to choke anybody out today, okay?

Mr. Warbird was still pretty agitated for the rest of the day. He went to drop momma and the kids off at the pool a few more times than usual, leaving me to watch his class and mine. I hardly got any teaching done. But I know better. He sits on the commode with his pants on and rests his mind. A bunch of times, Mr. Warbird also had to go to the other side of the building to the faculty work room to make copies. Copies he should have made early this morning instead of sitting there moaning and wringing his hands, or better, yesterday afternoon after school let out. You know, when unagitated teachers prepare for the next day so they can stay in class and milk the education magic for every single second.

But then came fifth period. That's when Mr. Warbird teaches algebra to a bunch of guys who don't want to be taught algebra. To be fair, they really don't want to be taught anything. To be even more fair, they really don't want to get out of bed and come to school. Ever.

About ten minutes into class, which involves Mr. Warbird

screaming at his students about various real or perceived infractions, slights, pimple squeezing, undone homework, inappropriate noises that may be burps or may be farts, or both at the same time, the new sub showed up. She's what you call a "hot body." I cannot speak to the substance of her intellect, although she was a girl in her mid-twenties and she didn't have a nose ring or a neck tattoo and she wasn't obnoxiously staring into a hand-held electronic device, so I gave her a whole lot of credit...and attention in certain places when she wasn't looking. I was hoping, very much, that she kept her lunch money in her cleavage. Miss Hot Body peeked into my classroom and asked if I was Mr. Warbird, and if I was Mr. Warbird that she had been asked to sit in on my class to observe.

Mr. Warbird shot out of his classroom.

And then, what I heard for the next thirty-five minutes, as it related to teaching the boring stuff on page 387 of the algebra book...and really...as it related to the profession of teaching as a whole in the United States of America, made me tear up, and then it made me want to kill Mr. Warbird.

I'll say this, too: if you're a principal or headmistress or headmaster of a school and you feel like some of your male teachers are starting to not love teaching algebra to kids with moderate to profound learning, behavior, and emotional disorders any more, then place a Miss Hot Body in their classroom from time to time.

Just don't take ours.

GOLF IS FLOG SPELLED BACKWARDS

Very early this morning Lamar appeared in the doorframe of my classroom wearing a golf glove on his left hand. I looked at him, and saw him smiling, but I didn't say anything. This handy human interaction technique was performed on purpose. I've learned that when you don't say anything to certain people and just look at them stupidly, and maybe even allow your bottom jaw to drop open and your eyes glaze over while you sort of focus on something in the upper corner of the room, that they'll often become dejected and disillusioned and downcast and walk away and go bother somebody else.

Lamar didn't walk away. He waved his left hand at me.

I said your golf ball is bouncing down the hallway. Run!

Lamar said he hadn't been playing golf. Lamar said that he was wearing a golf glove in honor of Michael Jackson.

I said I'm pretty sure Michael Jackson didn't play golf. I also related to Lamar my knowledge of contemporary times. I told Lamar that I knew Michael Jackson occasionally wore a glove, sure, but it was covered with diamonds. I also said, feigning humility, that I don't remember, however, which hand he wore the glove on.

Lamar was pretty sure it was his left hand.

I said let's go with that.

Just then Mr. Warbird came in for the day and said to Lamar that his golf ball was bouncing around in the boy's commode.

Lamar huffed.

I immediately adopted that stupid expression again.

Lamar stormed off.

I like working in teams of two. The Lamars of the world don't have a chance.

MOM'S NIGHT OUT. FROM LAMAR

Very early this morning Lamar appeared in the doorframe of my classroom and before I could tell him to go bother Mr. Warbird or Miss Velvet, Lamar told me he was very upset with his mother.

I made the mistake of asking why.

Lamar said his mother had won the free trip to Costa Rica at the school's big fund raiser thing and Lamar said she said she was taking some girlfriends with her to Costa Rica instead of him.

I asked Lamar to spend a few moments conjecturing why his mother might do something like that.

Lamar said he didn't know what conjecturing meant, so he wasn't going to do it.

I said adults need some time to themselves every once and a while.

Lamar said if she would take him that he'd let her go to the beach with her friends and that he would stay in the room and watch movies and eat the stuff in those little refrigerators.

I told Lamar that he just noted, himself, personally, from his own thinking brain, two valid reasons why she won't take him. I shouted...Way to go, *Lamar!*

Lamar asked me if he just conjectured.

I told Lamar he's wising up, which is even better.

TEST LOGIC

Very early this morning Lamar appeared in the doorframe of my classroom and told me that because he didn't study last night for today's big civics test that he shouldn't have to take it.

The vigorous conversation that took place for the next ten minutes between me and Lamar even got me confused. I never knew Lamar knew so much about how he's protected on something like this by the Constitution of the United States of America.

ARE YOU POOPY?

My guys in first period, even on a Friday morning, plop into their desks at the start of class with poopy expressions on their faces. I feel it's my duty to report this to them.

Even before I finish saying this sentence, in a particularly obnoxious voice...Y'all sure do seem like you're in a poopy mood...I can already see them rolling their eyes. This morning, Brainerd rolled his eyes and slapped a hand on the desk as if he's finally had enough. There are a lot of early mornings during the school year.

Fabio was the first to speak up in defiance. He said he didn't like the word *poo*py. It was too much like the nasty word, and since I had been using the word poopy all year Fabio said he'd appreciate it if I came up with another word. Fabio didn't disagree that they were always poopy early in the morning, however.

I thought about it for a moment. *Poo*-ty, I said. Y'all sure do seem like you're in a *pooty* mood?

I thought Brainerd might jump up onto the ceiling.

Fabio chuckled, satisfied with the new description, and then fixed his hair with both hands as if his head were covered with ants.

Lucy grunted.

Lamar said that word was just as lame as the last one. Lamar said he was in a good mood, actually. It's Friday, he said, and in a few hours he'd be free to be whatever he wanted to be. Poopy or pooty or whatever.

I asked him what that might be.

Lamar said he'd be baiting a fishing hook with worms.

REVERSE MARKETING

For some time, Headmistress Lynyrd Skynyrd has been nagging us in the faculty meetings about how we handle it when she and her chimpanzee poke their heads in our classroom when she's giving a tour to prospective parents.

The fussy little discussion item is never listed on the agenda, but she brings it up every time anyway. Headmistress Lynyrd Skynyrd said she wants a *student* to speak up and tell the parents what they're working on, not the teachers. I hope she didn't see me roll my eyes and blow out a hurricane of hot air, because that ain't ever going to happen. Teachers know their students better than anyone…even their parents and therapists.

I tried it for a while anyway. The look on Headmistress Lynyrd Skynyrd's face would change considerably, from salesmanship perky to extremely pale, right there in front of the prospective parents, after I'd ask everyone...anyone?...to tell Headmistress Lynyrd Skynyrd what we were working on...you know...just a few seconds ago.

No one wanted to tell her. They'd lift their heavy heads and look at her, with mildly inquisitive zombie-like expressions, but wouldn't say anything.

So then I went back to telling excitable tour groups what we were working on. The dissertations were so inspiring I wouldn't have been surprised if the parents whipped out their checkbook right there. And here's an extra thousand for the teacher's Christmas party, too!

So then Headmistress Lynyrd Skynyrd went back to telling the teachers in the faculty meetings that she wanted us to go back to insisting that the students tell prospective parents what we were working on. She said that when the students describe the activities that prospective parents really like that a whole lot more.

This morning I went back to asking everyone, anyone, to tell Headmistress Lynyrd Skynyrd and the prospective parent, a smiling gentleman in a spiffy golf shirt that actually shined, what we were working on...you know...just a few seconds ago?

The look on our headmistress' face changed considerably, from salesmanship perky to extremely pale. Sorry, I thought. You really should know better by now.

A CAT GUY, HUH?

I think Mr. Warbird might be losing his mind. His wife moved to New York a long time ago and he'll go a couple of weeks without seeing her. He says he loves her and that she saved him from a life of pain and loneliness...but airplane tickets sure are damn expensive.

He really is determined the finish out the school year like the dedicated professional he is.

Mr. Warbird recently celebrated a birthday with a zero at the end of it, which made him a little reflective in a way that makes him mumble what he thinks are profound utterances. He also says he and his wife are trying to make a baby, but it's hard to make a baby when her genitals are in New York and his genitals are way down here in a southern state of disuse.

The other day I overheard him tell Miss Velvet that he had been watching *Portlandia* episodes and it had affected him. Mr. Warbird has pictures of his two cats on his cell phone. He shows me these pictures at various times during our busy day. They're curled up next to his face. They're curled up on the shirt he's about to wear to school. They're curled up on the pillows he uses to rest his head after a wearying day at school. In one photograph, all three of them are reposing on his lonely marriage bed. I think Mr. Warbird might be losing his mind.

It gets worse. For me and the cats.

I finally asked him if the cats had names.

Excitedly, Mr. Warbird said they did! Their names were Mittens and Skrittles.

Skittles? Like the candy?

Mr. Warbird was instantly offended. *Skuuur*-it-tuls, he said, angrily.

So, I said, you have told others about these cats and they, too, have pronounced the name incorrectly. I can tell.

Skrittles, he said.

I told Mr. Warbird that if I ever saw the cats walking down the street I would eat them. With some French fries.

This announcement really provoked him.

Mr. Warbird said he'd never let them out where they'd just start walking down the street because he loved them so much.

I sensed Mr. Warbird, in his internal turmoil, didn't get that I was kidding. Pretty much making it up as I went along. These two cats didn't look like they'd taste good anyway.

And then Mr. Warbird finally told me something profound. He said their names really aren't Skrittles and Mittens.

No?

He said their real names are Madelyn and Molly. He just calls them Skrittles and Mittens when his wife's not around.

I stood there gawking at Mr. Warbird. Now I know who's really about to go completely crazy. It's Mittens and Madelyn and Molly and Skrittles...and me.

WHAT MY MOTHER DID ON SPRING BREAK

I asked the wide-awake folks in first period what they were doing during spring break next week.

Brainerd said his mother was going to get her tooth numbed.

LOVE ENERGY

Mr. Warbird has a huge group for fifth period algebra, so he has to teach the class at a bunch of desks he's set up in the commons room. There's even a white board out there so he can write all that squiggly algebraic hieroglyphics where they'll see it and be amazed at how easy algebra really is.

Only if you're the vodka-soaked Russian scientist who invented it.

Anyway, I heard one his students, a guy named Irving, start moaning about how he was worthless and how his family was worthless and how he hated them and how they hated him right back...and then Irving started in on some things that happened to him in sixth grade he was still mad about.

Mr. Warbird let Irving drone on, and then he offered up some advice about forgetting grudges and toxic hate and the people who make you do your homework: good and loving parents.

I listened as Mr. Warbird slowly worked it back to himself...and then to his wife who we've never met. All we have is a picture of her in her wedding dress on Mr. Warbird's desk next to a mug of broken pencils and dry pens. Mr. Warbird said to Irving in a powerful voice...that he will not allow his beautiful wife to spend any energy hating *any*thing...because that takes away the energy....*she* should be *using*...for loving *me*.

There was a long and profound silence.

Finally, Abraham spoke up. He said in a powerful voice...Mr. Warbird, you really are an enormous fag.

Todd Sentell

THE TEACHERS IN THE HALL

While I was busy teaching fifteen really good vocabulary words...allure, antiquity, appraise, cleave, depreciate, facet, facsimile, impervious, nondescript, quandary, repose, scintillate, scrutinize, synthetic, and transmute...Miss Kentucky knocked on my door and motioned for me to come out into the hall.

When another teacher knocks on the door and motions for you to come out into the hall, right in the middle of class, and if she's got a weird grin on her face, you know it's going to be good.

Miss Kentucky was teaching Spanish to a bunch of high school guys in the next classroom. She asked me to step in there and take a good whiff.

I stepped in there and took a good whiff. In just one good whiff I smelled butts, armpits, greasy hair, and school uniforms that had not been recently washed. A cornucopia, in other words. I came back out, and without saying a word, held my hands over my mouth and nose to indicate that I felt her pain.

Miss Kentucky said in her Kentucky accent...That's *so* wrong on *so* many *lev*-ulls. Then Miss Kentucky asked me to go in there and deliver a quick and forceful hygiene lecture from a real man's perspective. She said they don't listen to her at *all*.

When another teacher asks you to deliver a quick and forceful lecture to their class it makes you feel like a guest speaker being paid a large speaking fee and you're filled with enormous professional pride. I stepped in there. One of the farters, Irving, moaned real loud...Oh, *God.*

I noted how badly the room smelled, and how it was tough for the awesome magic of education to take place when you subtlety try to kill your Spanish teacher with your body odors.

None of them disagreed. They actually seemed proud that I noticed their strategy. They were maybe even a little smug. At least they got Miss Kentucky to leave the room. I'll have to give them that.

I asked them do they frequently, like every day, scrub with soap and warm water...their exhaust systems?

Most of them said they did.

I asked them were they not embarrassed with their gleeful farting?

Nope. One of them said he thought Miss Kentucky likes it because she laughs so hard when we do it.

In the hallway, I heard Miss Kentucky giggle.

I asked them did they know that after several days...that if you don't shampoo your hair for several days...that it starts to stink? Your greasy hair?

To a man they said they did not know that.

I asked them to shampoo their hair tonight.

To a man they said they probably wouldn't.

I gave them a long, hard, man-to-man, hygienic look. I said...Listen up! Wash your asses and your hair and stop farting in class so much. And then I walked out while they applauded.

Miss Kentucky taught the last minutes of class from out in the hall. She wouldn't go back in there. I finally had to shut my door. Not because of the smell. To lock someone in.

Lamar wanted to change classes so he could go fart with the rest of them.

GAME ADVICE

Every Wednesday afternoon Miss Velvet supervises controlled chaos in an after-school activity called "Game Club."

Game Club is held in the school's game room. This is the room where that kid named Diego used to go to masturbate. I assume he's found another secret place in which to masturbate because Diego seems like he's persistent and creative.

The game room has a big couch in it and some tables and chairs and a couple of TVs hooked up to hand-held software game controllers. There are also a bunch of board games whose parts have all been mixed up a long time ago...but they play the games anyway.

Miss Velvet had to go do something this afternoon so she asked me if I could run Game Club. She said the school pays her twenty-five bucks for forty-five minutes, but that it usually stretches to an hour and half because most parents are always late picking their kids up anyway.

After two kids nearly killed each other in an attempt to be the first one to play a Super Mario video game that had a Salvador Dali-like effect on me, I sort of hid at a table in the back of the room. I started reading signs that have been glued or taped or tacked to the walls in the back of the room. They had a mesmerizing effect on me, too:

- Use appropriate humor
- Use good timing
- Bounce back
- Speak up
- Try!
- Learn about others
- Join in!
- Once is enough
- LIGMO...let it go and move on
- Stay cool
- Try not to arouse
- Participate
- Make a good impression
- No policing
- Go with the flow
- Stay cool
- Be kind
- Be flexible
- Chat with friends
- Listen
- Stay coherent and on topic!

By the time Game Club was over, Ferrari was asleep on the floor under a blanket. Diego had not masturbated, but had won all the Super Mario competitions instead. Two kids were quietly doing homework, and one girl was staring into space. She had actually been staring into space pretty much the whole time.

I asked her if she was okay.

The rest of the kids said that's what she does in Game Club and for me to freakin' deal with it.

TRS YOU?

Clutch's mom knocked on the classroom door this morning, right in the middle of class, and asked if I could come speak to her in the hall real quick. Clutch wasn't in class, so I figured she was making the rounds and telling all of Clutch's teachers the news. Good or bad news I had no idea.

I walked out there and shut the door behind me. She had a funny look on her face. I figured I was about to get some bad news, but Clutch's mom said she just wanted to give me a hug because Clutch had always been afraid to write creative pieces and she said I had made it fun and easy for him and she was thankful for it. She was tearing up a little bit. We hugged again.

She said I bet you're wondering where he is...I said I was...and she said he's at the psychiatrist all day being analyzed and tested. And then she handed me a form and asked me to fill it out and to put it in this envelope and put it in the mail as soon as I could.

I said I would. We almost hugged again, but didn't. She touched me on the arm.

When I got back in class I could tell that Clutch's best buddies...Peetie, Kells, and Red...were worried that something bad was up for Clutch. I told them Clutch was being held by a foreign government and was laughing at the lameness of their torture techniques. They looked at each other and smiled. Clutch is their mute hero.

I unfolded the sheets and glanced at the lists. It was a TRS, a teacher rating scale, "for ages 12 to 21 as part of a behavior assessment system for children." It asked if the child never, sometimes, or always:

- Reads assigned chapters
- Breaks the rules
- Visits the school nurse
- Is usually chosen as a leader
- Shows interest in other's ideas
- Has trouble staying seated
- Seems lonely
- Listens to directions
- Acts strangely
- Deceives others
- Has trouble keeping up in class
- Throws up after eating
- Annoys others on purpose
- Complains of shortness of breath
- Acts without thinking
- Has trouble getting information when needed
- Seems to take setbacks in stride
- Tries to do well in school
- Tries to bring out the best in people
- Is sad

- Is easily distracted from classwork
- Threatens to hurt others
- Seems out of touch with reality
- Gets into trouble
- Says, "I don't have any friends"
- Worries about what other adolescents think
- Cannot wait to take turn
- Had headaches
- Analyzes the nature of the problem before starting to solve it
- Uses other's things without permission
- Is afraid of getting sick
- Is creative
- Congratulates others when good things happen to them
- Seeks attention while doing schoolwork
- Is negative about things
- Does not pay attention to lectures
- Babbles to self
- Has to stay after school for punishment
- Has poor handwriting or printing
- Says, "I'm afraid I will make a mistake"
- Loses temper too easily
- Gets sick
- Calls out in class
- Tracks down information when needed
- Is a "good sport"

- Uses the Internet effectively for schoolwork
- Makes suggestions without offending others
- Says, "I hate myself"
- Has a short attention span
- Teases others
- Has strange ideas
- Steals at school
- Complains about being teased
- Worries
- Has poor self-control
- Complains about health
- Asks to make up missed assignments
- Responds inappropriately when asked a question
- Recovers quickly after setback
- Makes decision easily
- Encourages others to do their best
- Acts out of control
- Is pessimistic
- Listens carefully
- Sees things that are not there
- Sneaks around
- Gets failing school grades
- Worries about things that cannot be changed
- Defies teachers
- Avoids other adolescents
- Is overly active
- Is unclear when presenting ideas

- Adjusts well to changes in routine
- Is well organized
- Offers to help other adolescents
- Is easily upset
- Eats too much
- Argues when denied own way
- Seems unaware of others
- Lies
- Does not complete tests
- Is fearful
- Makes friends easily
- Complains of pain
- Completes homework
- Is clear when telling about personal experiences
- Complains when asked to do things differently
- Works well under pressure
- Says, "please" and "thank you"
- Disrupts other adolescent's activities
- Says, "I want to die" or "I wish I were dead"
- Is easily distracted
- Picks at things like own hair, nails, or clothing
- Disobeys
- Complains that lessons go too fast
- Refuses to join group activities
- Bullies others
- Quickly joins group activities
- Interrupts others when they are speaking

- Is able to describe feelings accurately
- Adjusts well to new teachers
- Has good study habits
- Gives good suggestions for solving problems
- Cries easily
- Has a hearing problem
- Seeks revenge on others
- Hears sounds that are not there
- Cheats in school
- Has spelling problems
- Says, "I get nervous during tests" or "Tests make me nervous"
- Plays alone
- Has stomach problems
- Eats things that are not food
- Communicates clearly
- Adjusts well to changes in plans
- Is easily annoyed by others
- Compliments others
- Disrupts the schoolwork of other children
- Has seizures
- Pays attention
- Says things that make no sense
- Smokes or chews tobacco at school
- Has reading problems
- Refuses to talk
- Calls other adolescents names

- Has trouble making new friends
- Eats too little
- Has difficulty explaining rules of games to others
- Gets upset when plans are changed
- Takes careful notes during lectures
- Is good at getting people to work together
- Says, "Nobody likes me"
- Has eye problems
- Hits other adolescents
- Falls down
- Uses foul language
- Has problems with mathematics
- Is nervous
- Is chosen last by other adolescents for games

I got to thinking that we adults might benefit from a rating scale, too. Never? Sometimes? Always?

SELF ETYMOLOGY

Today the guys in first period had a vocabulary test. We had been studying the words for a long time, and today they were asked to write a sentence using the words. The words were: meteoric, precocious, succinct, sylvan, virtuoso, articulate, garb, inherent, zany, and parody.

Lamar slapped his hands on the test and screamed he wasn't taking the test.

I said...let me guess...because you didn't study for it you feel like you shouldn't have to take it?

Lamar screamed...That's damn *right!*

Brainerd was already scratching out answers. So was Lucy. As fast as they could go. Fabio had a panicked expression on his face. Fabio inquired that might I had forgotten to announce we were having a vocabulary test today?

I reminded Fabio that we've been going over the words for about a week...every day...and I've been reminding you about the test every day...for about a week...and yesterday I gave you some sample sentences with the words. Remember, I told Fabio, that I said you could even use my sentences if you wanted to...to ensure a particularly easy grade of A-plus.

Fabio increased the intensity of his panicked expression.

Lamar turned around a smiled an evil smile at Fabio.

By this time, quiet, mute, extremely irritable Lucy, was ready to turn in the test. I took it from her and looked it over. In her hard-to-read handwriting, Lucy wrote: People who have autism speak succinctly sometimes. My shyness is an inherent part of me. I have trouble speaking articulately to other kids sometimes.

I looked at Lucy. Nice job, I said. Really. Well done.

Lucy wouldn't look up at me, though. She didn't say anything, either. She was too busy pulling hairs out of her arms again.

TIME OUT!

Today, I said to my civic scholars, I'm going to deliver a fun and fascinating lecture on horology!

Lamar instantly went nuts.

Todd Sentell

I let him go nuts for a while. I finally wrote the word on the white board...HOROLOGY.

Lamar yelled...That's not the way you spell it!

Everybody told Lamar to shut up. Including Nesbit, who's no longer afraid of Lamar either.

I told everybody that horology was the science of time and timekeeping and that people who study time and time zones and whatnot were called horologists. Even watch repair guys. Horologists. I knew Lamar would go nuts again.

Lamar went nuts again.

I said that time does two hugely important things for the human civilization. I told Lamar that I'd like for him to join us as a member of human civilization, as opposed to representing right now, baboons.

He comically clamped both hands over his mouth.

I told them that time keeps us organized and productive. I waited for Lamar to say something. He didn't. I said that if I were to say to Lamar that I would buy him anything he wanted...and that I would come over to his trailer park on Saturday and pick him up on Saturday...imagine if we didn't agree on a time because Saturday lasts twenty-four hours and begins real late on Friday night and ends real late on Sunday morning. I looked at Lamar about as sarcastically as I could.

Lamar screamed...I don't live in a trailer park! *You* do!

So if I tell Lamar I'll be by his trailer park at three in the afternoon, I told the class, that gives Lamar a point in time to prepare for. In other words, I said, he can organize the rest of his time better by knowing a time of arrival instead of wandering around for twenty-four hours worrying about it. What if we said school lets out sometime in the afternoon and you had to worry about it all day. That's not productive.

Lamar asked me what time it was.

I looked at my watch. I told him he had forty more minutes of this to endure.

Lamar asked could he take a time-out.

I said sure.

As Lamar was walking out I told him to be a good horologist...and to take his *time*.

Lamar, in the hallway, very publicly, went nuts again, vividly describing to a couple of kids sitting in the hallway taking time-outs of their own, what we were talking about today in civics class. We were talking about time-wasting *whores*, Lamar shouted.

Mr. Warbird yanked open his door and yelled at me...What the hell are you *teaching* them over there!

JESUS AND HITLER AND ABIGAIL AND IRONY

Other than Nesbit being wigged out about how Lamar and Brainerd constantly make faces and noises at each other in civics class, and other than Nesbit constantly going through medication changes and medication adjustments, I just can't understand why he started beating his forehead on his desk while I'm reading to them this morning a fascinating story from my recent copy of National Geographic about Civil War illustrators. They could have listened to a story about koala bears, but they voted for Civil War illustrators.

When I asked Nesbit why he was beating his head on the desk he screamed that everyone in here...*deep breath*...LOOKED LIKE JESUS!

Lamar started laughing. Brainerd got mad at Lamar because he was laughing at Nesbit and Brainerd liked Nesbit. Lamar got mad at Brainerd because he was mad at him for laughing.

I said to Nesbit...Uh, do what?

Then Nesbit said that if I don't leave him alone he was going to give me...*deep breath*...THE HITLER SALUTE!

Nesbit, with my calmest and most understanding urging, went out to the commons room to take some more deep breaths and search for a reasonable reality in his head that might get him through the rest of the civics class. Lamar does not look, or act, like Jesus. No way. Neither does Brainerd.

A couple of hours later, in between classes, a calm Nesbit showed me a book he was reading. The book was about Abigail Smith Adams, the wife of the second president of the United States. As Nesbit tapped on the picture of Mrs. Adams on the cover, he said...She sure is one ugly looking woman.

I gave Mrs. Adams a fair and unspoken review, but I had to wince.

Nesbit shook my hand and trotted to his social skills class.

WITH LIBERTY AND JUSTICE FOR ALL

There's a lower school girl with a slender, athletic build, with huge brown eyes, whose name is Taffi, who hits, scratches, kicks, spits on, spits at, snarls at, and cusses at other human beings when she's not involved in the wondrous process of education. The weekly recipients of her violence are teachers, counselors, administrators, and her fellow students.

The way she weaves cuss words into phrases is imaginative and natural and mildly admirable. She should be a script consultant to Quentin Tarantino. One time, Mr. Warbird had to wrap both arms around her when he heard her in the counselor's office busting lamps while a counselor was off to the side, cringing. Taffi called him a rapist bastard son of a bitch racist rapist. On a field trip one time, during the picnic portion of the beautiful day of communing with nature, she stabbed her father in the top of the hand with a fork. In front of everybody. One day she punched Bugs in the face. It was the only moment in my life I sort of felt sorry for Bugs.

One of her teachers told me one day...Oh, but she's brilliant.

I said, Who *cares?* She's a killer in training.

I was proctoring an assessment test one day for a few of the lower schoolers and a few feet away from Taffi a young fellow made a noise in his throat, with no intention of being disruptive, and without thinking Taffi zipped her pencil at his head. I'm pretty sure that pencils have sharp ends on them that can stick into a person's eyeball. Taffi turned around and looked at me like it was the most natural thing to do at that moment...with those big brown eyes...to zip a pencil at a kid's head. I didn't say a word. I waited for her to politely ask me if I had another pencil she could use.

She comes back to school in the days after her terrorizing as if nothing ever happened. Others come back to school the next days, too, limping. Some with visible bruises. Others with scraped shins.

Taffi's teacher told me Taffi's family has a lot of money.

I asked the teacher if these people, other than their tuition payment, were giving a lot of their money to the school.

The teacher said she really didn't know.

Taffi kicked out the back window in her nanny's Mercedes SUV. Taffi beats her sister up. One day we all got an e-mail from our admissions lady that this morning Taffi witnessed her beloved nanny being fired by her father...so go easy on Taffi today because it upset her.

Right. Go easy on her.

You get tired. Teachers get soul-deep weary. That's why we have that look on our face sometimes. Teachers get tired of being bullied by little children and a school who doesn't protect you, or anybody else, from them.

She's a runner, too. Not on the school's track team, but a kid who at least once a week runs and hides somewhere in the building. Or runs out of the building and hides in bushes or hangs out way up in the parking lot, just standing there in the wide open space as if she went up there to smell the air. A lot of important people get involved in trying to find Taffi when she runs and hides. When she runs and hides it stops school for a lot of other kids, and for their parents who pay a lot of money to the school.

Taffi's very presence in our school is unfair to everybody. There are places better equipped for violent, unpredictable, fourth grade girls who may weigh sixty pounds. We are not that kind of school. But we are because we seem to need the money.

This morning, during the reciting of the Pledge of Allegiance...there she goes. She zipped away from those who were neatly assembled for our every-morning tradition...and up the steps at the corner of the gym...and there she goes along the mezzanine toward the high school side of the building...you could just see the top of her head...and there goes Headmistress Lynyrd Skynyrd running after her...and there goes Miss Manhater running after the headmistress.

Two counselors go running after Taffi, too.

Walkie-talkies began squawking.

... with liberty and justice for *all!*

The thrill of the chase got Lamar freaked out. While I was walking with him to our classroom, he proposed a scenario where he would be allowed to run around the building and if he found Taffi that he would tackle her and hold her down until the police arrived, like he's seen on police shows. Instead, I asked Lamar to sit in my classroom and spend ten minutes or so calming himself down and not saying anything at all. Lamar said he's always wanted to be a policeman, and then he wanted to be an FBI agent.

Lamar really didn't want to sit quietly with me in my classroom or shut the heck up for more than three seconds while so many others were running around the building looking for Taffi while they squawked on walkie-talkies. But he had to sit in here anyway.

As I was organizing the top of my desk by fiddling around with the pencils and pens and peppermint sticks in my pencil mug, I was also carefully watching Lamar. I took an absent-minded sip of coffee. All of a sudden Lamar's eyes widened and he pointed toward the floor. Lamar said...Uh, there's a goddamn human under your desk!

I scooted my chair back a little bit and looked under my

desk. I had forgotten about Taffi, but she was right there at my feet, curled up like a little animal.

Lamar said...Uh, who is it?

As brightly as I could, I chirped...*Hi*, there, *Taffi!*

She squeezed away from me. She had in her hand a pair of scissors. Not the kind of scissors with the round tips, but a real pair of scissors. Teacher scissors. Adult scissors. The kind of scissors that might slide right through your skin and into an organ you really need.

I asked her, politely, to hand me the scissors and come on out of there...okay?

She squeezed in there some more.

I leaned down and made eye contact with her. I worked in a good long dramatic pause. I said something to her I knew would appeal to her immediately and totally. An immediate and total appeal to her love of schoolhouse madness and disorder and chaos and mayhem and violence. I said if she didn't hand me those scissors that I would have Lamar lick her on the face with his enormous green tongue.

Taffi handed me the scissors. She crawled out and jumped up and down on her toes a couple of times, smiling. She hugged me sweetly, and then went over and hugged Lamar, and then skipped out of my classroom, still smiling a sweet smile.

Lamar was wide-eyed.

I am the adult in the room. I am an adult and a teacher who doesn't mind going home after a tough day feeling disrespected or confused. That's okay. That's the way it goes a lot of days. But I'm not going home with a pair of scissors in my lung stuck in there by a psychopathic fourth grade girl we keep enabling. We are not that kind of school. I'm fairly sure.

Lamar was still wide-eyed and noted that that was a pretty freakin' wild ass moment.

I breathed out, and then took another sip of coffee.

Lamar, out his particular wild blue yonder, said…I'm *much* more worried about why *tur*tles cross the road, Mr. Sentell.

I leaned my head back and gargled my coffee in his honor.

FRIEND ME?

The school's admission lady just e-mailed everybody to ask who took a book out of her office and hadn't given it back in a long time and that she wanted it back. The book was written by a learning disorders guru fellow who knows all about what we do and see every day. The name of the book is titled, "It's So Much Work to be Your Friend."

I wonder what teacher stole the admission's lady book. It wasn't me. I've already got one. A long time ago, Lurlene gave me a copy.

WHAT I PROBABLY MIGHT NOT DO THIS SUMMER

After all the end-of-the year awards were given out, and after all the speeches were made at the end-of-the year ceremony, Lamar's mother bopped up to me while I had a huge amount of free food in my mouth. Lamar bopped up to me, too.

Lamar's mother, Monique, asked with a big, pleading

smile if I'd be willing to come to their home this summer and tutor Lamar on study skills and manners! I looked around for a second to see if she was in on a joke or something.

Lamar was smiling and bopping his head up and down, too. He was all for it.

And then Lamar introduced me to his brother. Lamar's brother seemed a little dangerous, too. Lamar's brother said he didn't need any more manners. Lamar's brother said that's why he doesn't have to come to this school, because he's okay on the manners, *man.*

Lamar asked me, with that special grin on his red face, if he needed to learn any more manners! Head still bopping. How much do you charge!

I told Lamar that my time would be complimentary. I said that means *free.*

*Ohhhh...*he said. I can afford *that!*

I told him I liked to think I might have a hand in saving the world from untold evil and agitation and I could see that our work together might result in me receiving the Nobel Peace Prize.

Lamar said...*Hell* yeah!

I said to Lamar that I've always wanted to win the Nobel Peace Prize. Really, I said. Who doesn't?

Lamar asked if he could have some of the money.

I said I think the award is a gold medal or something. A big gold coin sort of affair. With a fellow's head on it.

Lamar said he'd help me melt it.

I looked deep into Lamar's manic eyes, just to confirm, maybe, hopefully, why I live to teach—just through Lamar, as a stand-in, standing there for every student I've ever had and will have. They're looking at me for answers, but they don't even know they're asking.

PART 4

CAREER CHANGE CONFIDENTIAL: MUSINGS ON MY OWN DEPARTMENT OF EDUCATION

In the rest of the world they do things different than what you been taught.

—Flannery O'Connor, *The Violent Bear It Away*

I LIKE THE notion of dumping the United States Department of Education and saving the country a lot of money, and then asking the fifty states to run their schools on their own. The thought of fifty American states—sovereign in educating their kids, maybe even in competition with each other—thrills my teacher's heart and soul, and the coach in me, too. Like our American football games, college and pro. The drive to avoid embarrassment is local, even personal.

I think I've figured out how we become educated. It's not that complicated. A teacher gathers his students in a classroom, shuts the door, and starts informing his students in the way he thinks the students will retain the information. The teacher's ultimate hope is that the students will use the

306

information in some way, too. As the teacher teaches, he also demands that the students use their manners with him and each other.

The teacher's principal, from time to time, pats the teacher on the back and tells him he's doing a great job and how much we value your work here. From time to time, the principal tells the teacher where he could improve an area or a technique or something else he might try that worked for her when she was a teacher for so many years. The principal knows how a teacher is performing because she walks into his classroom from time to time and sits in a desk and watches him do his job. Principals are constantly asking their teachers in conversations here and there…Tell me what's happening in your classroom these days. They get pacing guides and curriculum schedules, but the great principals love to see your face light up when you explain what great things are happening in your classroom these days.

Then, the teacher's principal, in every staff meeting, tells her teachers that the headmaster or county superintendent or the United States Secretary of Education or the president of the United States is aware of all the great work we're doing and he wanted you all to know it. From time to time, one of those people attends a staff meeting and tells us himself. Which would be nice.

The parents of the students constantly stress the value of education and good manners, sometimes not in that order, because a great parent knows that people notice if you have good manners long before they can tell if you're educated. Great parents are not afraid to say the right thing and they are not afraid of the reactions of their kids. Great parents, when it comes to school issues and feelings and attitudes and desires, hand out tough love when needed. Great parents do not distract great teachers by pestering them with unreasonable and idiotic e-mailed requests, or conversations, or by sneaking around the teacher and going to the principal with their unreasonable and idiotic requests. Thank you.

Students have to be tested in some way to see if they retained the important information. There's no other way. It's going to be some kind of test...some kind of quantification. A number that's produced, or a letter: F, D, C, B, or an A. Plus or minus or right there in the middle. After that, it's really up to the student to keep that information in their brain, not the teacher's, although we sort of never forget because we love and respect the information we teach and it makes us happy to think about it every waking moment of our dang lives.

Becoming educated is a state of mind: the student's. Becoming educated is always and ultimately up to the student and always will be. So who is second-in-command of education? Teachers, of course. We've been there for students all along, learning a few things ourselves:

- Being a parent doesn't make you a better teacher. Being a teacher makes you a better parent.
- Those savant students who know as much as you do about the subject you teach sure do keep you sharp.
- I found out pretty quickly, even though I tried, that you can't fix a kid's learning, behavior, or emotional disorders right there in third period while you're talking about

the Battle of Gettysburg. I got some good advice from Lurlene one time on that one when she said...Fix the behavior; not the kid. You don't have time to do any real fixing, she said, although we're all trying anyway. That's the job of their therapist. If their parents care enough to get them one.

- The five most powerful words you can say to a student, a struggling student or otherwise, are: I'm proud of you. When you say this a lot, and always at the right times and with a hand on their shoulder and while you look them in the eyes, students will improve in their academic skills, and sometimes even their emotional and behavioral disorders seem to lighten. At the same time, as a teacher, your silent mantra should be: Don't give up. I'm proud of me, too.

- Some teachers really are crazy. I worked with a teacher who, during responsibilities outside of classroom teaching, was never where he was supposed to be. He always showed up late to faculty meetings. He hardly ever went to parent-teacher conferences. After a while I got over my anger and became mesmerized by him. I was finally convinced he didn't care what other people thought of him and that he wasn't worried about getting fired. Not one bit. He had a great smile, even though he had green, broken teeth, and he knew his subject and had been teaching for years and the kids loved him. Other than the kids, this fellow teacher was the next most fascinating person I've ever spent the day in the schoolhouse trying to figure out what made him so nuts.

- The moment when their eyes light up and they say this is great stuff and they mean it...that's it. That's why you teach.

- So you want to become a teacher? I'll bet you're good at telling stories; you like to inform; you're probably real organized and real well read; and you're probably pretty decisive and confident in yourself. But how will you handle yourself when a kid is rude and disrespectful to you? Every day? Sometimes six or seven at a time...at the same time? How about when a parent is rude and disrespectful to you when you've done nothing to deserve it?

- So you still want to become a teacher? I'll bet you're the kind of person who would make up your own mind about becoming a teacher. Good. You'll make a great teacher.

- And you're willing to spend your own money. You love to go The School Box, even online. You love the way the place looks and smells. It's like a toy store for teachers. You feel creative and engaging and dedicated the moment you walk in. The teacher's section at Dollar Tree ain't bad, either. I learned early that kids will kill for stickers. Not other kids. You. They will rush your desk like the Pamplona running of the bulls for a sticker that says they did a good job.

- They're out of control! If you're a control freak, after about two days of your first substitute or full-time teaching job, in any grade and in any kind of school, you won't be a control freak any more. That hideous personal character flaw will be burned right out of you forever and replaced with the awesome ability to manage your anger and irritation with anything and anyone. You'll quickly learn how to pick your skirmishes, battles, and even your wars. You'll like yourself again; trust yourself again; you'll ooze a special confidence and common sense and logic and fairness and understanding and empathy; and other people who know you real well will notice the wonderful change in you.

- When defiance or laziness or apocalyptic disinterest clogged everything up, all I asked of my students was to give it a try. Do *one* little thing, then. Ask *one* question. Offer up *one* discussion item. Write *one* sentence, and see if you live through it. And when none of those things worked, we'd just try again the next day. I told them I'd be right back in here tomorrow...that I would never give up on them or learning or just sitting here talking. They'd usually moan...*Thank* you.

- My best lecture wasn't about some great moment or thing or person in history or in art or in literature. It was a super short and super effective lecture, and I gave it to only the pathologically defiant. I gave it to those students who would constantly and untiringly argue and disagree and debate the air around them…while they were in the comfort and understanding and controlled environment of a schoolhouse. I guess it really wasn't a lecture. It was actually a question. I'd ask the defiant student, When you get pulled over by the police one day, and you will, what are you going to do when he asks you to get out of your car? Really, what are you going to do at that insanely critical moment in your heretofore insanely defiant life?

- When a student says you're his favorite teacher, don't qualify it or poo-poo it or tell him you're uncomfortable with it. Enjoy it. Life's too short not to accept that you've reached a kid in some way—academically or as a teacher-entertainer.

- There a lot of parents who hold their kids back academically, emotionally, and socially through their own narcissistic reasons I will never understand.

- The class periods and full days and weeks and months and semesters when their eyes don't light up and they never say this is great stuff makes you wonder why you teach. Lurlene gave me some good advice on that, too. She said…Don't take it personally.

- There are very few teachers and parents who are confident enough in themselves to give out tough love to kids and teenagers. The ones who *are* confident enough give it to themselves every day, too. That's how they back it up.

- I'm not a sex therapist, but I guess I look like one. In a parent-teacher conference, parents generally want to hear all you're willing to tell them about their child. But I think I speak for all teachers when I say that we don't really want to hear everything a mother wants to tell us about herself. Her very private sexy self. One time, in a conference, when it got a whole lot creepy and seemed like it was going to get even creepier, I finally held up my two hands and formed the "time-out" sign at the mother. And then I said to her...T-the-heck-M-I! The lady looked at me like *I* was crazy.

- Not quite the alumni magazine. For years I've bought a certain publication at the gas station up the street that contains fresh mug shots of those recently arrested. The tabloid-style newspaper is called "Just Busted." I always wondered when I'd see a picture of someone I knew or, God forbid, of someone I was related to. The moment finally came, and it was a picture of a former student who was arrested for impersonating a police officer. I brought the Just Busted issue to school to show a fellow teacher who once had the guy, too. He said, without a pause, that years ago he should have been arrested for impersonating a student.

- In another issue I spotted a picture of a mother of a former student. She used to come to conferences geeked up on prescription pills and wobble around in her chair and say things no one could understand, but we just kept on talking anyway so we could get it over with and get out of there. She was a good looking gal; real rich, too, who dressed in some mighty sexy clothes for parent-teacher conferences. I was always legitimately fearful that one, or both, of her big boobs were going to flop out of her blouse and knock over her enormous water bottle. She was arrested for destruction of public property.

- At the beginning of the spring semester one year, a helicopter parent team came to meet with all of their eighth grade son's teachers. The couple said we're tired of helicoptering and enabling and pretty much doing all of his work for him. It's sink-or-swim time, they said, and we've told him so, too. He knows we're meeting with you today. I liked this. I liked this a lot. My fellow teachers and I winked at each other. And I liked their son, too. He was oblivious to the educational fun around him, but he had good manners and he was respectful. I just never knew he was alive some days, even though his eyes were open and I could see him breathing. I often thought about tossing a hissing firecracker at him to help increase his level of interest in what we were doing. I'm sure he would have looked at the shredded firecracker on his desk, looked at me, looked back at the shreds, and then looked at the clock on the wall to see how much longer he had to endure sitting in a class not doing or saying anything. All that without blinking. Anyway, so we all let him sink or swim. He chose to furiously tread water. He made it out of eighth grade just fine. I don't know how the parents turned out. I'm assuming they got on with their lives and were enjoying themselves.

- If you want to have the same mental and physical energy at the end of the day that you started out with, you have to eat a big breakfast and then a small, non-fatty snack once an hour and drink a lot of water all day. Once you get into the routine it's easy. In other words, if you're never hungry or dying of thirst starting in homeroom until you leave, you're doing it right.

- Manners! One day, right in the heat of a parent-teacher conference, it finally happened: a mother answered her cell phone and started yakking into it as if she was the only person in the room. We all looked at each other, dumbly. I finally said to the mother, with a wave of my hand...*Please*. Take your *time*. She did.

- One time I had a mother say to me about her son...Well, good luck with him, she said, because he's one *straaaaange* little guy. He really was one strange little guy, so I wasn't shocked at all when she muttered those words to me. But, mom, *right in front of him and his pals?*

- In my time teaching, I discovered four students who had been cutting their upper arms. Three were girls and one was a boy. One girl's cuts were clean, gaping-open, long cuts, as if they were performed by a surgeon. I noticed the lowest cut on her upper arm one morning, and when I lifted the sleeve of her short-sleeve shirt to reveal the rest of the cuts, I gasped. Then she screamed that she wanted to go to a goddamn mental hospital! Right now! She even knew the name of the hospital and what street it was on. I said in an odd voice...Okay, you got it. Another teacher started dialing the girl's mother. Another teacher dialed the front office. I knew about that mental hospital. I had a college roommate who spent some time there. Later, he earned a Ph.D. in philosophy...and later he became a monk. I swear. A monk in a monastery. I'll never forget that one night...the future monk, driving his souped-up BMW at well over one hundred miles per hour, with me holding on in the passenger seat, and with both of us bathed with flashing blue lights, almost outran a South Carolina State patrolman.

- My parents, I'm fairly sure, don't believe the stories I tell them from time to time about my school day.

- Listen to the advice of the savvy veteran teachers and administrators about teaching kids. I've learned that nearly every bit of it is valuable...usually just a few minutes later.

- Probably because I'd leave my copies in the teacher's toilet, the kids found out I subscribed to the *National Enquirer.* Kids know what this highly informative news publication is because they see it, and gawk at the headlines and gawk at the arresting photographs of the huge beach butts of movie stars on the cover as they're sneaking candy and gum onto the conveyer belt in aisle three. But they thought this was pretty cool—a teacher, you know, who was interested, professionally and personally and recreationally, in a wide variety of things. They also learned that I played the lottery from time to time. Can't win millions of dollars if you don't play, I'd tell them. Of course, they'd always want to know what I would do if I won. My answer...my sincere answer...freaked them out. I told them I would build my own school.

- Then learn how to lip read. There are always a few inquisitive students who watch you while you're chitchatting with other teachers at lunch or while you're watching them play four square. Sometimes these information seekers are still in the building after school's out, working with other teachers on various things, and they'll walk in on you in your classroom while you're talking with another teacher and you can tell they know they've bopped in on something pretty juicy. One time, a girl finally came up to me and asked me what are ya'll always talking about! I told her we were always talking about *you* guys...the students. I asked her what she thought was the second biggest thing teachers talk about. She had no idea. I said...*Food*.

- I think students of all grades should take P.E. every day—K through 12—and every year of their school life they should be required to take additional classes called "Manners," "Common Sense," "How to Have an Intelligent Conversation With Anybody," "Table Etiquette," and "Understanding Teachers."

- Want to utterly find out what a kid is interested in? Then offer that grand ol' schoolhouse tradition, "Show and Tell," any time they want it. I did. Any time they wanted to bring something in and show it to us and tell us about it I'd stop what we were doing and prop my feet on my desk and sit back and get wowed. Within reason, of course. I told them they couldn't bring in their little brother as that would get me in even more trouble. Anyway, a lot of kids took me up on it, and their bug-eyed classmates learned about all kinds of things, while I, sneakily, learned a whole lot about the kid standing behind The Lectern of Speaking. One time a girl brought in a shrunken head.

- I hear rotor blades. One time it got so bad with a helicopter mother that the school's headmaster wouldn't allow her to come into our building and the mother was no longer allowed to e-mail any of the teachers or approach them outside the building. If she felt she needed to send an e-mail, which she did tens of times a day in pink letters to every teacher her son had, the headmaster told the mother to e-mail him only. Not even to the assistant principal. The headmaster wasn't done. It was that bad. The headmaster had the crazy mother's husband meet with him and all her son's teachers and he tough-love told the poor guy that your wife is crazy and we're done with your crazy wife and your crazy wife is actually holding your wonderful son back and that now your crazy wife was your responsibility, completely and forever. In that meeting I watched a sane grown man, who I really liked, put both hands over his face and bawl…and tell us he couldn't control her anymore either. I figured the next time I saw the mother and the husband they'd be on the Dr. Phil Show. The son was actually doing pretty well.

- This would be a great place if it weren't for the fascinating crazy people. In another school there was an exasperating mother who roamed around the building during the school day, sometimes carrying around her little dog. Sometimes she wore her pajama pants. She never paid attention to her hair, but she did her son's homework perfectly. Nobody could do their jobs because she'd demand a parent-teacher conversation right then and there. We'd often find her aimlessly rifling through her son's locker. Sometimes she'd complain in detail about her husband to you. She repeated all of her stories. I got the husband story one time, two days in a row, word for word. She never knew when to stop talking. You literally had to walk away from her. It was finally time for action. We agreed that the first teacher to see her walking around the building would e-mail all the other teachers that she was in the building. I learned at lunch one day where everybody hid or what they'd say to her if they got caught out in the open. If you were a fly on the wall when that woman moped into the building you would have thought all the teachers had horrific urinary or bowel afflictions.

- Everywhere I've ever taught the students finally figured out that I would toss them a piece of candy when they said something nice about my hair. When you fling rubber chickens at kids while you sport a nice hairdo...well...that's like something out of David Lynch movie. Candy has a grandpaw feel to it. The cash register ladies at the Publix near where I live, as they'd tally up big bags of candy every other week or so, finally asked me what I did for a living. I told them, proudly. One of them asked me what makes me give out the candy. I said when they say something nice about my hair. The cash register lady looked at my hair. It was particularly poufy that morning. She said you sure must have a lot of patience.

- Patience for what? The patience thing really mesmerized me. Every time you told someone who didn't know you were a teacher they'd tilt their head to the left like a dog looking at a piece of abstract art, and a glazed expression would wash over their face, and then they'd mutter...You sure must have a lot of *pay*-tience. I finally figured it out. Most people think that all kids are maniacs and constantly give you trouble. A lot of kids are maniacs. A lot of kids are not maniacs. I've had classes of kids who were so engaged and respectful and mannerly that my heart would flutter when I was teaching them. I'd get revved up in the very best way. Sometimes I told them that if they wanted to cut up a little bit it was okay with me. They never would. One day I demanded that Honoria make a funny noise—that she had to make a funny noise or else she'd be in trouble. I thought she was going to faint. One day she did faint, of course, but because of something else. Her brain turned off because it really did get full.

- One of my proudest teaching moments came when I gave a little professor-type kid the perfect nickname. His existence on Earth begged for a nickname and I believed I was placed on Earth with the one mission of coming up with his nickname. I was profoundly moved by this revelation. I was shocked that it wasn't his real name already. Anyway, I'd been noodling over my final selections for some time...*weeks*...and the day came when I officially bestowed my decision upon him in class in front of his classmates. Everybody freaked out with its dead-on accuracy. The victim was pleased with it, too. He thought it was perfect. Later that day at lunch I was sitting at the teacher table and I told my teacher buddy, Gary the math teacher, to look over at the kid and while he was looking at him that I was going to utter the perfect nickname I came up with for him. Gary started looking at him and then he said...Okay, *say* it. I said...Winkelberg. Gary said...Good *Lord* that's *per*fect. He really is a total Winkelberg! I breathed again into Gary's left ear...*Wink*elberg. I was so proud.

- Just because you tell school stories to your best friend, who begs you for them, doesn't mean you're making fun of your students, their parents, or what you do. It just means you enjoy telling your best friend interesting things he'd never know on his own. That's what teachers do. We educate people about things they'd never willingly learn on their own. Raise your hand if you've ever, on your own, read the Constitution of the United States of America. It's not that long. Raise your hand if you think you might last ten minutes with Lamar without either one of you ending up injured or dead.

- I made a big deal out of the infamous vexillology week every year for an ultimate and sneaky and specific reason that some students understood: the diligent, unrelenting use of a certain word in your life...*Why*. Always go deeper by asking why.

Why? Why? When they made their "flags of me," they had to explain what the green on their flag meant, or what the picture of a bug meant to them, personally. Why does it mean that to you? Come to think of it, why would you be rude to so-and-so? Is it so-and-so, or is it just kids with zits you don't like? Go deeper by asking yourself *why*. There really is a reason for everything, and it takes some thinking and hard work to learn the reason. When you get down to the real and ultimate *why* something happens, then you'll finally understand how everything in the world works, even your own behavior and mind. Just by studying flags.

- Got glyphs? Sometimes students are just as fascinated with your handwriting as you are with theirs.

- Name calling. It feels good when your friends and family call you "Teach." And when you commit to extracurricular activities, and some students call you "Coach"...that's a pretty good feeling, too.

- Think of the angriest you've ever been in your life. There will be that student and that moment in your career where the student perfects the moment of apocalyptic disrespect, and you, the teacher, think that all of a sudden you're in a waking nightmare. You cannot fathom how the student thinks it's okay for them to make you question your existence on Earth...right in front of everybody else in class. But it happens. My apocalyptic moment came one day, and I was so dumfounded by this fellow that I read his student file that afternoon. I really spent some time with it—his file was thick—and wondered how he wasn't already in prison by killing two particular people in his life who were supposed to love him and take care of him. After that, I was still firm in my class expectations—behavior and academic—but I looked for any and everything I could do that would prompt me to pat him on his back and to make him feel like he mattered. Sometimes in life the people you end up despising the most are people you've never even met.

- School wasn't so bad. My best friend and I have known each other since the first days of ninth grade and we've been pals ever since. We even live down the street from other now. We both admit that our four years of high school together was the best time of our lives. We loved the bump and shuffle of school. The characters. The mindless pranks. The quirky teachers. I guess I still do.

- I taught a workshop one time at a statewide conference of teachers on how to be a successful teacher your rookie year, and I told them that you don't really have to love kids to be a great teacher...you just have to understand them. All the teachers in the room agreed with me. That was a real nice moment. I couldn't believe I had actually hit on some remarkable, agreed-upon truth in a profession I was real green at. One woman was asleep, with her mouth hung open, so I'll never really know if she agreed or not.

- Being fascinated helps, too. If you're a teacher and you're genuinely fascinated with children, teenagers, and young people and what they say and do and how they interact with you and each other, then you'll always have fun at work, every day. This is why some people teach until they croak and why most policemen police for a long time, too.

- A couple of years later I taught another workshop at the conference to a room of teachers about how I got a bunch of unmotivated and uninterested and nearly illiterate kids to write stories and essays. To write something every week by Friday. I told them I borrowed this one from the working world, especially the newspaper news room. Every Monday the kids got a fun subject to write about, a low word count, the opportunity to be edited by me, and then I would read their work, out loud, in my goofy announcer voices, to everybody else every Friday. My God, did it work. The first couple of Fridays were horrifying to the students, but then they finally got whacked each week by a sense of pride and Fridays became the most looked-forward-to day of the week. Not because it was the last day of the week. It became the proudest day of the week because they learned that hard work and a dedicated routine always has a payoff.

When you see emotionally fragile kids pat each other on the back—literally pat each other on the back—because they loved each other's stories, it's hard not to get teary-eyed right in front of them. Every Friday.

- The unexpected result of mischief is sometimes just as funny. Just to keep it even more interesting, wear the same clothes to work every day for several days in a row and you'll finally come to the horrifying conclusion that no one, including your fellow teachers and your students and the janitor, is paying attention one bit to what you wear to school every day. For male teachers, however, you'll find that after two days your students and colleagues will notice that you haven't been shaving the left side of your face.

- The time spent driving home from school was long enough to go over the day, every day, and figure out what I could have done better...where I truly screwed up...and sometimes where I did a pretty brilliant job. It was also the best time to grieve, and even weep, for what you saw and experienced that day. I never wore sunglasses while driving until I became a teacher.

- Brood and ruin your mood. I finally got smart and learned that too-many cigars and brooding for way too long every evening at home, was not the way to take the edge off what a teacher experiences. It was not the way to refresh. It's exercise—open-mouth breathing, sweat-spewing, body-changing exercise. That's what ultimately does it. I started training for marathons and ran in a bunch of marathons and half-marathons and in those hard-core, military style obstacle course races, one of them with Mr. Warbird leading the charge to not be burned alive, electrocuted, or to drown in creeks, lakes, or huge pools of freezing mud or ice water. I boxed at the local Police Athletic league and got kicked around, but while I changed my body and teacher's mind for the better. Some of my students caught on and asked why in the heck would I subject myself to all that. I never told them the real truth. But I did let them punch me in my stomach as hard as they wanted and anytime they wanted. You can know your subject and teach it like an expert, but if you want to impress young scholars, let them punch you in your new rock-hard gut and enjoy the satisfaction of being their teacher-hero in the most unconventional way. This used to drive Lurlene crazy and she told me to stop but I never did. Old Burrell thought it was brilliant. At his old school, six or seven hundred years ago, he said he used to kick kids out of class by dragging them into the hall while they were still in their desks. That was back in the good ol' days, he said, and parents thanked him for it.

- Gut check. I got in trouble with Lurlene for something else, too, among one or two million other things. If a guy got in trouble in class, instead of kicking him out, I had him do twenty push-ups. Some of these kids were pretty good athletes and they'd call my bluff. They'd pop off a quick twenty, and then crank their head up and look me right in the eye and ask for twenty more. One of these guys popped me in the gut one day, too. I kept it together for as long as I could, while I think I was lecturing about Abraham Lincoln or somebody, and then excused myself and went to the teacher's bathroom to see if my liver had come out my navel. Actually, my left kidney came out my right ear, too.

- This same fellow started hallucinating in class one day. He said there were black spiders all over the top of his desk. Everybody else in class craned their necks to see...nothing. I told him he was free to trot up to the school nurse's office if he wanted to. He wouldn't do it. He said he was going to Marine it out. He did. Classes lasted nearly two hours at this school and he Marined it out. With the thumb and the index finger of his right hand he methodically pinched the heads of about two hundred spiders. Then he was okay.

- I'm not hallucinating. When you put in a few years in different grades and in different subjects and with different kids at different schools, you will finally come to the stunning conclusion that you've seen it and heard it all. Really. All of anything and everything. But you forget something over

and over and over: there's always the next
class period.

- Eat your vegetables: get a survival tool.
Spike's mother always had a certain look on
her face on field trip Saturday mornings
when she watched Spike fly up the bus
steps...before I eased shut the squeaky doors
behind him. It was an expression that
evoked deep, unspoken gratitude toward a
teacher. She was saying to me with her
freckled face...Thank you so much for
cooking up this Saturday field trip business
because, although we love Spike as much as
parentally possible, he is the quirkiest and
most physically and mentally exhausting
child on the face of the earth who has ever
popped out of my womb, and speaking for
me and my husband, thank you so much for
giving us several hours of peace and
solitude and sex time and please feel free to
take as long as you like today even though I
don't even remember where you all are
going. I liked her. I always winked at her
before the doors shut. A wink that said back
to her...I love him, too. Spike loved the
museum gift shops and the Army/Navy
stores more than the museums we went to.
He always brought along enormous wads of
his own money, stuffed in both pockets. I
stopped anywhere he wanted because I like
those places, too. So did everybody else.
From a display case, he'd pick out a
flashlight or a pair of binoculars. After Spike
told the salesman he'd take it, he'd ask me

for my cell phone and call his mother. Spike would always hunker over to the side somewhere, mumbling, and then he'd screech...Macaroni and *cheese!* He'd hand me back my phone and pay the shopkeeper. At another Army/Navy, he'd find something else. I'd automatically hand him my phone. I could hear his mother squawk for a moment and then Spike would screech...A *pig* rib and some *cole*-slaw! It was a weird and wild retail ritual, one of many from his repertoire that forever fascinated me and his loyal fans. All his mother wanted to know was if he had a good lunch or an early afternoon dinner. After he convinced her he ate something other than Skittles, Spike could buy almost anything he wanted.

• There's great sport in lying to kids, but you really have to know when and where and how. It's actually pretty easy to get good at it. On a Saturday field trip, we were eating our lunch on the grass outside of a BBQ joint in a real rough patch of town. After a few Saturday trips, and even on weekday field trips, we discovered that the best BBQ joints are always in the rough patches. While we were eating, a fellow shambled up to our group. He's what you'd immediately recognize, on a field trip to any small town in America, as a local character. This fellow made some kids nervous. Some kids were fascinated. The fellow was at least seven feet tall. He started to preach some Jesus to us. I angled him off to the side and preached a little of my own Jesus to him, with all eyes on me, and then I reached into my pocket and gave him five bucks. He went on down the sidewalk and preached some Jesus to some other people eating BBQ sandwiches. Back in the bus, as everyone was fighting over their sleeping spots and while I was getting the cold bus cranked up, Spike slinked up to me and asked me why I gave that man some money. I told Spike the man was the mayor of Columbus and that, God bless, he had recently fallen on hard times. Spike munched on that for a moment, and then he turned around and screeched to everybody in his leprechaun voice...Hey, *y'all!* That man was the president of the United States and he had recently fallen on *hard times!* Spike patted me on the back and said...God bless you, *too, Todd.* You're an *awe*some role model for *all* of us!

- I miss Spike so much.
- Ever since going to school started thousands of years ago in Greece or Rome or China or wherever, the funniest thing you'll ever see in class, and always has been, is watching an attentive scholar keep from falling asleep. In my experience, I discovered there are about one hundred and forty-eight ways that students attempt this, and they're all hilarious. I think it's perfectly okay to stop class and get everybody to help watch the agony. It's about the only agony of another person you can witness that makes you feel so unguiltily gleeful.

- For attention, scream like a caged animal. One day I thought a kid named Merle needed a bit more attention from me, so I wrote him a note that said: No matter what we're doing at the time, make a real funny noise at 1:40, and then I folded up the note and handed it to him in the middle of class. Merle read it, and the most satisfied expression washed over his face. I winked at him, and then comically looked over at the clock on the wall and did some goofy-looking things with my eyebrows. I winked at him again, and then went back to pontificating about the horrors of the Civil War. The other kids in class were visibly jealous that Merle got handed a note by the teacher and that Merle seemed pretty darn pleased about the contents. Merle was a perpetually angry little fellow and everybody hated his guts right back. At 1:40, Merle made a lecture-shattering noise that was not from this earth. I had forgotten about our special agreement. I about fell off my stool.
- Only three questions tonight! The homework dilemma was never a dilemma for me. Why create more fuss and disappointment. I just tried to get as much work done as possible in the time I had them in a classroom with me.
- I never had a parent complain that their child wasn't getting enough homework.

- The parents who complained all the time about homework were the parents doing the homework.

- Sometimes I gave out homework just to see, usually through handwriting and grammar and punctuation analysis, the sneaky ways parents who did the homework would try to make it look like their child did the homework. Other teachers did the same thing and it gave us even more fun things to laugh and cry about.

- Sometimes your personality brings out the worst in some students...and then in other classes, if you haven't changed a thing, it brings out the very best in some students. It's not the subject matter, but that can help or hurt, too. If a student just doesn't like you, who also hates learning about the Civil War, then you'll have a civil war to fight every day. It's pretty nice when both combatants finally reach a lasting truce, especially when the battle begins on the first day of class.

- If medication can make a kid a better student and human being, once all the side effects are tamed and if the medication can actually be afforded within the family budget, then why not? I've never worked with a teacher who thought parents or their child were failures, or weak, because they gave their child medications to help them become a better student and human being.

- You inherit krazy from your teachers. When somebody would create some mischief, I'd say that thing you just did *I* invented in third grade. I'd say you can't pull anything on me because I invented it all, with the help of some of my other misfit school pals, and passed it down to all school kids in America. Some kids knew I was kidding, but the more mischievous kids believed me. I was their mentor and they didn't even know it.

- That's exactly right. Teachers get a couple of weeks off around Christmas and a week off for spring break, usually during April, and two months off in the summer. Sometimes a whole week off at Thanksgiving. And your point is?

- Teachers are underpaid. We are. We are horribly underpaid. And your point is?

- Talk therapy. The best principals know what you deal with every day. Without interrupting, the best principals will listen to you for as long as you need them to.

- Dawg gone. I stayed in touch with Lurlene. She really could bring you up to date on anything and everybody pretty much instantly. Nothing ever got by her. One time she told me...Oh, by the *way*, Pam's fat nasty little *dawg*, *Bloo*-tow, finally exploded and is now with *Jee*-sus. I said to Lurlene I'm sure there was some wailing and teeth gnashing. Ye *gods*, Lurlene said, there were conniption fits and freak outs and the questioning of how *life on Earth* and the awesome process of edu-*kay*-tion could continue without that *dawg* in the building. When they heard the news, Lurlene said, a *num*ber of the *chill*-ren had to be taken out of the building on stretchers. Lurlene said that...I my-*self* had to lie down on the carpet while my *own* palpi-*ta*tions ceased.

- I really miss that Lurlene, too. She was something.

- Sneaky seeking of knowledge. I'm always amused when a student asks me while they take a quiz or a test if spelling counts. Of course, that's the reason many of them are here. They have dyslexia. I say it counts...sure...spelling always counts in school and in life, but here's how we handle it on quiz day. Hop up from your desk and whisper the answer to me. I'll write down your answer on your quiz. Most of the time, I found out, whispered answers were correct. Most of the time, though, the kids didn't whisper the answer, but shouted it, and if the other kids were paying attention they got a dang freebie.

- Sales knows no hours. The people who know the most about a company's faults and good parts are the salesmen. The people who know the most about a school's faults and good parts are the teachers. In other words, when you're the person actually providing the product to the customer you'll be amazed about how much you come to know about everything and everybody, and you're usually exactly right.

- They may not drop from the tree at all. On the Saturday field trips I led, I had an uncle come along one time and an adult family friend of a student on another trip. Parents were always invited. Word got around about our awesome excursions where we didn't have to fly back from somewhere to make car pool. On every trip, Smucker's dad would come along, too. Smucker Senior really was an exact, but older copy, of Smucker Junior. Pudgy, with a quick smile, freckles, a ready-for-anything attitude, and an intense interest in history and museums and in eating BBQ. Smucker Senior would kindly follow my instructions and listen to my announcements and laugh at my obnoxious humor, and was always imbedded in the group, just a foot taller or so than the others, rather than hanging off to the side like the other adults who'd come along. On the rumbling, coma-inducing bus, Smucker Senior would fall asleep like everybody else. One time, on our way home after our day of controlled adventure, I looked into the huge rear-view mirror above my head and saw that Smucker Junior was sprawled out on a seat with his legs hanging out into the aisle, and then there was Smucker Senior sprawled out in the seat on the opposite side of the aisle from his son with his legs hanging out in the aisle. I remember giggling to myself...Man, this is way too much fun. Smucker Senior was an insurance salesman.

- Really? Yes, really. After a few weeks of school, Lurlene would ask the teachers to call the parents of all their students new to the school. I liked that. Not an e-mail, but a call on the phone. Just to check in after a few weeks and let them hear our voices. So I learn pretty quickly that you need to say everything's okay real early in the conversation because one time a mother said to me...When I see the school's number my heart leaps out of my throat! That day I said everything's fine. I understand. I said your son's doing fine and it's a pleasure having him in class. He's been polite and respectful. She said I appreciate that. I heard her let out a huge breath. And then she said...*Really?*

- Home is where the salaciousness is. Old Burrell loved to visit with me nearly every day after all the kids had gone home. I would hear him shuffle across the hall and I would stop what I was doing and lean back in my chair and get ready for it. Old Burrell told the kind of stories particular to old men: tales of very personal yore. It was told to me one day, by Old Burrell, that the state of Alabama has an interesting history, too, particularly Phenix City. Old Burrell said he grew up in Columbus, Georgia, across the Chattahoochee River from that famous den of iniquity, so he knows a whole lot about Phenix City. They had every kind of crime you could think of over there, Old Burrell said. Dope, gambling, murder, loan sharking, larceny, car theft, kidnapping, extortion, book making and *loose women!* Old Burrell was convinced the police were in on it, or doing it themselves. And then Old Burrell gave me a bona fide crazy wide-eyed glistening teeth look, and says...and black market *bay*-bies. Who says future-looking teachers aren't interested in history, too.

- The sella mortis. Of the millions of curriculum nights there's one that I'll remember forever and they were all pretty dang memorable. In the third period session for a class where I had six kids, six parents came in, and without prompting, sat in exactly the seat where their child sits. There were twelve desks in The Cozy Room of Learning. I stood there, dumfounded. I finally told them what just happened. I had to. They were as amazed at me. A couple of the parents, however, were visibly unnerved by it. They looked at the desk they were sitting in, and then lifted their hands up off of the desktop, as if it was covered with germs.

- L*ooo*k int*ooo* my *eye!* In all my years, the maddest I ever saw a kid get was after another kid looked at him. All Lamar did was look at Brainerd. A perfectly normal thing you'd do during the day. Folks look at each other from time to time. Brainerd achieved a level of bonkers never before seen in the history of kids going to school, which I believe goes back thousands of years. Lamar had that kind of power. It was palpable and undeniable and maybe somebody someday will harness it to pull sunken battleships to the ocean surface or to zap meteorites apart way out in space.

- Of all the principals and assistant principals and dean of academics I worked with, even a headmaster or two, the best ones had a genuine sense of humor. The rabbis, too. Right after the final bell rang one Friday afternoon, the eldest rabbi in the school said over the intercom, in a comic announcer's prosody...*And the an*swer to this morning's *trivia* question *is*: Ben Ga-*zzara* in Tales of Ordinary *Mad*-ness! I stopped for a moment and thought, *Dang it, I never heard the question this morning.* I bumped into the rabbi on my way out of the building and told him I was disappointed I didn't hear the question, you know, if substitute teachers can participate in the ol' Friday trivia contest? The rabbi looked at me funny, and then said...There *ain't* no contest. I just do that every Friday afternoon for fun...for like the last thirty years. I started laughing. Really laughing. He was, too. With my hand on his shoulder I said to the rabbi...Man, that's funny. He said: I know. You're the first person who's ever said anything about it.

- Meetings can be productive. Old Burrell used to fall asleep in faculty meetings. Chin on his chest. Face contorted in a late afternoon nap nightmare. Bushy eyebrows twitching like bacon frying. Each week, watching Old Burrell dream about old times was an enormous source of entertainment for me outside the classroom. I thought about asking Lurlene if we could have a faculty meeting every day but the other teachers would have killed me.

- Chalk talk. When I was a student in high school and in college, instead of paying attention to what they were teaching, I paid more attention to how the teachers taught and managed their schedule and their students and how they decorated their class rooms. How they dressed and the awful cars and trucks they drove were a source of great hilarity, too. Most of them were of the old-school way: teacher...piece of white or yellow chalk...green chalkboard...and a textbook. I don't believe that classroom technology has made us smarter. Old-school style teachers—supremely engaging and caring and knowledgeable teachers with chalk-coated fingers—make us smarter. Sometimes you don't even need the textbook or a chalkboard.

- The power of nice. Students who are exceptional athletes are treated better, *especially* if they put up good grades and have good manners. Students who do some great work in extracurricular activities are subtly treated better, or differently. The special treatment is subtle and it happens. I'm guilty of it, I admit.

- Just say the words. Mom, you can moan and whine in my face because you're mad your son has only an A-minus in my class; you can scorch me with hideous e-mails packed with misspelled words glued together by idiotic grammar and capitalization insanity; but if you end every conversation and every e-mail by thanking me for all I do...then I'm okay with it.

- The one thing parents can teach their kids is manners. Teachers are there for the undeniable academic pleasures of advanced placement trigonometry, and we teach manners, too, when we can work it in, and we do work it in, but manners are the ultimate domain of parents, and even grandparents. So when a kid has bad manners, I deal with the kid's bad manners right then and there, but silently blame the parents for wasting my time, the time of the other kids in class, and their own kid's time.

- Teacher bites back with tough love. In a parent-teacher conference that was three weeks late, I sat across the table from a dad who I knew was a furry. Furries are adult human beings who dress up as various animals and animal-like creatures in fancy costumes and dance around and chase each other and have frisky relations while they still have their costumes on. Their costumes have flaps with snaps in sexy places. I know all this because I was told by a teacher whose broad study of her professional and personal subjects included a whole lot of partying with fascinating people when she was younger. While the other teachers were talking, I gazed at the man and went through a number of costume selection scenarios. I had him as a Dalmatian...then a squirrel. A chicken, maybe. Then I thought that what he did on his own time, if it's not illegal, was his business, so I quit figuring out what animal he was, although a sloth seemed about right. All I wanted was for him to start getting his son to school. And when he got his son to school for more than two days in a row before he didn't get him to school for a few days again, I hoped that he would arrive on time for at least five days in a row. I told the dad that we'd take it from there... from 8 'o clock until you finally picked him up. Five days in a row at the official picking-up time would be nice, too.

- Technology keeps the peace. I guess you could say a DVD player hooked up to a TV screen in the corner of the classroom is technology. It didn't make any of us smarter, but it made me feel like a teaching revolutionary. One day I figured if they came into the classroom with a movie *already playing* that they would scoot to their desks and start the class period off without bickering at each other, dropping their books on the floor because they love the loud noise that makes, or trying to sneak candy out of The Globe of Happiness. My idea sort of worked. They typically did only one of those. Anyway, I played Civil War documentaries, *Nacho Libre*, *The Outlaw Josey Wales*, *School of Rock*, *Dorf on Golf*, and *The*

Right Stuff, among a number of other mesmerizing, teacherly selections. They loved it. Every single student loved the idea. Of course, the time came when we had to turn the movie off and get to work and to some chicken chucking. But the dramatic exhibition of hard work and good behavior was always rewarded by giving them the last few minutes of class off so they could repeat Nacho's famous toast eating scene or watch our hero Lone Watie say, "Endeavor to persevere!"

- Who needs coffee? One day a fellow teacher told me, during a particularly chaotic day in the schoolhouse, that she doesn't mind the chaos. She said she *likes* it. I admitted to her that I did, too.

- Parent trap. I'll never understand how a mom or dad would never attend—not one—of their child's basketball or soccer games or track and field meets. I will never understand it.

- I don't recognize her anymore. The best description of a student's positive progress I ever heard in my teaching years was when a teacher would say to another teacher about someone...She's a completely different human being...He's a completely different human being. This pronouncement usually came after some time, and a whole lot of work from all parties, but it's exactly what you see a lot of times, months and years later: a different and better human being. Grades are never mentioned.

- A kick in the head. One of the schools where I subbed and taught longer sessions for sick or infant-nursing teachers asked me if I'd help coach the girl's soccer team. Naively, I said what the heck. It was a sudden shock to learn that most of the sixth, seventh, and eighth grade girls on the team had never played organized soccer before. They were cute and all in their new cleats and bubbly, pre-season attitudes, but I also found out, very quickly, such as in the first seconds of our first practice, that most of the girls had never experienced someone raising their voice at them. Running laps and sprints was new to them, too. Someone blowing a whistle real loudly in their vicinity freaked them out. Someone pretty much telling them what to do and exactly when to do it was extremely unnerving to most of them. Their eye rolling and bickering and questioning and whining and mood swinging and complaining was brain melting—for four afternoons a week for two and a half months. But the head coach and I never stopped blowing our whistles and raising our voices and telling them how to play and practice the character-building game of middle school girl's soccer. We got through the season without too many tears, mine and theirs, and finished second in our school's sports league. I was proud of them. But I have to admit: After the last game of the year, before I started for home, I sat in my truck, and while breathing a sigh of relief that would have filled the Goodyear blimp, I questioned, out loud, my existence on Earth.

- Just run somewhere. At another school I was asked to be the track and field coach of the middle school and high school kids. We didn't have a track or access to another school's track. During practice I had to get real creative. I had to use what I had, and that was having them run around in a nearby parking lot, dodging their own mothers, nannies, fathers, and driver services, who used the parking lot as a shortcut for when they came to pick up their track and field stars.

- They weren't UFOs. I taught Lamar how to fling a discus and put a shot. During our Olympic-level training (at least for us), he never whined or moaned or debated or bickered or complained. He went to track meets with the rest of the gang and competed and socialized between flings and puts with athletes from other schools, special education and mainstream. It was a glorious time. He was glorious. There's no other word to describe Lamar when he was acting like a human being. But during the bus rides back to school he wasn't always glorious, especially when I wouldn't stop for him at every Burger King or McDonald's or Dunkin' Donuts or strip club.

- So real you can see it change the color and texture and temperature of the air in the room. Every once in a while I'll read or hear people saying that ADD or ADHD or hyperactivity ain't real! That the dang kid can't control herself and she just needs her a good whippin' is all! ADD and ADHD and hyperactivity are real, all right, and they're some of the most powerful forces in human civilization. Just like ignorance in adults.

- Oy vey. I substituted a lot and taught long supply jobs in the special education section of a school for Jewish kids, as well as in their mainstream classes, pre-kindergarten through eighth grade. On my first day, in homeroom, a little sixth grade girl with a wild head of hair asked me if I was Jewish. I said I didn't know. She looked at me funny, and then cocked her head. Then she asked me if I was a Christian. I asked her…How do I know if I'm a Christian? She made an even funnier face this time. I said why do you ask. She asked have I ever asked a question just for the sake of asking a question. I gave her my most serious face, which took a few moments to make, and then said…Uh, *no*.

- Mitzvah me. One day I was walking down the hall toward the teacher's lounge to get a cup of coffee and one of the school's rabbis was running down the hall behind me yelling my name. He trotted up to me, huffing, and asked could I sub for him next Tuesday. I was sort of stunned. I said you know I don't speak Hebrew. He said that's okay! I said you know I'm not Jewish. He said that's okay, too! I said I have no idea what you actually teach and how you teach it. He said he'd have it all written down for me on a piece of paper he'll leave on his desk! I still wasn't convinced I wouldn't set the religion back a few thousand years, so I said are you absolutely *sure?* He rubbed the flesh of his chin. He was the only rabbi in the school with a lot of rabbis who didn't have a beard potentially full of barn swallows. He said...Ya know, maybe I should consult the authorities on this one. I said that's probably a good idea. The next Tuesday I didn't set the religion back a few hundred years, but learned a few good things myself about how to be a better human being. By default, some things I had already been working on. With some encouraging success.

• Get ready for your close up. One day at a school I noticed a camera up in the corner of a math classroom. I noticed a camera in the corner in another classroom on another day. Some classrooms didn't have cameras. I never asked why. Anyhow, one day I was back in a classroom with a camera and I started to feel conscious of my gestures. When my arms got away from me or when my hands went above my head, I wondered who might be watching, and what they were thinking, and how loudly they were laughing at me. I started wondering if there was a microphone in the camera, too. But I was more worried about my gesticulations than what I was saying: How much were my arms and hands waving around? Heck, I just don't keep track of them. I also knew I had that oblivious teacherly habit of pacing back and forth in the front of the classroom while I pontificated, too. One day I went to visit another substitute teacher in another classroom that had a camera. We were both enjoying our free periods. While we were chitchatting I asked if she knew she had a camera in her room. She turned around and looked up at the camera. And then she turned around and looked at me with very wide eyes, and whispered, Oh...*shit.*

- I think the classroom is a sacred place. It's a good and wonderful and otherworldly place to me, and it should be respected and honored and used and enjoyed by everyone who wants to learn something. Every morning before the first student walked across the threshold, I imagined what might go on in my classroom and those thoughts always inspired me and made me feel lighter and happier. Every day before I turned off the lights and walked out to go home, I looked around the room for a few moments and remembered what went on that day, right there, and right over there. Everywhere I taught I did that. Every time I left my classroom for the day. I still do.

- Got alektorophobia? One day late in the year, the headmaster said to me...Hey, I hear you're doing some clever things in your classroom! *Clever,* huh. Works for me, too, I thought. Anyhow, I think "clever" means

you've come up with a not-too-radical
solution to something nagging you. Student
disinterest and not interacting with each
other nags me. I really wanted my students
to know they could talk during class—to
talk about whatever was on tap that day, or
something close to it. I wanted to interact
and converse and debate and inform. And if
they did that with me and each other, they'd
get the chicken until somebody made an
even better comment or asked a better
question. After almost a full school year, of
course, there were certain folks who became
upset, and way-too vocal themselves, that
their kid didn't get the chicken chucked at
them that day or week or at all. Sorry, mom.
The opportunity to say something
intelligent is a daily offering, and has been
since the first week of school. When the
chicken got retired early, I went back to the
same toy section of my grocery store and
bought a nine-inch long rubber lizard with
sharp teeth and big eyes and bright green
speckles and started flinging it around when
good discussion items and questions and
comments were offered up. The kids
thought I was crazy. A rubber lizard?
Compared to our wiggly plucked hero?
After a couple of days, Spike came to me
privately and said the lizard was lame as hell,
Todd. I told Spike if I snuck the wiggly
plucked chicken back in that Lurlene would
kill me. Spike said he'd take a punch for me.
Anyhow, it worked, that little rubber

chicken from the grocery store toy section. It did exactly what I'd hoped it would do...provoke class discussion with a sense of fun and moderate creepiness. The opportunity to get the chicken chucked at them electrified kids who would otherwise not be electrified in a history class. The whole idea was totally unique to American education, I'm pretty darn sure. So now I have a new word: it's alektorophilia. It's Latin or Greek or French or whatever for people who love chickens. It's also my new word for those who think of clever ways to get a student's attention: alektorophiliacs. Isn't that ultimately what we do...get their attention...and hope they love and remember what they learn next?

- I really would build my own school if I won the lottery. First, I selfishly admit, I'd have the truck fixed in a bunch of places, and then have a doctor un-deviate my septum, and then I would give wads of money to my family and friends and important charities, and then I'd build it. I already have the campus laid out in my mind and the school colors chosen (four of them) and have even got the name of the school all figured out, too. I know what our mascot would be: a ferocious animal, but not a chicken. I know who I'd hire to teach, and who I'd hire to run the school. It wouldn't be me, though. I'd hire myself to teach. That's a whole lot more fun. And I know who I'd hire to run the lunchroom: my favorite four waitresses at my local Waffle House: Marie, Christine, Sylvia, and Shenanigans. I swear that's what it says on her nametag: Shenanigans. These four, who I've patronized and pestered for years, know how to dish out the good food and the sass and the mischief and the unending, unrehearsed, and unbridled smothered and covered country gravy-style repartee. The kids would be totally freaked out by *these* lunch ladies. Totally. And sometimes that's okay...at my new school, where we would learn everything, even things that make us giggle.

- I'd build a boxing gym, too, at my new school, but I didn't tell them that.
- One day a student asked me why we go to school. She said, I have always wondered why we have to go to school and be educated. She was a good girl, but school wasn't her thing. She didn't make everybody else miserable about it, though, like a few others who didn't dig the wonderful grind. She was kind and respectful, fairly quiet, too, but when she spoke up she usually offered up some thoughtful zingers. I turned away from the chalkboard, paused for effect, and said...So we can become articulate. That's really it. So you can become articulate. She chewed on that for a moment, and then said, But can I become articulate on my *own* and not go to school? Sure, I said, but you wouldn't have great teachers and your friends to support you every day to make sure you're doing it right.

- Where are they now? I really wish I knew. I really do, but I remember every one of my students and everything they said and did and that keeps me feeling satisfied and sentimental. Kids with learning, behavior, and emotional disorders aren't real good at staying in touch. They're real good at staying in touch while they're *in* class, that's for dang sure, but after they graduate or get kicked out or just stop coming to school one day or go off to another school and are never heard from again, that's when you have to get back to the kids who need a great teacher the most. They'll always be right there in front of you, waiting for you to perform the best job on Earth.

- Special delivery. I miss Lamar, I admit. Every once in a while I go through the box where I keep the odd trinkets and bizarre drawings and pretty good doggerel poetry he created just for me. I'll gaze at his creations and chuckle. I think about him all the time, and about that time he'll call me. I've got his number and his name plugged into my cell phone: LAMAR is calling again. There's a cosmic-karma relationship thing going on with Lamar that I'm too afraid to question. I think about him. He calls. I usually take in a deep breath, and then click the green button. Lamar's most recent news is that he got a job driving a delivery truck. He says he's making twenty dollars an hour. I told him that's more than a lot of teachers make. He giggled. Lamar asks about a few of his old teachers. I tell him what I know, which is always pretty interesting. And then Lamar says in a certain tone of voice...Mr. Sentell, those were the best days of my *life!*

- And some of the best days of my life, too, in the most strange and wonderful ways.

ACKNOWLEDGEMENTS

At the thought of this, she was flooded with gratitude and a terrible pang of joy ran through her. "Oh thank you Jesus, Jesus thank you!" she cried aloud.

The book struck her directly over her left eye.

—Flannery O'Connor, *Revelation*

THIS MIGHT BE a first in the history of world literature: an author extends his deepest gratitude to…a *song*. A piece of music that lasts only two minutes and five seconds. It's a sweet-hearted song called "Little Martha," a guitar instrumental plucked by Duane Allman and Dickey Betts of the Allman Brothers. While writing this book, I must have listened to that song well over a thousand times, because it produces in me the perfect mood to write about kids, whether they're calmly going about class business or not calmly going about class business. Heck, I'm listening to it right now, and see in my mind Levon looking into the classroom window at me, grinning. I *still* think kids are the most important people on Earth.

My thanks to *Edutopia*, the web site of the George Lucas Educational Foundation, and the foundation's Samer Rabadi and Betty Ray, who understood, and enthusiastically supported, why I was posting vignettes from this book, instead of original thoughts, in response to the web site's various schoolhouse topics. Thanks, too, to the web sites *Education Week* and *Education Week Teacher* for their support.

Over the years I posted the vignettes because I'd much rather show what goes on in the classroom than try to explain it. Once you shut the classroom door and begin the period some mighty powerful things occur. Every day. I think people need to know about them.

I am so grateful to the many great teachers—subs and full timers—I've worked with over the years. So many have become close friends. I can't wait to get there, every day, because I also get to be with my teaching and coaching pals. A school is a building full of like-minded, hard working, and smart-thinking people, who laugh at the same things and finish each other's sentences. They're called teachers. You know who you are, and I appreciate you so much for your good advice, camaraderie, and friendship.

My best friend and his wife would make good teachers, but after hearing my schoolhouse stories I figure they'll pretty much stick to what they're doing. Jeff and Feryal Hendricks have always been right there with me during a large part of my publishing life, begging for wondrous and heartbreaking and hilarious stories only a teacher and coach could tell.

And to my parents, Jack and Joan Sentell, champions of learning and education, who gladly and proudly made it possible for me to go to the finest high school in America, Woodward Academy, where I joined a class of characters who, to this day, have not changed a bit. It's scary to think we may have gotten even better at who we are.

My thanks to the Georgia Independent School Association who, during the writing of this book, allowed me to teach my revelations to a packed workshop of other teachers around the state during an annual conference about how to teach special education students, and mainstream students, to write remarkable fiction and nonfiction and how to effectively self-edit their work. To see a bunch of teachers applaud another teacher for his great new secrets was quite a moment in the history of American education.

As always, my thanks to Ken Coffman and Stacey Benson at Stairway Press, who are deeply and forever supportive of writers who have stunning stories to tell. Their love of this book was felt from the beginning.

And finally, to my past and future students...who may act sometimes like it's a big game, but know deep down it's not. School is the best thing that'll ever happen to you. Sometimes, though, you come to that realization after you're done.

So now, go teach. You'll never be accused of not working hard...ever again.

ABOUT THE AUTHOR

He returned to his journal and presently the screams subsided.

—Flannery O'Connor, *The Comforts of Home*

TODD SENTELL WAS born in Atlanta and raised in Georgia. Teaching kids with learning, emotional, and behavior disorders was an apocalyptic career change for him. For many years before he became a schoolteacher he sold something real expensive to a dwindling market of ootsie-tootsie rich people under tremendous quota pressure during a global economic meltdown. Compared to teaching that job was easy.

A two-time award winner for magazine journalism, Todd is a long-time contributor to *Golf Georgia*. His articles have also appeared in *Racquet*, *Golf Illustrated*, *Atlanta*, *Fairways & Greens*, *Dossier*, *Flag Research Quarterly*, and *Cheers!*, the newsletter of the Flannery O'Connor Society. His golf fiction has appeared in *The Golfer*, *Atlanta GolfLife*, and *Orlando GolfLife*.

Todd is the author of the critically acclaimed novels, *Toonamint of Champions*, and the *Stairway Press Collected Edition of Toonamint of Champions and Why Golf is so Exciting! A Novelty!*

Todd is a recognized master at teaching special education and mainstream students how to write remarkable fiction and nonfiction prose, and how to understand and appreciate all forms of art and artistic personalities. Todd is also one of Georgia's most distinctive folk and abstract artists. He has never won a marathon.

SERIOUS SCHOOL BUSINESS

*The author with his butt-kicking third
grade cross country coach, Mr. Meadows*

CPSIA information can be obtained at www.ICGtesting.com
Printed in the USA
LVOW10s0845240115

424201LV00003B/351/P